Unjust Legality

UNJUST LEGALITY

A Critique of Habermas's Philosophy of Law

JAMES L. MARSH

ROWMAN & LITTLEFIELD PUBLISHERS, INC.
Lanham • Boulder • New York • Oxford

ROWMAN & LITTLEFIELD PUBLISHERS, INC.

Published in the United States of America
by Rowman & Littlefield Publishers, Inc.
4720 Boston Way, Lanham, Maryland 20706
www.rowmanlittlefield.com

12 Hid's Copse Road
Cumnor Hill, Oxford OX2 9JJ, England

British Library Cataloguing in Publication Information Available

Library of Congress Cataloging-in-Publication Data

Marsh, James L.
    Unjust legality : a critique of Habermas's philosophy of law / James L.
Marsh
      p.   cm.
    Includes bibliographical references and index.
    ISBN 0-7425-1260-6 (cloth : alk. paper) — ISBN 0-7425-1261-4 (pbk. : alk.
paper)
      1. Sociological jurisprudence   2. Law—Philosophy.   3. Critical theory.
    4. Habermas, Jürgen—Contributions in law.   I. Title.

    K370.M37   2001
    340'.115—dc21   2001019017

Printed in the United States of America

♾ ™ The paper used in this publication meets the minimum requirements of
American National Standard for Information Sciences—Permanence of Paper
for Printed Library Materials, ANSI/NISO Z39.48–1992.

To William Kunstler and Ramsey Clark,
whose lives as lawyers manifest and exemplify
the just practice of law
in an unjust society

Contents

Preface

In a book such as this, it is important to lay out the context, historical and personal, in which and from which I am writing. As the reader will discover, I am very profoundly positively influenced by Habermas. In fact, Habermas, along with others such as Ricoeur, Marx, Hegel, Kierkegaard, and Lonergan, is one of the major influences on my thought. But, as the reader will also discover, I am also profoundly critical of Habermas, and the reasons for that, insofar as they refer to my previous personal development , need to be articulated.

But, first, a few words are in order about Habermas in his historical and social context. Today, at the beginning of the twenty-first century, Habermas is undoubtedly one of the world's top four or five philosophers and social theorists. His thought has caught on increasingly in the United States, so much so that any major graduate program that claims to be serious about contemporary continental philosophy and social theory has to have at least one critical theorist on its faculty. That was not true twenty years ago. Such a state of affairs owes much not only to Habermas but also to the success of his students and disciples, such as Thomas McCarthy, in spreading the word.

With these gains, however, has also come cost, mostly the taming of critical theory so that it conforms to the limits of academic, liberal discourse in the West. It has become apparent to many of us involved as active participants in critical theory that Habermas is no longer interested, if he ever was, in undertaking a radical critique leading to a transformation of late capitalist society. Rather, at best he is concerned with beating back the effects of illegitimate intrusion of market and administrative power on the life-world, effects that he calls "colonization." But capitalism kept within its own proper economic sphere is apparently unproblematic, nonexploitative, the best we can do. Critical theory in his hands and those of most of his U.S. disciples has become a progressive form of liberal theory, able and willing to dialogue with, and learn from, the likes of Dworkin and Rawls but no longer interested in "that wild man" Marx or even an earlier, much more radical critical theorist such as Marcuse.[1]

I find all of this unfortunate and reprehensible, not only because I think the project of radical social critique and transformation is necessary, desirable, and feasible but also because Habermas's own theory has radical implications from which he backs off. Simply put, the theory of communicative action in *Between Facts and Norms*, developed into a theory of democratic law, implies radical democracy—full economic, social, and political democracy. Showing this is one of the main aims of this book. By contrast, late, welfare-state capitalism, to which Habermas remains committed, is an inadequate, contradictory, halfway measure. A great deal of the interest and story of *Between Facts and Norms* is Habermas's heroic effort to square that circle, law rooted in democracy and capitalism. It is my contention that he does not and cannot succeed.

The liberal, pro-capitalist stance has been manifested *in actu* by Habermas in his support of the Gulf War and the war in Yugoslavia, both unjustified, unjust, imperial interventions. While his support for the Gulf War seemed somewhat restrained, apologetic, and cautious, his support for the Yugoslavian intervention was aggressive, enthusiastic, and even contemptuous of dissenters. Habermas, in the latter part of his life, seems to have become, or at least to approach having become, an enthusiastic apologist for late state capitalism in all its viciousness at home and abroad. And he has adopted these stances on foreign policy in spite of his very conscientious liberal stances on political debates within Germany, such as discussion of the Holocaust. But it is increasingly evident that such liberalism, for all its genuine moral-political substance, is insufficient.[2]

These stances are inconsistent with, and fly in the face of, Habermas's best insights—for example, into the necessity for unfettered communication in the public sphere freed of the influence of money and power and the necessity for legislative, administrative, and judicial spheres to be similarly free of such unjust intrusion. There insights rest on, and flow from, many others, such as the theory of communicative action, his account of historical materialism, his theory of modernity and defense of a legitimate form of modernist reason against postmodern critique, his account of the life-world–system distinction, his theory of morality, and his account of the system of rights. Above all, he has brought a methodological consciousness to critical theory which we dare not reject.

To move beyond Habermas, as I and others are trying to do, we must be sure that we have measured up to and absorbed his positive achievements and insights. And yet, after doing that, or trying to do that, and because we have done that, we regret to say that Habermas's theory falls painfully short of what it could be and should be. Instead of championing a radical, transformative social theory that takes on late capitalism in all of its pomps, Habermas has capitulated to it and even become, at times at least, its apologist.

In my own efforts to develop such a transformative, genuinely radical theory, I find myself moving toward a new critical theory, based upon Habermas but going beyond him.[3] Such a new critical theory has several aspects: a much fuller, more positive appropriation of Marx, earlier critical theory, and sources of Western Marxism such as Bloch, Gramsci, and Benjamin; exploration of the cognitive, existential intersubjective human subject including but going beyond Habermas's linguistic subject; a linking of a formal moral with a material ethic of content; a linking of right with good, duty with happiness, deontology with teleology; a critique of capitalism not only as colonizing but also as exploitative in its own inner workings, marginalizing, tyrannizing, and dominating, interpreting racism, sexism, and heterosexism as distinct from, but related to, classism; and a critique of capitalism as imperialistic, extending beyond the borders of the North into the South, into the Third World.

Let us focus a bit on two of these aspects, the link between formal and material morality and the link between right and good, duty and happiness, deontology and teleology. Both of these are comprised in my three-level social ethic, developed in *Critique, Action, and Liberation*, of right, morality, and justice. The level of right calls on me to obey the exigencies of communicative action as spelled out in a principle of universality, U, which leads to and grounds the basic principle of discourse ethics, D. The principle of universality states that any legitimate norm requires that all concerned can accept the consequences and side effects its universal acceptance can be anticipated to have for the satisfaction of everyone's interests (and that these are preferable to any other alternative). D states that only those norms can claim to be valid that meet (or could meet) with the approval of all concerned in their capacity as participants in a rational discourse. U and D cannot be denied without self-contradiction or arbitrariness. If, for example, I try to deny U, that it should meet with universal acceptance on the basis of the better argument, I implicitly contradict the content of what I affirm explicitly. If the claim is not rational, then what is arbitrarily asserted can be rationally questioned or denied.

The level of right, however, proves to be insufficient, for the issue arises concerning the requisite material and social conditions such that people can participate equally and freely in communicatively active, moral, political discourse. Equal opportunity to participate that is more than merely formal and verbal demands approximately equal material and social conditions, such as wealth, income, education, housing, food, and medical care. Accordingly, the principle of generic consistency, or PGC, is affirmed: act in accordance with the generic rights of others as well as yourself. Negatively, this principle implies that I ought to refrain from coercing or harming recipients of my actions. Positively, the PGC implies that I ought to assist others to have freedom and well-being whenever they cannot otherwise have them and I can help them at no great risk or cost to myself. Accordingly, if I see a person drowning in a lake as I am walking by and I am a good swimmer, I have an obligation to save that person.

On the level of morality, moreover, the PGC implies freedom as self-development, or FSD. Because freedom and well-being are both dispositional and occurrent, habitual and present in individual actions, any choice must imply the willing of the basic conditions and dispositions that are necessary for the essential unfolding and realization of the project of being a self. Self-development is the freedom to develop myself through my actions. It is a process of realizing my projects through activity in the course of which I develop my character and other capacities. I develop myself when I engage in political activity over a period of time, or learn to be a pianist, or go to graduate school in philosophy.

Because, however, freedom in the full sense is positive and not merely negative, because it implies the capacity to realize one's choices, and because control by one group over the enabling conditions of self-development implies a domination incompatible with freedom, self-development implies equal positive freedom. Such a freedom implies and includes the right of each individual to the enabling conditions, material and social, without which individual purposes cannot be realized. Among the material conditions are means of subsistence, labor, and leisure activity. Among the social conditions are cooperative forms of social interaction; reciprocal recognition of each one's free agency; and access to training, education, and other social institutions.

The levels of both right and morality, form and content, lead into and imply four principles of justice, unity of form and content, in the light of which we can evaluate social institutions:

1. Everyone's security and subsistence rights are to be respected.
2. There is to be a maximum system of equal basic liberties, including freedom of speech and assembly, liberty of conscience and freedom of thought, freedom of the person along with the right to hold prop-

erty, and freedom from arbitrary arrest and seizure as defined by the
rule of law.
3. There is to be (a) a right to equal opportunity to attain social position and offices and (b) an equal right to participate in all social decision-making processes within institutions of which one is a part, as
well as (c) an equal opportunity for meaningful work.
4. Social and political inequalities are justified if and only if they benefit the least advantaged and are consistent with just savings but are
not to exceed levels that will seriously undermine equal worth of
liberty or the good of self-respect.

One implication of my principles of right, morality, and justice is the
injustice of both capitalism and state socialism. Both violate the orientation to full communication present in U and D. State socialism openly
represses any kind of dissent, and late capitalism covertly represses it
through such mechanisms as campaign financing, largely supplied by the
rich and corporations; media subservient to capitalism; and different
kinds of selection mechanisms operative in government, such as limiting
the range of options considered and forming committees largely sympathetic to the corporations they are overseeing.

Both state socialism and capitalism are also incompatible with equal
positive freedom on the moral level. If such freedom is to be realized, it
requires access to means of self-development as they are present in political power, production, and culture. Because they allow some to own, control, and derive the primary benefit from the means of production, power,
and culture, both capitalism and state socialism essentially violate the
imperative of equal positive freedom.

Both state socialism and capitalism violate all or most of the principles
of justice. Both systems violate the principle of equal opportunity to
make decisions in the economic arena, and both violate the fourth principle because the levels of income and wealth exceed the limits of equal
worth of freedom and self-respect. Democratic socialism, however,
involving ownership of firms by workers; full economic, political, and
social democracy; a minimal welfare state; a market forbidding
exchanges between capital and labor; and local, regional, and national
planning associations to coordinate and plan investments, disperse
funds to needy, deserving firms and individuals, and monitor abuses,
does satisfy the principles of right, morality, and justice.[4]

Another consequence of my principles of right, morality, and justice is
solidarity with the poor and oppressed. For insofar as people are exploited, dominated, and marginalized by an unjust racist, sexist, heterosexist,

classist capitalism, then I have to hear and respond to their cry and side with them against the oppressor. There is a preferential option for the poor, marginalized, and oppressed that can be argued for philosophically.[5]

Such is the context of my own personal development, out of which I write this book on Habermas's philosophy of law. The reader can easily see that there are many agreements and many disagreements with Habermas. For the most part, however, these will be in the background of my argument with and against his position in this book. When I have recourse to my own arguments and claims, they will be used to complement and strengthen the main argument of this book, which is one of *immanent critique:* using Habermas's own theory, values, and principles, do his arguments, conclusions, and implications of his arguments measure up in a fully consistent and comprehensive way with his own best, true insights, or do they fall drastically short ethically, legally, and socially-theoretically?

I argue that they fall drastically short. The system of rights, democracy informed by law, and the ideal of communicative action cannot be realized fully, adequately, and consistently in late capitalist society. At their best, Habermas's arguments point beyond themselves toward a qualitatively more just, fully democratic, socialist society. At their worst, they lead to uncritical, dogmatic capitulation to an intrinsically unjust society that should be ruthlessly criticized, resisted, and transformed. Capitalism in its essential functioning is flatly contradictory to the rule of law, full democracy, and the full flowering of communicative action in the public sphere and the formal political sphere of the state.[6]

In order to critique Habermas's position adequately, I have found it necessary to lay out his argument in detail as it unfolds chapter by chapter in *Between Facts and Norms.* Whatever the reader thinks of my critique, which I hope she will find stimulating and challenging, I hope that she will find my interpretation of Habermas's thought to be fair, clear, and comprehensive.

Finally, I wish to thank my assistant, Ryan Gable, for an excellent job of word processing this manuscript, and my department and university for a full year off in order to write it.

NOTES

1. See James L. Marsh, "What's Critical about Critical Theory?" in *Perspectives on Habermas,* ed. Lewis Edwin Hahn (Chicago: Open Court Press, 2000), 555–65.

2. On Habermas's support of the Gulf War, see Jürgen Habermas, *The Past as Future,* trans. Max Pensky (Lincoln: University of Nebraska Press), 5–31. On his

support of the war in Yugoslavia, see his "Bestialität and Humanität: Ein Kriegand der Grenze zwischen Recht und Moral," in *Die Zeit,* April 29, 1999,1, 6– 7. Ulrich Rippert, "How Habermas Defends the Balkan War," World Socialist Web Site, www.wsws.org., June 5, 1999, 1–6.

3. Marsh, "What's Critical about Critical Theory?" 555–65.

4. See James L. Marsh, *Process, Praxis, and Transcendence* (Albany: State University of New York Press, 1998), 211–13; and James L. Marsh, *Critique, Action, and Liberation* (Albany: State University of New York Press, 1995), 113–76.

5. Marsh, *Critique, Action, and Liberation,* 174–75.

6. There have been several books published after the appearance of *Between Facts and Norms* that deal with, or draw on, it in different ways. None of these includes the detailed, analytic interpretation and critique in this book. Such books include James Bohman, *Public Deliberation* (Cambridge: MIT Press, 1996); David Ingram, *Reason, History, and Politics* (Albany: State University of New York Press, 1995); Michael Rosenfeld and Andrew Arato, eds., *Habermas on Law and Democracy: Critical Exchanges* (Berkeley and Los Angeles: University of California Press, 1998); William Rehg, *Insight and Solidarity: A Study of the Discourses on Ethics of Jürgen Habermas* (Berkeley and Los Angeles: University of California Press, 1994); Lewis Edwin Hahn, ed., *Perspectives on Habermas* (Chicago: Open Court Press, 2000); and Peter Dews, ed., *Habermas: A Critical Reader* (Oxford: Basil Blackwell, 1999).

For the most part, these books, while insightful and helpful in many respects, adhere to Habermas's reformist, pro-capitalist stance on democracy and law and his support of capitalism. The exceptions are Ingram, who argues for workplace democracy and offers a critique of capitalism as unjust in principle; William E. Scheurman, "Between Radicalism and Resignation: Democratic Theory in Habermas's Between Facts and Norms," in *Habermas: A Critical Reader,* ed. Dews, 253–77; William Forbath, "Short-Circuit: A Critique of Habermas's Understanding of Law, Politics, and Economic Life," in *Habermas on Law and Democracy: Critical Exchanges,* ed. Rosenfeld and Arato, 272–86; and many authors in Hahn, *Perspectives on Habermas,* critical of Habermas's reformist, pro-capitalist stance. Interestingly enough, Habermas in his reply in *Habermas on Law and Democracy,* 381–452, chose not to respond to Forbath's critique and did not choose to reply to any of the contributors to *Perspectives on Habermas* after initially agreeing to do so. Whatever the motives for these refusals, they constitute an interesting limit so far on responding to those who question his reformist framework.

Many of the other efforts are useful and illuminating, but to the extent that they share the reformist framework of the master, they are limited. James Bohman, for example, in *Public Deliberation* has plausible proposals for shifting to a dialogical model of democracy over against Habermas's discourse model and for the notion of "capacities" as useful in describing the abilities that citizens need to participate effectively as equals in public dialogue. But in saying that radical democracy "no longer means the total transformation of society; rather it means a piecemeal project of reforms that builds upon the constitutional achievements of the past" (20), he gives in to the worst mistakes and limitations of Habermas himself. My questions to Bohman are, why does he call his proposal "radical democracy" at all?

(Habermas makes a similar mistake), and are not Bohman's democratic dialogue and capacities as effectively short-circuited and blocked by capitalism as other forms of democracy? There is more to capitalist injustice than colonization and an inadequate welfare provision that can in principle be reformistically handled. Like Habermas, therefore, Bohman understates empirically the depth and variety of capitalist injustice and thus ends up in an implausible, harmonizing unity between capitalism and democracy.

1

Toward a Critique of
Habermas's Philosophy of Law

In *Between Facts and Norms* Habermas has shown, in a way that he has not done since *Legitimation Crisis*, the concrete, social, political, and legal implications of his theory of communicative action. As we know from *The Theory of Communicative Action*, Habermas is committed to democracy. What he has done in *Between Facts and Norms* is to show that such democracy is possible and actual in modern democratic states.

I am not sure that I would agree with the assessment of a well-known critical theorist that *Between Facts and Norms* is Habermas's greatest work.[1] That honor belongs to *The Theory of Communicative Action*, I think, and it would be as much of a mistake to accord *Between Facts and Norms* that honor as it would be to thus rank Hegel's *Philosophy of Right* over against his *Phenomenology of Spirit*. Nonetheless, like *Philosophy of Right*, *Between Facts and Norms* is a great, marvelously synthetic, original, path-breaking book that erects the philosophy of law on a new, much more sophisticated and comprehensive foundation.

To say that *Between Facts and Norms* is an achievement, however, is not to deny that it is, as Marx has shown *The Philosophy of Right* to be, a flawed achievement. When I first read *Between Facts and Norms*, it seemed to me to be very insightful, yet more and more I have the sense that Habermas and I do not live in the same social world. That impression, of course, does not necessarily speak against Habermas. This chapter will attempt to articulate the basis for this ambivalent reaction and to defend my radical interpretation of the social world as more adequate than Habermas's reformist version. I will first reflect on some of the general contours of my argument with and against Habermas and then move into my argument with *Between Facts and Norms*. This chapter outlines in a provisional way the argument of this whole book.

On the one hand, *Between Facts and Norms* is correct in discussing the many-leveled tension between facticity and validity; the co-originality of private and public autonomy; the overcoming and sublating of liberal and republican accounts of law into a procedural paradigm of law; the correlation between different aspects of the constitutional state and forms of rationality (for example, the legislature with justification, the judiciary with application, and the administrative with pragmatic, strategic forms of rationality); and finally the claim that law is a medium whereby communicative power is translated into administrative power. On the other hand, we live in a racist, sexist, heterosexist capitalist society that is at odds structurally not only with democracy but also with justice and with human well-being. In New York City, where I live, one can see the victims of capital—the poor, the unemployed, and the homeless—grow daily more numerous; the division in income between rich and poor is worse than in Guatemala. I live in a country in which democracy is for sale. Western capitalist democracies are, or seem to be, more and more democracies for the few, for those who can afford them, leaving the vast majorities both underrepresented politically and underprivileged economically. Such a state of affairs seems to be in flat contradiction with the proclaimed universality of Habermas's proceduralist paradigm of law, which posits that everyone should have an equal right to participate, make her interests known, and share power.[2]

An initial reaction to *Between Facts and Norms,* therefore, is to say that Habermas seems to be insufficiently bothered about this state of affairs and that he should be. He seems not to share, for example, the kind of prophetic outrage that Jacques Derrida expresses in *Specters of Marx* about the New World Order. This initial impression, however, is somewhat unfair, as *Between Facts and Norms* struggles with this sensed incompatibility. Like Fukayama and apologists for the capitalist order, Habermas is haunted by the specter of Marx. Maybe, finally, Marx is right about the fundamental irrationality and injustice of capitalist democracies, early or late.[3]

The tensions and contradictions of *Between Facts and Norms* are on at least two levels, normative and hermeneutical. On a normative, moral level, Habermas's vision is contradicted by the reality of late capitalist society. On a hermeneutical level, Habermas is inaccurate insofar as he continually underestimates, understates, and ignores the deep pathology and irrationality of capitalist democracy.

My basic claim is that *Between Facts and Norms* is fundamentally, internally contradictory. Its moral and political reach exceeds its grasp insofar as that vision cannot be realized or even approximated in a society that is as fundamentally unjust, unequal, dominating, and exploitative as ours is. The clearest indication of that contradiction is Habermas's statement (407–8) that both the liberal paradigm of law, developed to defend the rights of the individual before the state, and the welfare paradigm, which grants welfare entitlements to secure such negative liberties, are rooted in a productivist image of capitalist society that legitimates the pursuit of private interests by autonomous individuals. Both views lose sight of the link between private and public autonomy and of the democratic meaning of a community self-organization; the proceduralist paradigm, in contrast, does see such connections and is thus preferable. It is nonreified as opposed to reified, communal as opposed to individualistic, democratic and communal as opposed to instrumental and strategic. Yet how is such a paradigm to thrive and be realized in a capitalist society that is as virulently productive as it ever was, as committed as ever to turning human beings into means for the sake of profit? The material underpinnings—racist, sexist, heterosexist, classist—of capitalist society seem to be at odds with the proceduralist paradigm. Habermas's procedural model hovers uneasily, like a Kantian postulate, above a capitalist society that is incompatible with it.[4]

Such a contradiction expresses itself in other contradictions in this and previous works of Habermas. One, equally universal and fundamental, is the contradiction between capitalism and democracy. Democracy as a free and equal community of human beings relating to each other mutually is in tension with a socioeconomic system that not only is undemocratic, unfree, and unequal in its own internal workings but also tends to expand outward, to the extent that it is a mature capitalism, and subjects everything to its sway. Thus the culture and the state tend more and more to be "capitalized," to serve the ends of capital, of which the dominant one is the extraction of profit.

By *capitalism* in this book, I understand a socioeconomic system in which one class owns, controls, and derives the primary economic benefit from the means of production, and another class, separated from the means of production and possessing only or mostly its own labor power to sell, can work only on capital's terms. Profit or surplus value, the amount of average, socially necessary time for which labor is not paid and which goes to the capitalist, is the overriding goal of such a society and tends to impose itself on all domains of society, economic, social, and political. Such surplus value represents the part of the working day that goes to capital and is over and above necessary labor time, which goes to the worker to reproduce the value of his own labor power. *Capital* refers, first, to the class of persons owning and controlling the means of production; second, to the process of investment, production, exchange, and consumption running through capitalist society (self-expanding value); and, finally, to the social relationship between capital and labor. Most of the time in this book, "capital" will have the first sense, the class of those who own and control the means of production.

The result of such subordination is a structurally based legitimation crisis, taking the form in the modern state of a tension between accumulation and legitimation. The state has contradictory goals: to secure capitalist accumulation in a way that more or less frustrates the economic and political aspirations of noncapitalists such as labor, women, blacks, and Hispanics; and to legitimate its decisions in ways that respect the demand of democratic participation, in which all interests and persons in principle have an equal voice, no question is in principle excluded, and a legitimate formation of general interests emerges. To the extent that full, free democratic discussion occurs, the prerogatives of capital are undermined. To the extent that capital prevails, false, manipulative consensus is substituted for true consensus in a way that violates democratic procedure, and a pseudocompromise between legitimate general interests representing the will of all and particular interests is substituted for a legitimate compromise between merely particular interests that cannot be generalized. A nation's legitimate interest in a reduction in military spending after 1989 (a "peace dividend") and an increase in spending for the poor, education, the inner city, and the environment gives way to capital's need to keep military spending as high as possible for the sake of profit and the necessity of keeping the Third World in thrall by maintaining a strong military enforcer of last resort.[5]

As the foregoing indicates, there is a sense in which one can show how on Habermas's own terms capitalism is unjust and systemically irrational and contradictory. At the same time, he understates both the injustice and the irrationality. As I have shown elsewhere, in addition to colonization of the life-world by system, which Habermas articulates, there is exploitation of labor, women, and racial minorities within the workplace by capital; tyranny (in Walzer's sense), in which one life-worldly sphere imposes itself on others (science and technology, for example, imposing themselves on spheres subject to moral, communicative action); marginalization and nonrecognition of the disenfranchised such as the poor, the unemployed, women, blacks, and Hispanics; and domination in many different spheres by capital over labor, black over white, men over women. Consequently we have five forms of injustice and irrationality rather than just one, and the capitalist firm is not innocent if all it does is refuse to colonize. Rather, domination and exploitation take place within the capitalist firm in a way that runs counter to the imperatives of communicative action.[6]

These issues I cannot explore further here. What emerges, however, as a more adequate picture of late capitalist society is one overriding corporate power center that operates nationally and internationally, inside and outside the public sphere, and whose fundamental telos is to twist the legislature, judiciary, administration, and public sphere to its own unjust, undemocratic ends. To think that one can have an adequately democratic society rooted primarily in the interplay between an informal public sphere and a formal legislative branch—an interplay that functions in a fundamentally undemocratic, unjust, corporate context—is as plausible as to think that in the nineteenth-century South in the United States there could be a democratic, free, nonracist public sphere, a lonely island in a sea of institutional racism. The picture is implausible both morally and hermeneutically, and another contradiction asserts itself in *Between Facts and Norms* between a public sphere in principle free from such corporate influence and one that is in fact structurally mired in it and, as I will show later, dominated by it.[7]

Habermas admits some of what I am saying factually, of course, but denies that such an admission invalidates anything about capitalist society in principle. Thus he says such crises can at most be explained historically: "They are not built into the structures of functionally differentiated societies in such a way that they would intrinsically compromise the project of self-empowerment undertaken by a society of free and equal subjects who bind themselves by law."[8]

Here another contradiction breaks out between merely factual claims such as this and other claims made in *Between Facts and Norms* and other works indicating that these are problems in principle. One example is the previously mentioned analysis of legitimation crisis as rooted in class conflict, albeit displaced onto the political sphere; another is the admission that corporate power is a major player within, and not simply without, the public sphere and the most that we can do is try and beat it back. Habermas's political sociology seems, therefore, to be at odds with itself and with his defense of the constitutional state.[9]

"The intention is to tame the capitalist system, that is to 'restructure' it socially and ecologically in such a way that the deployment of administrative power can be simultaneously brought under control."[10] This move is as inadequate, I have already suggested, as trying to tame racist economic and political power without doing away with it in the South. A further contradiction that emerges, therefore, is that between an accepted reformist stance toward capitalism, which stance undermines and contradicts communicative action itself, and a rejected, radical, revolutionary stance necessary to be fully consistent with the imperatives of communicative action. As Habermas himself says, "we have lost confidence that these conditions can be changed by revolution."[11]

Habermas's reformism compromises his own best insights into communicative action and amounts to an adaptation to late capitalism in a way that vitiates the universality and consistency of communicative action. As a result, critical theory culminates not with a bang but with a whimper. The tension between facticity and validity turns into a contradiction between facticity and validity, and, much like Hegel again, elements that are genuinely incompatible in principle, capitalism and democracy, are seen as compatible in principle. The danger is, therefore, that insights in principle pointing beyond capitalism as a form of life and bringing it into question lead to a justification of it. Ideology critique turns, in Habermas's work, into a modernist form of ideology, "why it is reasonable and realistic to live with late capitalism and love it, or at least accept it."

Up to this point I have been reflecting on problems and contradictions that run through *Between Facts and Norms* as a whole. Now I propose briefly to go into more interpretive and argumentative detail by reflecting in turn briefly on the genesis of rights, the legislature, the administration, the judiciary, and the public sphere. Although much of Habermas's argument is insightful and true, his basic valid model of a democratic polity founded on law cannot be realized in other than a truncated, contradictory way in capitalist society. To be faithful to and realize his own best insights, Habermas needs to be a socialist in a substantive sense.

Habermas's genesis of rights proceeds on two levels: a horizontal level on which a law-abiding community is constituted, and a vertical level on which the state is generated. On the horizontal level, he affirms (1) a basic right to the greatest possible measure of equal individual liberties, (2) the rights flowing from being a member in a voluntary association of consociates under law, (3) basic rights resulting from actionability of rights and from individual legal protection, (4) basic rights to equal opportunities to participate in processes of opinion-and-will-formation in which citizens exercise their political autonomy and through which they generate law, and (5) basic rights to provision of living conditions that are socially, technologically, and ecologically safeguarded in order for citizens to have equal opportunities to utilize the civil rights listed in 1 through 4.[12]

I am going to focus on the last two, that is, the provision of equal opportunity to participate and of living conditions. Habermas seems to restrict equal opportunity to political autonomy in a way that arbitrarily limits the universality of communicative action. Why would not and should not a group of citizens constituting themselves decide to extend equal opportunity to economic and social spheres, full economic, cultural, and political democracy? One advantage to such a move is that it eliminates the tension between political democracy and economic oligarchy. Second, equal opportunity without at least a rough material economic equality—that is, a right to education, medical care, leisure time, food, shelter, and healthy working conditions—is a chimera. Equal opportunity is asserted formally in the political sphere but is contradicted materially by a lack of real, effective equal opportunity.

Third, Habermas in his principle of welfare provision asserts some right to material provision, but any adequate implementation of this norm is incompatible with capitalist class society in which enormous differences of wealth and income and, consequently, in educational opportunity, exposure to culture, and so on are possible and actual. In the United States, for instance, the top 1 percent of the population has about the same amount of wealth as the bottom 95 percent. The average CEO made as much as 209 factory workers in 1996, up from 42 in 1980. Such statistics indicate that late capitalist society is moving further away from the equality necessary to sustain real democracy, not closer to it.[13]

Taking principles 4 and 5 together, therefore, we see that they are not only factually but also in principle incompatible with capitalist class society. By Habermas's own standards, that society is unjust. A tension emerges between these principles, which point beyond capitalist society, and Habermas's reformist accommodation to that society. Such an argument is reinforced by Habermas's claim that "public discourse requires a background of political culture that is egalitarian, divested of all educational privileges, and throughly intellectual."[14] Merely beating back or taming colonization is insufficient if the inequality in wealth and income within the economic sphere is left untouched. Yet as long as this sphere keeps to its own turf, it remains innocent for Habermas.

Because the horizontal generation of rights is flawed, the vertical generation of the state is similarly flawed; the validity of the former is a necessary condition of the latter. The principle of popular sovereignty, for example, states that all political power derives from the communicative power of citizens operating equally, freely, and mutually. Yet because equal opportunity remains all or mostly formal, and not real, the principle of popular sovereignty is violated actually and in principle. The same is true of the principles of political pluralism, guaranteed autonomy of the public sphere, competition among political parties, and majority rule. As indicated by the current situation in the United States, where both major parties operate as wings of the "business" party, none of these principles can operate freely, democratically, and equally if principles 4 and 5, the freedom principle and the welfare principle, are violated. The principle of the legality of administration implies that administrative power regenerates itself from communicative power of the citizens operating in common. Since such communicative power implies real opportunity and material equality, such regeneration cannot happen, and, therefore, the administrative power flowing from it and legitimated by it cannot be established. Because a judiciary supposed to apply the law fairly and equitably is chosen in a legislative and administrative context that is flawed, the judiciary will similarly be flawed.

Finally, since principles 1, 2, and 3 (which posit the greatest possible individual liberty, membership in a community, and adequate legal protection) require real democracy resting on genuinely equal opportunity and genuinely fair legislative, administrative, and judicial processes, these rights cannot be realized adequately. As a result, liberty, community, and equal protection mean something different for the rich, whites, males or for the corporation than for the poor, labor, blacks, women, and Hispanics. As I will show later empirically, this is more than an empty fear.[15]

Directly or indirectly, horizontally or vertically, each of the rights elaborated by Habermas is in tension with capitalism. The state as presumably generated by decisions among free and equal subjects acting democratically is incompatible with class unfreedom and inequality that minimizes or somehow puts such democracy out of play. Once enacted, the constitutional state cannot run in other than an inadequate, contradictory way in a capitalist class society. It requires real socialism, full economic, social, and political democracy, as its material, real embodiment, not just Habermas's formal socialism, "the set of necessary conditions for emancipated forms of life about which the participants themselves must reach an understanding."[16] A tension arises even here between Habermas's formal socialism and late capitalism, insofar as the set of necessary conditions for emancipated forms of life are incompatible with such capitalism. Habermas's formal socialism points toward real socialism; formal democracy toward real democracy; a truncated, merely political democracy toward full economic, social, and political democracy; his arbitrary acceptance of the capitalist status quo toward a full questioning of that status quo that respects more adequately the imperatives of communicative action.

Up to this point, my argument has been largely conceptual, partly to show that the democratic, constitutional state is not just factually but also in principle incompatible with this socioeconomic system. Empirical, socioscientific analysis supports the conceptual argument and makes it very clear why I think that Habermas and I do not live in the same social world.

Congress, for example, is overwhelmingly unrepresentative. Women make up 51 percent of the population but less than 7 percent of Congress, African Americans are 14 percent of the population but less than 7 percent of Congress. Occupational backgrounds are skewed toward the upper class. Lawyers, a small percentage of the population, constitute 50 percent of both houses; bankers, investors, entrepreneurs, and business executives compose the next largest group. There are almost no blue-collar persons or other ordinary working people in Congress.[17]

Because of inequity in campaign financing, we have the best Congress money can buy. In the 1992 elections, business interests outspent labor by more than five to one. In both major parties millions of dollars came from special interest groups or political action committees. Because campaign financing is so heavily dependent on the wealthy, access to political power remains dependent on campaign contributions. Members of key committees such as defense, finance, and transportation regularly receive millions of dollars from corporations that they oversee. In 1988–90, the top nine Senate recipients of donations from weapons makers and the top ten House recipients, together receiving $2.2 million, were all members of committees that dealt with defense contracts. Is it any wonder that there was little or no peace dividend?

In six years members of Congress took $36.5 million from the banking industry. In return, bankers were granted deregulation and bailout legislation that will cost the U.S. public $500 billion. Because of lack of representation, lack of access, and lack of influence, labor, women, the poor, the unemployed, and indeed most of the bottom 60 to 80 percent of the population do not come close to having their interests represented in a way that even approximates Habermas's procedural ideal or constitutional state.[18]

The reality is similar in the administrative and judicial arenas. From the beginning of the U.S. Republic, the top leadership positions—the presidency, vice presidency, cabinet, and Supreme Court—have rested primarily in the hands of wealthy white males, and the remainder occupying these leadership positions come from the upper middle class. Almost all U.S. presidents have come from the top 10 percent of the population in wealth and income. Government and business elites are linked by familial, institutional, professional, and social ties and often meet in very powerful foreign policy groups such as the Council on Foreign Relations

(CFR) and the Trilateral Commission. President Ford appointed 14 CFR members to his administration, and President Carter appointed 17 members from the Trilateral Commission. The CFR has advocated in the last fifty years a strategic nuclear arsenal, escalation in Vietnam, a sharp escalation in military spending, and a harder line toward the Soviets in 1980; the Trilateral Commission advocated a rollback in democratic participation because it was perceived as threatening the capitalist status quo. All of these positions were adopted by whoever was in the White House.[19]

The judiciary has similar problems. In class background and political proclivity, Supreme Court justices are more often identified with the landed interests than with the landless, the slave owners rather than the slaves, the industrialists rather than the workers, the exponents of Herbert Spencer rather than Karl Marx. The Court's personnel are drawn mainly from the class of corporate lawyers. Such political proclivities, class origins, and process of selection apply more or less all the way down to the very low levels of the judicial system.

Is it any wonder, then, that rather than getting an application of norms that would satisfy Habermas, we get one that is skewed toward the wealthy, whites, and males rather than the poor, blacks, and women? One form that such unjust application takes is a double standard. White-collar crime committed by the wealthy costs the nation $100 billion a year, a figure that excludes antitrust violations like price-fixing, which may cost another $160 million. This cost is much more than that of street crime. Yet white-collar crime is rarely prosecuted, prosecution often does not lead to convictions, and the penalties are much less frequent and costly than for street crime. The savings and loans defendants involved in the 1980s scandals who actually went to jail spent less time there on average than car thieves, and they served their sentences in perfectly comfortable minimum-security prisons. The 2,729 people on death row at the end of 1993 were overwhelmingly poor, black, or Hispanic. As of 2001, this figure had risen to 3,600.[20]

Now Habermas, to his credit, recognizes factually some of these problems. He is less adequate in seeing that these empirical difficulties manifest problems in principle. One final mechanism that he proposes as a way of dealing with these issues is the public sphere, that domain of informal discussion and opinion making that should in principle function independently of corporate power: "Only in an egalitarian public of citizens that has emerged from the confines of class and thrown off millennia-old shackles of social stratification and exploitation can the potential of unleashed cultural pluralism develop."[21] Yet Habermas, empirically honest again, admits that corporate media are internal to the public sphere and are major players within it: "A third group of actors are the journalists, publicity agents, and members of the press. . . . They are members of mass media which are more complex and more expansive . . . and more centralized." And a little further on: "The image of politics presented on television is predominantly made up of issues and contributions that are professionally produced as media input and then fed in via press conferences, news agencies, public-relations campaigns, and the like."[22] Habermas continues:

> Collective actors operating outside the political system or outside large organizations have fewer opportunities to influence the content and views presented by the media. This is especially true for messages that do not fall inside the "balanced," that is, the central and rather narrowly defined, spectrum of established opinions dominating the programs of the electronic media.[23]

The dominant players in the public sphere are corporations like NBC, CBS, and ABC, the *New York Times,* and the *Washington Post,* which are themselves out to make money and whose major function is to defend capitalist moneymaking as a way of life and help to create a hegemonic control favoring capitalist priorities over others. The income of these media comes primarily from advertising revenue supplied by other corporations, and their privileged source of information is government and corporate representatives and experts. The intended and functional effect, therefore, is to marginalize to some degree points of view that would contest such hegemony. Alternative forms of media, such as Pacifica Radio and Z *Magazine,* receive much less funding, have fewer subscribers, and have a harder time getting a hearing. The accumulation-legitimation crisis, therefore, is not just in the political sphere but also in the public sphere, and it is structural, not just accidental or contingent.[24]

How does Habermas respond to such a state of affairs? One way is estimating how the public sphere can have an influence on the political sphere; here there are three possibilities. Two of these pertain to a public sphere at rest, in which initiative comes from officeholders and political leaders and the broader public is excluded from, or does not have any influence on, the process of decision making; in the second, the public sphere is mobilized because the support of certain groups is needed. These are the normal cases, and the mass media simply go along and are content to receive their materials from such government procedures and practice strategies that lower, rather than raise, the discursive level of communication.[25]

Thus, for the most part the public mass media act contrary to their normative self-understanding. Only in abnormal crisis situations, the third possibility, is the situation different: "In a perceived crisis situation the *actors in civil society* thus far neglected in our scenario can assume a surprisingly active and momentous role."[26] At this point, the argued-for tension between facticity and validity becomes a full-fledged contradiction between capitalist facticity and communicative validity. The contradiction between capitalism and democracy, already present in the genesis of community, state, legislature, administration, and judiciary, is present in the public sphere as well. That which in Habermas's eyes acts as a final guarantor and ground of democracy turns out to be as much a part of the problem as it is a part of the solution. Late capitalist society, by his own admission and measured according to his own norms, operates normally and for the most part undemocratically and unjustly.

Habermas over the years has shown himself very resourceful in answering the criticisms of such groups as feminists, communitarians, systems theorists, and hermeneutical theorists. I am sure that he has similar weapons in his arsenal to answer me, even though I am less an anti-Habermasian than a disillusioned Habermasian. His theory of law is promising enough, but it is flatly contradictory to the social conditions of late capitalism. The best way to overcome my disillusionment is for him to become fully consistent with himself and his own best insights. Habermas should become a genuine, substantive, radical democrat.

All of this is not to deny that *Between Facts and Norms* is a valuable work. One of its most valuable aspects is its realism about the possibility of social change. Using such realism, Habermas could criticize my position as utopian. Ethical consistency, however, requires that realism not mean accommodation in the long run to structural injustice. Such accommodation is Hegel's mistake and Habermas's temptation, for which Marx properly takes Hegel to task and for which I have criticized Habermas.

In a structurally unjust society such as ours, the most adequate form of realism has to be oriented toward long-range social transformation, not accommodation. Such radicalism is realistic because it rests upon contradictions in the present pointed out by Habermas, such as economic, rationality, motivation, and legitimation crises; works with social movements provoked by colonization; works within a public sphere that, though flawed, can be the basis for a long march through institutions; and incorporates gains in social learning institutionalized in the modern state such as democracy, human rights, and welfare rights. Habermasian reformism and interpretation can be used, contrary to Habermas's intentions, in a nonreformist, revolutionary manner. In this way even the contradictions of *Between Facts and Norms* become rich and fruitful.

NOTES

1. I am referring here to a private remark by David Rasmussen at a fall 1995 meeting of the Society for Phenomenology and Existential Philosophy.

2. Noam Chomsky, "Rollback II," *Z Magazine*, February 1995, 22.

3. Jacques Derrida, *Specters of Marx*, trans. Peggy Kamuf (New York: Routledge, 1994), 13, 37, 81–85.

4. Jürgen Habermas, *Between Facts and Norms*, trans. William Rehg (Cambridge: MIT Press, 1996), 407–8.

5. Jürgen Habermas, *Legitimation Crisis*, trans. Thomas McCarthy (Boston: Beacon Press, 1975), 68–75.

6. James L. Marsh, *Critique, Action, and Liberation* (Albany: State University of New York Press, 1994), 238–40, 271–72. Since writing *Critique, Action, and Liberation*, I have more explicitly thematized domination as a fifth kind of injustice.

7. Habermas, *Between Facts and Norms*, 171, 175, 308, 373–79.

8. Habermas, *Between Facts and Norms*, 386.

9. Habermas, *Between Facts and Norms*, 373–79.

10. Habermas, *Between Facts and Norms*, 410.

11. Habermas, *Between Facts and Norms*, 467.

12. Habermas, *Between Facts and Norms*, 122–23.

13. Holly Sklar, "Imagine a Country," *Z Magazine*, July-August 1997, 65.

14. Habermas, *Between Facts and Norms*, 490.

15. Habermas, *Between Facts and Norms*, 168–86.

16. Habermas, *Between Facts and Norms*, xli.

17. Michael Parenti, *Democracy for the Few*, 2d ed. (New York: St. Martin's Press, 1995), 220.

18. Parenti, *Democracy for the Few*, 204–7, 221–22.

19. Parenti, *Democracy for the Few*, 203–4, 289–92.

20. Parenti, *Democracy for the Few*, 120–24, 308. Mark Lewis Taylor, *The Executed God: The Way of the Cross in Lockdown America* (Minneapolis: Fortress Press, 2001), 36.

21. Habermas, *Between Facts and Norms*, 376.

22. Habermas, *Between Facts and Norms*, 376.

23. Habermas, *Between Facts and Norms*, 377.

24. Noam Chomsky and Edward Herman, *Manufacturing Consent* (New York: Pantheon Books, 1988), 1–35.

25. Habermas, *Between Facts and Norms*, 379–80.

26. Habermas, *Between Facts and Norms*, 380.

2

The Tension between Facticity and Validity

I begin this chapter by reflecting on some pertinent items in Habermas's preface to *Between Facts and Norms* and then proceed to the first chapter, "Law as Social Mediation between Facts and Norms." The discussion will reflect on the book's major claim, which is that modern democratic societies can establish in principle a mediation between *facticity*, or the actual, factual acceptance and practice of conforming to laws and norms, and *validity*, the legitimacy of such laws and norms established or able to be established through recourse to communicative action.

At the same time, tensions emerge in Habermas's text between that claim and other empirical or normative claims implying or explicitly positing social forces that endanger, compromise, or overwhelm such a mediation. The issues dealt with in this volume are thus joined in the very first pages of Habermas's discussion. Is such a mediation possible or likely in late capitalist, democratic societies, or are we confronted with an irreconcilable contradiction between capitalism and democracy?

PREFACE

After indicating in outline form the organization of chapters, Habermas indicates that he is operating on the basis of a "moral-practical self-understanding of Modernity," one attached both to universalistic moral consciousness and to the liberal ideal of the constitutional state.[1] His discourse will attempt to reconstruct this self-understanding in a way that resists scientistic reductionism and aesthetic assimilation. The dimension of a proceduralistic reason expressed in cognitive, evaluative, and normative validity is all that we have left to evaluate and criticize existing unreason. Such a reason continually puts itself on trial and, in relation to such a reason, there is neither a higher nor a lower reality to which we could appeal (xl–xli).

The first point to be noted here is that Habermas's procedural-formal interpretation of modernity is not as unproblematic as he seems to imply. Different thinkers have agreed with him that procedural rationality is certainly a crucial dimension of modernity but have argued that such a reason needs to be linked to universal content in a way that Habermas thinks is not permissible. He is inadequately dialectical here. The dogmatism of merely particular, life-world contents as not redeemable universalistically is juxtaposed to a formalistic universalism. He misses the possibility of a dialectical linking of form and content in which universalistic principles of content emerge. Rawls's two principles of justice are one example; my four principles of justice are another; Ricoeur's blending of Aristotelian and Kantian ethics is another.

Habermas then goes on to show why, in relation to his procedural notion of reason, Marx's philosophy of history is thoroughly discredited. Marx's theoretical error is to have mistaken the socialistic project for the design of a concrete form of life. One should, however, conceive socialism formalistically as the set of necessary conditions for emancipated forms of life, "about which the participants themselves must reach an understanding" (xli). Ironically here, as we shall see, socialism in this formal sense is compatible with the most vicious kind of capitalism. Marx, at least, would not take kindly to such a redefinition of his project.[2]

Moreover, if this democratic understanding is merely formal and procedural, as Habermas says here, what are we to say of the necessary material prerequisites for equal, full, democratic participation? Do we not need a material principle, a principle of content, to spell out such prerequisites and the way they are to be provided? Otherwise we have mere formal opportunity and mere formal democracy, contradicted by a lack of effective opportunity and real, full, participatory democracy. Is Habermas insufficiently materialistic here?[3]

I resist the opposition between a merely formal socialism, compatible with the most vicious kind of capitalism, and a socialism of content that attempts to design and impose a total form of life. Following the dialectical mediation of form and content described above, we can talk about a socialism that is both procedural-democratic and content laden, in the embodying of a material principle of content, but still abstract and universalistic and that leaves open the full concrete shape of a society—for example, its mix of ethnicity, religion, race, custom, and language.

As Habermas notes, the victory in the Cold War between East and West is not without its problems. "Just when it could emerge as the *sole* heir of the moral-practical understanding of modernity, it [the West] lacks the energy to drive ahead with the task of imposing social and ecological restraints on capitalism at the breathtaking level of global society" (xlii). The liberal, modern West zealously respects the systematic logic of markets and is on guard against overloading the power medium of state bureaucracies. What is conspicuously absent, however, is a care for the social solidarity that is actually endangered. Politics in western societies has lost its self-confidence before a terrifying background of environmental pollution; nuclear blackmail; racial, religious, and ethnic wars; issues of immigration; and the struggle for the distribution and allocation of scarce resources. Behind the hackneyed rhetoric of democracy, timidity reigns. Even in established societies, existing institutions of freedom are not above challenge, but Habermas suspects here that the unrest has a deeper source, "namely, the sense that in the age of a completely secularized politics, the rule of law cannot be lived or maintained without radical democracy" (xlii). Again, here is a stunning admission with which I agree, but not in the sense that Habermas intends. Radical democracy, for me, is full economic, political, and cultural democracy in which capitalism is transformed and overturned. Habermas's sense of radical democracy is much more limited; namely, that private subjects enjoying equal liberties and exercising their political autonomy in common achieve clarity about justified interests and standards and agree about the relevant aspects under which equals should be treated equally and unequals unequally.[4]

Habermas's radical democracy, therefore, is pretty tame; his radical rhetoric is in tension with his commitment to a liberal, capitalistic status quo. But what if even this liberal version cannot be realized fully without overcoming capitalism? If, for example, capitalist control of media is essential to maintaining capitalistic hegemony, how can subjects achieve clarity in the face of manifestly skewed, biased presentations by mainstream media? We will pursue this issue further throughout the book, especially in chapter 7, on the public sphere.

While we have to credit Habermas for not giving in to a defeatism that is all too present, he gives in to his own kind of defeatism before advanced capitalism, concluding that the best we can do is tame and try to control it, not transform it. As a result, ethical-political reason functioning democratically has an extremely limited reach. The most that it can do is to try to democratize the public sphere and the legislature and indirectly affect the judiciary and administration; there is no possibility or even desirability of democratizing corporations and banks and changing their intrinsic injustice, domination, and exploitativeness. If this is not defeatism, I do not know what is.

"But moods—and philosophies in a melancholic 'mood', do not justify the defeatist surrender of the radical content of democratic ideals" (xlii–xliv). These are noble sentiments, and truer even than Habermas realizes. Even his defeatism does not justify the surrender of genuinely radical ideals. Could it be that his own self-contradictory liberalism, not wishing to go all the way with reason, contributes to this defeatism in himself and others? Does a socialist version of radical democracy offer a third alternative to unalloyed, cynical, postmodern defeatism and contradictory, liberal defeatism that claims to be hopeful but in fact gives in to the worst excesses of capitalist modernity?

LAW AS MEDIATING BETWEEN FACTS AND NORMS

The task of mediating between facticity and validity occurs in four different areas for Habermas. The first is the tension between the factual agreement of a community on a set of norms, laws, and policies and the ideal of validity possible in the unconstrained exercise of communicative action. The second is the tension between a taken-for-granted life-world consensus and the questioning of that arising in a modern communicative and strategic context. The third is the tension between law as factually, coercively enforcing obedience and law as being grounded and legitimated in communicative action. The fourth is the tension between a communicatively, constitutionally structured state and community and systems of money and power that interfere and impose their priorities from without, a "colonizing" of the communicative life-world.

Habermas contends that all four of these tensions are in principle compatible with capitalism, susceptible of mediation in a liberal rendering of capitalist modernity. I argue that there is a fifth tension, between capitalistic injustice and the moral demands of communicative reason. This tension is in fact a contradiction, is not resolvable, exacerbates the other four tensions, and points toward a future, fully just liberation based on a radical interpretation of modernity. This interpretation brings the liberal reading out of contradiction with itself, saves it from itself, realizes it. The radical interpretation saves Habermas from himself.

I agree with Habermas in his general attempt to redeem modernity and in his corresponding critique of postmodernism. He goes wrong, however, in his liberal, self-contradictory reading of modernity, which does not do justice to, and compromises, his own best insights. It may be that his impassioned defense of modernist reason against postmodernism motivates him to understate the pathology of modernity, rooted fundamentally in capitalism.[5]

Habermas begins his discussion of the first tension by reflecting on the difference between meaning and validity. Meaning as expressed in propositions is something general, identical with itself, publicly accessible, transcending individual consciousness, and ideal. In this sense, meaning is distinguishable from the particular, episodic, and merely private.

Meaning is also distinct from validity. Not only do we conceive universal propositions or concepts, but we also pronounce these right or wrong, true or false, moral or immoral, just or unjust. After I conceive Newton's laws or the theory of relativity as possibly true, I engage collaboratively with a community of scientists in a process of verification. When the experiments performed confirm the hypothesis, then it is true. It has ideal universality; it is true for any time or place, for any community, for any group of scientific observers (9–13).

Influenced by Peirce, Habermas then constructs the notion of any ideal, intersubjective validity, based upon the counterfactual concept of the final opinion, a consensus reached under ideal conditions. Validity claims raised here and now, in this community, can "overshoot" local standards of validity and truth, that is, standards that have been established in each local community of interpreters (14). The justice of racial segregation in the southern United States, for example, was brought into question by Fanny Lou Hamer being unwilling to give up her seat on the bus. The de facto segregation in the South was highlighted and brought into question in the light of the universal validity claims operative in the entire national and international speech community. The tacitly assumed equality between and among participants in the speech community calls into question the factual inequality between white and black.

The tension between facticity and validity built into the use of language is and can be a fruitful tension. Any factual consensus can be questioned. If it is a just consensus, then the questioning will confirm it; if it is an unjust consensus, arrived at through illegitimate coercion, exclusion, or violence, then communicative action can overturn it. This first tension between facticity and validity seems to be the most basic. Other tensions are built upon, and emerge from, it. Upon it rests the possibility of democracy, law, and justice in modern industrial societies.

A second tension is that between life-world and communicative action. The actual life-world is to communicative action as background to theme, implicit to explicit, taken-for-granted basis to action emerging from the basis. The life-world, we might say, in its perceptual linguistic meaning-fulness is the condition for the possibility of communicative praxis. Communicative praxis, on the other hand, is that which utilizes, thematizes, actualizes, and contributes to this life-world as a context of meaning. The discovery of electricity is now part of the taken-for-granted context of my life as I go to the bathroom, take a shower, and begin to shave.

When we consider the life-world in communicative theoretical terms, it has at least three aspects: naïve familiarity with an unproblematic background; validity of an intersubjectively shared world; and a blend of determinate and indeterminate, indefinite and limited, undefined and defined. A new worker in an office, for example, enters into a situation where there is unproblematic background knowledge: the validity of the enterprise, the availability of technical resources, the presence of certain customs. When she is asked to pick up sandwiches for the immediate group in the office, she may be unaware of the taken-for-granted custom that this task falls upon the newest members of the group. She may wish to question the premises and assumptions in a way that is in principle unlimited. Why is such a custom legitimate? Who began it? Why should she do it? What if she is one of two new workers and the other is male; is there sexism underlying the request? When she questions one of the assumptions, then something becomes a *theme* of discussion in relation to her *situation* in the world, her immediate relationship to her office mates. The indeterminacy and porosity of the life-world manifests itself not only in the unlimited range of assumptions, values, and attitudes that can be brought into question and thematized but also in the indeterminacy, perceptual and linguistic, of the life-world. The worker is in an office in a building, on Wall Street, in New York City, and so on.

When we proceed to a more concrete, serviceable concept of the life-world as sociologistic, three different aspects emerge. *Culture* is the stock of knowledge from which participants in communicative action supply themselves with interpretations in order to come to an understanding of the world. I draw on the history of modern art from impressionism through cubism to abstract expressionism to understand the recent work of Frank Stella, Nancy Graves, or Judy Pfaff. *Society* is the legitimate order through which participants regulate their membership in social groups and thereby achieve solidarity. The Constitution was used by the United States in this way to handle the crises of Watergate and Irangate. *Personality* is the sum of the competencies that make a subject capable of understanding and judging, speaking and acting, communicating and asserting his own identity. Certain abilities, traits, and competencies define me as Jim Marsh, American, Catholic, philosophical, neo-Marxist.[6]

Because the background knowledge upon which communicative action draws is tacit and taken for granted, the tension between facticity and validity is leveled out as far as that background knowledge itself is concerned. Archaic societies reduce the tension between life-world and communicative action by an authority that is at the same time compelling and binding. Once modern societies emerge, however, this solution is no longer possible. In the course of social evolution, the risk of dissension increases with the scope for taking yes/no positions on recognizable validity claims. Here the basic validity claims relate to truth about claims concerning the external world, sincerity concerning the relation of the uttering subject to its own claims, and appropriateness or rightness concerning the relation of one subject to another. Is it right or appropriate to order you to do something?

As social complexity increases, pluralized forms of life and individualization of life histories develop, while zones of unquestioned, overlapping life-worlds and shared background assumptions shrink. As disenchantment occurs, socialized belief complexes fall apart, under differentiated validity aspects, into thematizable content of a tradition that has come into question. When processes of social differentiation require multiplication and specification of tasks or roles, on the one hand, communicative action escapes narrowly circumscribed boundaries. On the other hand, social differentiation implies and requires the self-interested pursuit of one's own economic success and political power and influence (25).

The problem that emerges in modern societies is how the validity and legitimacy of a social order can be stabilized once communicative action becomes autonomous and strategic action oriented to self-interest begins to differ from communicative action oriented to reaching understanding. In premodern societies self-interested action was always limited by, or fused with, a normative order. In societies organized around a state, legal norms are already superimposed on a mature normative infrastructure, but even in these traditional societies the law fed upon the self-authorizing force of a religiously sublimated social realm. In medieval society, for example, the notion of a higher law was rooted in a sacred fusion of facticity and validity. The law made by the ruler was subordinated to the Christian natural law administered by the church (25–26).

In modern capitalistic societies, there is a danger that the integrating capacity of communicative action will be overtaxed, because traditions present in the life-world function less and less as the source of integration, and because forms of communicative action have become pluralized into aesthetic, moral, and scientific domains. Moreover, the role of strategic action is expanding in relation to communicative action; these are split into two distinct spheres, and we have a modern version of the facticity-validity split. For self-interested actors, all features of a situation are transformed into facts that they evaluate in the light of their own preferences. Actors oriented to reaching understanding, on the other hand, rely on a jointly negotiated understanding of a situation and interpret the relevant facts in the light of intersubjectively recognized validity claims. Consequently, norms suitable as socially integrating constraints must meet two contradictory conditions. They must, on the one hand, present de facto restrictions that alter relevant information and willingness to act in such a way as to compel people to behave in the objectively desired manner. On the other hand, they must have a socially integrating force by imposing obligation on the addressees (26–27).

At this point enter modern law, which at its core "consists of private rights that mark out the legitimate scope of individual liberties and are thus tailored to the strategic pursuit of private interests" (27). Modern law provides a system of rights that lends to individual liberties the coercive force of law. As coercive, such law has a factual dimension about it—"Do this or do not do this or else." As a system of rights, such law can be legitimated and redeemed through recourse to communicative action (27).

Because human beings are fundamentally oriented to communicative action, no society can be adequately or completely legitimated by recourse to coercive law. Nor is legitimation possible simply in terms of rights tailored to success-oriented action alone. Either the legal remains embedded in an encompassing social ethos and is subordinate to the authority of suprapositive or sacred law, or individual liberties are supplemented by rights of a different type, rights of citizenship geared no longer simply or primarily to strategic action but to autonomy in the Kantian sense. Since the former is no longer likely or possible, then the latter is the only possibility. The coercive law tailored for the self-interested use of individual rights can preserve its socially integrating force only insofar as the addressees of legal norms understand themselves as the rational authors of these norms (33).

Modern law in the modern state uses both strategies that have emerged historically to counter the risk of dissension and the risk of instability built into communicative action, strategies of circumscribing communication and of giving it free play. On the one hand, the state's guarantee to enforce the law offers a functional equivalent for the stabilization of behavioral expectations by spellbinding authority. Modern law allows convictions to be replaced by sanctions that leave open the motives for compliance with rules while enforcing observance. On the other hand, the combination of positivity and legitimacy in modern law takes into account and allows for the possibility of the unleashing of communication that exposes all norms and rules and principles to possible questioning. "Members of a legal community must be able to assume that in the free process of political opinion-and-will-formation they should also authorize the rules to which they are subject as addressees" (38).

Now I confess to finding something quite appealing and even correct about this claim made by Habermas. He is on to an important point about the relation of law to communicative action, democracy, and the dilemmas of modernity. I would distinguish here, however, between a radical interpretation of this claim and Habermas's liberal version. Can the legitimation deficit be made up if modern capitalistic societies and states are caught up in a contradiction between accumulation and legitimation, ultimately rooted in, as Habermas himself admits, class structure? For legitimation to obtain fully, would not that contradiction have to be removed in principle? And would not that removal imply overcoming the class nature of modern capitalistic societies?

This accumulation-legitimation tension, I take it, is not reducible to the first three: facticity-validity within communicative action, life-world and communicative action, and the communicative and coercive aspects of modern law. The accumulation-legitimation tension is a systematic contradiction within modern societies, and, as such, it indirectly indicates as well the moral problems with capitalism as an *essentially* unjust society. The morally consistent conclusion for Habermas to draw is that in a class-dominated, class-divided society, the moral demands of communicative action will not and cannot be fully realized. He comes close to this conclusion in *Legitimation Crisis* but backs away from it thereafter.[7]

The accumulation-legitimation crisis is an instance of one specific kind of crisis tendency in late capitalism, along with economic and rationality crises on the side of systems identity and a motivation crisis on the side of social identity. Capitalism will fall prey either to recessions and depressions (economic crises); to an economic crisis mediated by the state, such as the state's inability under President Carter to control unemployment and inflation simultaneously (rationality crisis); or, on the side of social identity, to a legitimation crisis or a crisis in motivation in that motives for accepting our socioeconomic system are falling away and new motives for resistance and critique are coming into play. *Systems identity* refers to society conceived in objectivistic terms as a well-running structure apart from human intentionality; *social identity* refers to society as forming conscious meaningful relationships within and between individuals and groups in that society.

In *Legitimation Crisis,* Habermas correctly expands Marxist crisis theory from economic crisis as the sole possibility of crisis to rationality, legitimation, and motivational crises. Another clear implication of this illuminating analysis, one which Habermas does not draw, is that capitalism is an essentially contradictory, tension-ridden socioeconomic system and that the way to resolve the tensions is to remove their basic cause, the class basis of capitalist society, and move to full economic, social, and political democracy.[8]

Yet, after *Legitimation Crisis,* for the most part (the accumulation-legitimation tension is mentioned in *The Theory of Communicative Action*),[9] this analysis of crisis drops out, and for it he substitutes the system–lifeworld tension. No reason or argument is given for such substitution, but the effect is to substitute a liberal, reformist reading of capitalist modernity for one that is radical, at least by implication, and one that does far more justice to the contradictory, messy, pathological character of capitalist modernity. Early, or earlier, Habermas is in tension with later Habermas here, and there is good reason to prefer the earlier, more progressive, more critical version. In any event, there is a gap in his argument with himself. His reasons for his change of mind, for what looks like a failure of nerve, are not given.

The final kind of facticity-validity tension, the tension between the lifeworld and system, is mentioned but not developed in chapter 1 of *Between Facts and Norms.* Habermas sees this tension as external; systems of money and power infringe on the legitimate legal order of modern societies and impose their alien logic. To expand on what he says, anonymous systems get in the way of the smooth functioning of democracy and full discussion between and among equals. Politics, for example, becomes the selling of the president through well-financed media campaigns; political action groups put pressure on the legislature to vote and enact laws that favor powerful, wealthy interests; foreign policy elites can decide to wage wars that may or may not be supported by the majority of the population; and universities, rather than being places to pursue the examined life, are seen by students and faculty as training grounds for making it in the corporate, administrative world. Universities become launching pads for Wall Street.[10]

Money and administrative power, Habermas suggests, are systematic mechanisms of integration that do not necessarily coordinate actions via the intentions of the participants but do so "objectively" behind their backs—for example, Adam Smith's "invisible hand" operating in the market. The economy, according to Smith, operates independently of, and sometimes contrary to, the intentions of the participants. The media of money and power are anchored via legal institutionalization in the life-world, which is then socially integrated through communicative action. Because law is just as entwined with money and administrative power as it is with communicative rationality, the legal system assimilates imperatives of diverse origins. Often enough, law provides illegitimate power with only a semblance of legitimacy. "At first glance, one cannot tell whether legal regulations deserve the assent of associated citizens or whether they result from administrative self-programming and structure social power in such a way that they independently generate the necessary loyalty" (40).

Incursion of system on life-world is certainly one form of capitalist irrationality and injustice, but what Habermas says does not go far enough. As a result, the first chapter sets us up for the essentially reformist solution that follows in the rest of the book. All that has to be done, can be done, and should be done is to beat back the colonizing effects of economic or administrative systems that have transgressed their natural boundaries, for, kept within their proper boundaries, these systems are rational and just. All of the discussion in *Legitimation Crisis* of crisis tendencies rooted in capitalism *as such* has dropped out. Late capitalism as a social system is essentially, in the mind of the later Habermas, benign. A critical theory that has its origins and inspiration in Marx ends not with a bang but with a whimper.

In other words, Habermas in this work makes it too easy for himself. He understates the pathology of late capitalism, while honestly, according to his own lights, facing up to the problems, even to the point of admitting empirically emergent tendencies that give trouble to his analysis. He understates that pathology not only in relation to his own earlier work but also by passing over at least four other forms of capitalist irrationality and injustice: economic exploitation in the workplace; tyranny of one life-world sphere over another; marginalization of the poor by the rich; and economic, political, and cultural domination—for example, rule by capital over labor in the workplace, or the enormous power of the rich and corporations in politics that keeps other, more progressive agendas from getting a hearing, or corporate media that give minimal or no play to viewpoints that challenge capitalist hegemony.[11]

These forms of injustice help to explain numerous phenomena, among them a massive and increasing rate of poverty, unemployment, hunger, and homelessness throughout the First and Third Worlds; a minimum of 20 million people die each year just from structurally induced starvation within the capitalist orbit. The rate of incarceration of blacks and of all races in the United States is several times higher than it was in South

Africa under apartheid. In the economic sphere, the top 2 percent in the United States doubled their income and wealth from 1973 to 1993, while those in the bottom 80 percent lost ground in terms of real income.[12]

Habermas understates such phenomena; his empirical basis is too narrow and superficial. But this empirical understating has an evidential and rhetorical point, namely, to give the impression that things are not too bad in the United States or Germany or other western capitalistic nations, that there is nothing amiss that a little reform and tinkering will not handle.

The empirical understating leads to an undertheorized account of capitalistic modernity. There is no mention, even to refute it, of the prison-industrial complex, a late-twentieth-century capitalist variant complementing the military-industrial complex. Prisons are used to warehouse blacks, Latinos, and poor persons, the majority of whom are arrested on relatively minor drug charges. Prison building was a major growth industry in the 1980s and 1990s in the United States, and corporations use prisoners as a source of cheap labor. Most big cities have very repressive law enforcement agencies, and beatings and killings by police officers occur with regularity. The destructive force of the death penalty is used disproportionately against blacks, Latinos, and the poor. And President George W. Bush, a self-described "compassionate conservative," presided over at least a hundred executions during his tenure as governor of Texas. How can we have serious discussion of law, morality, and democracy in western capitalist countries without discussing the prison-industrial complex? And yet the topic never sullies Habermas's pages, never interferes in the unfolding of his argument for an essentially just capitalist modernity. Such a complex is in blatant contradiction with Habermas's principles of moral and legal justice.

That capitalism is an economy of death is also shown by the military-industrial complex. The military functions as an enforcer of last resort, ensuring that the capitalist structure of worldwide exploitation continues unabated and that military spending continues at a very high rate, in spite of the tumbling of the Berlin Wall. The peace dividend has essentially failed to materialize, and the very high profits from military spending continue to pour into the coffers of capital.[13]

Let us, then, consider briefly the other forms of injustice not mentioned by Habermas. The first, and in some way the most basic, is the exploitation of labor by capital. If abstract labor time is the source of the value of the product as measured in money, then the profit based on surplus value, the value appropriated by the capitalist, can only come from surplus labor time, for which labor is not paid. Surplus value cannot arise in the sphere of circulation because exchange of equivalents occurs there. Consequently, it can arise only in the sphere of production. Here there are three possible sources of surplus value: instruments of production, materials of production, and labor. The first two, however, can only transfer their value and do not create new value. Labor, therefore, is the sole source of surplus value.[14]

Of course, value theory, on which the above argument is based, is not everybody's cup of tea and is contested by Habermas. I show elsewhere why I think such contestation is mistaken.[15] The point about exploitation, however, can be made independently of value theory. Massive statistical evidence, as I have already indicated, shows huge increases of wealth and income among the very wealthy, while the income of the bottom 80 percent of the population declined in real terms from 1973 to 1993, at a time when the productivity of labor rose. Such transfer of wealth and income occurs nonconsensually in a way that violates the imperatives of Habermas's communicative ethic; working people witness a transfer of wealth and income without their consent, and such wealth and income have been created chiefly through their own labor.

According to sixteen social health indicators, such as child abuse, child poverty, high-school dropout rates, and the gap in salary between rich and poor, U.S. social health fell steadily from 1990 to 1997. In 1997, the last year for which comprehensive data are available, the United States declined 1.3 percent to 46 out of a possible 100. Three indicators in 1997 reached their lowest level since 1970: health insurance, food stamp coverage, and the gap in income between the richest fifth and the poorest fifth. While gross domestic product grew by 113 percent, the income gap grew worse by 35 percent. It is not hard to conclude that the so-called Clinton boom was based on a deepening recession for the nonwealthy.[16]

That such a pattern of wealth-and-income transfer occurs as a general rule in the capitalist world can be shown even more graphically when the relation of the First World to the Third World is considered. In the 1980s there was a *transfer* of $200 billion dollars from Latin American to North American banks and corporations; yet during the same period the number of poor in Latin America grew by 40 million, an increase of over 50 percent. Third World populations are impoverished generally by the capitalist, with only a small capitalist elite benefiting significantly. Whether in the First World or the Third, labor and the poor are mere means to capitalist profit.[17]

Linked to exploitation in late capitalism is domination by capital over labor in the workplace. Labor does not willingly and consensually submit to the discipline of the workplace, but because it fears starvation, it does its work on capital's terms and because the sphere of production, as opposed to the sphere of circulation, is manifestly a science of coercion, as Marx makes clear:

> The sphere of circulation or commodity exchange, within whose boundaries the sale and purchase of labour-power goes, is in fact a very Eden of the innate rights of man. It is the exclusive realm of Freedom, Equality, Property, and Bentham. . . .
>
> When we leave this sphere of simple circulation or the exchange of commodities, which provides the "free trader vulgaris" with his views, his concepts and the standards by which he judges the society of capital and wage labour, a certain change takes place, or so it appears, in the physiognomy of our *dramatis personae.* He who was previously the money-owner strides out in front as a capitalist; the possessor of labour-power as his worker. The one smirks self-importantly and is intent on business; the other is timid and holds back, like someone who has brought his own hide to market and now has nothing else to expect but a tanning.[18]

As I will show more fully later, domination is shown not only in the workplace but also in the political realm, in which the rule of money imposed by corporations, political action committees, and special interest groups conspires to enforce a corporate agenda on the rest of the country in a way that violates the letter and spirit of democracy. In political campaigns the rule of money ensures that hardly anyone who challenges even in a mild way the hegemony of capital can get nominated or elected. In Congress the role of political action committees representing the rich and capital ensures decisions favorable to business and not so favorable to the rest of the population. Culturally, in the realm of media, advertising by big business exerts a constraint on news and programming, ensuring that views criticizing business hardly get a hearing and those sympathetic to business are disporportionately represented.[19]

A third category of injustice, in addition to exploitation and domination, is tyranny. I am using this term in Michael Walzer's sense of the illegitimate imposition of one sphere of the life-world (the social and natural environment of which we are aware in a first-person way) on another. Walzer's main example, although not the only one, is the imposition of the rule of the wealthy and corporations on politics and other spheres for which it is inappropriate: I may be the dumbest of human beings, but because I am a millionaire, I can buy intelligent politicians. I may be the least attractive of men, but because I am wealthy, I can buy for myself the most beautiful of women. I may be culturally stupid, but I can buy works of art. I may be the most tasteless of sponsors, but my being the head of a powerful corporation enables me to influence program content on radio or television.

Wealthy individuals or corporations intervene in spheres that are, or should be, only accidentally related to money. Why should money rather than political wisdom determine who gets elected? Why should money rather than being loving, intelligent, and caring enable mé to court and marry a beautiful woman? Why should money rather than artistic talent and taste give me access to works of art and influence over program content?[20]

A fourth kind of injustice is marginalization. Critical social theory here takes account of the concern for the marginalized often made much of by postmodernism but contextualizes that concern in a normative and hermeneutical framework that postmodernism disallows. Because profit is valued over human beings and because labor-saving technology is employed more as capitalism develops more and comes into its own, a tendency develops to produce a surplus population. Marx states the general law of capitalist accumulation as follows: "The greater the social wealth, functioning capital, the extent and energy of its growth, and therefore also the greater mass of that of the proletariat and productivity of its labor, the greater is the industrial reserve army." Capitalism structurally produces unemployment, poverty, homelessness, hunger, and disease. These are the effects of the original relationship of domination in the workplace, in which the worker is hired not for her own self-satisfaction and profit but for the capitalist's. From this relationship all bad things follow. Capital is a Moloch on whose altar the poor and oppressed are sacrificed.[21]

Who can doubt that this law continues today with increasing virulence and ruthlessness? Growing rates of poverty, unemployment, homelessness, and hunger make this clear. What is changed from the days of Marx's time is the much greater role of the state in mediating, or, one might say, administering, this general law of capitalist accumulation: the attacks on labor unions in western capitalist countries throughout the 1980s and 1990s, tax breaks disproportionately benefiting the rich and contributing to a redistribution of wealth upwards, and military spending that is unnecessary in terms of real human need.[22]

Exploitation within the workplace, tyranny, marginalization, domination, and colonization are best seen as expressions of an essentially unjust capitalist system. Here validity is not simply in tension with facticity but in flat contradiction to it. Habermas, however, by not recognizing such injustice as a distinct level, gives the impression that all contradictions can be smoothed out and resolved into a harmonious capitalist present and future.

Nevertheless, *Between Facts and Norms* seems to catch something about

capitalist modernity. Habermas gives us a way of theorizing law in relation to communicative praxis, democracy, and systems of money and
power. Yet he fails to see the way the positive aspects of capitalist modernity contradict *essentially* the negative aspects. This contradiction cannot
be smoothed out by a liberal adaptation to capitalist modernity, by simply
pushing back into their proper orbits the influence of money and power.
What Habermas's book actually reveals—the contradictory nature of capitalist modernity—is different from, indeed in contradiction to, what he
intends to reveal about the benign character of this modernity. But this
contradictory revelation makes *Between Facts and Norms* a more valuable
book.

Moreover, and finally, I reject the internal-external dichotomy between
system and life-world. Since Habermas projects no revolutionary transformation of corporations such as NBC and CBS, which dominate the
public sphere; they are essential in his liberal version of capitalist modernity, and in behaving the way they do, they are not acting beyond their
own proper domain at all. To have an effectively functioning public
sphere, these corporations would have to be eliminated, become
nonessential in a way that raises difficulties for his defense of the status
quo. By this external-internal contrast, Habermas again makes it too easy
for himself.

NOTES

1. Jürgen Habermas, *Between Facts and Norms*, trans. William Rehg (Cambridge: MIT Press, 1996), xl–xli. Page numbers in parentheses throughout this
chapter refer to this book.

2. John Rawls, *A Theory of Justice* (Cambridge: Harvard University Press,
1971). Paul Ricoeur, *Oneself as Another*, trans. Kathleen Blamey (Chicago: University of Chicago Press, 1992). James L. Marsh, *Critique, Action, and Liberation*
(Albany: State University of New York Press, 1995).

3. See my argument to this effect in *Critique, Action, and Liberation*, 132–47.

4. Marsh, *Critique, Action, and Liberation*, 166–76, 313–30.

5. Jürgen Habermas, *The Philosophical Discourse of Modernity*, trans. Fred
Lawrence (Cambridge: MIT Press, 1987).

6. Marsh, *Critique, Action, and Liberation*, 245–47. Jürgen Habermas, *The Theory of Communicative Action*, vol. 2, *Lifeworld and System: The Critique of Functionalist
Reason*, trans. Thomas McCarthy (Boston: Beacon Press, 1987), 136–44.

7. Jürgen Habermas, *Legitimation Crisis*, trans. Thomas McCarthy (Boston:
Beacon Press, 1975), 92–94.

8. Habermas, *Legitimation Crisis*, 1–17, 47–94.

9. Habermas, *Critique of Functionalist Reason*, 344–45.

10. For the university as an example of colonization, see Marsh, *Critique, Action, and Liberation,* 254–60.

11. See *Critique, Action, and Liberation,* for my development of these forms, 266–89.

12. James L. Marsh, *Process, Praxis, and Transcendence* (Albany: State University of New York Press, 1999), 266–97. Holly Sklar, *Chaos or Community* (Boston: South End Press, 1995), 17–34. Jack Nelson-Pallmeyer, *Brave New World Order* (Maryknoll, N.Y.: Orbis Books, 1992), 202.

13. Marsh, *Process, Praxis, and Transcendence,* 172–73, 280–82.

14. Marsh, *Critique, Action, and Liberation,* 267. Karl Marx, *Capital,* vol. 1, trans. Ben Fowkes (New York: Vintage, 1977), 125–31, 258–69.

15. James L. Marsh, *Post-Cartesian Meditations* (New York: Fordham University Press, 1988), 234–35 n. 33. Marsh, *Critique, Action, and Liberation,* 392–94 n. 8.

16. Paul L. Street, "The Economy Is Doing Fine, It's Just the People That Aren't," *Z Magazine,* November 2000, 30.

17. Marsh, *Process, Praxis, and Transcendence,* 266–67.

18. Marx, *Capital,* 280.

19. Marsh, *Critique, Action, and Liberation,* 280–82, 291–308. Marsh, *Process, Praxis, and Transcendence,* 303–8.

20. Marsh, *Critique, Action, and Liberation,* 168. Michael Walzer, *Spheres of Justice* (New York: Basic Books, 1983), 295–303. Karl Marx, *The Economic and Philosophic Manuscripts of 1844,* ed. Dirk Struick, trans. Martin Milligan (New York: International Publishers, 1964), 165–69.

21. Marx, *Capital,* 798.

22. Marsh, *Critique, Action, and Liberation,* 270–74.

3

On Mediating Private and Public Autonomy: The Genesis of Rights

Let us briefly recapitulate. In chapter 1 I developed a hypothesis, whose basic thesis is that there is a contradiction between basic tenets of Habermas's philosophy of law and his support of capitalism. In chapter 2 we reflected on the tension between facticity and validity, showing that to defend this tension as a fruitful one, Habermas has to understate the pathology of capitalist modernity; conceptual consistency is achieved at the cost of empirical adequacy. Moreover, we saw another facticity-validity tension develop, that between justice and injustice. This is not a tension between reconcilable opposites, but between contradictories, in relation to which we have to choose.

Chapters 2 and 3 of *Between Facts and Norms* are, like the portions already discussed, a flawed achievement. Chapter 2, "The Sociology of Law and the Philosophy of Justice," reflects the disagreement that occurs between third-person, objectivistic versions of the sociology of law and first-person-oriented versions of the philosophy of justice. This debate finally works itself out in a tension between system and life-world, briefly mentioned in the first chapter of *Between Facts and Norms* and familiar to readers of *The Theory of Communicative Action*.[1]

For Habermas, both approaches are inadequate and need to be mediated. A two-tiered conception of society and law and justice is required. On the one hand, approaches such as Luhmann's that emphasize, or reduce all to, system are in the end not able to account for certain phenomena, such as the communicative interaction between and among action subsystems like economy and state and the necessity, finally, for citizens to have recourse in a first-person, life-worldly way to ordinary language to resolve disputes and mediate between subsystems. Theorists of justice like Rawls, on the other hand, do not do sufficient justice to the reality of systems, the way they are institutionalized, and the unsettling side effects the colonization of the life-world by system can have on a society attempting to function democratically and justly.[2]

What is necessary is a two-tiered conception of society as encompassing both system and life-world. This conclusion, defended earlier in *The Theory of Communicative Action,* will not be surprising to devoted readers of Habermas. Law in modern societies acts as a bridge between system and life-world. Rooted in the life-world, law institutionalizes systems of money and power that are inevitable in modernity and that can function beneficially or destructively. This claim about the function of law in modern societies is an important insight; it has implications unforeseen and unappreciated by Habermas. Law will not be able to mediate adequately between unjustly institutionalized capitalist systems of money and power and the life-world. Habermas too quickly and too easily elides the distinction between system and life-world as such and unjust institutionalization of systems, between just and unjust systems of money and power. Law could only perform its mediating function adequately in a society that is just in principle, a fully democratic socialist society (75–76).[3]

In the course of his discussion of the sociology of law and the origins of injustice, Habermas says that only reform is possible and legitimate. The passage is worth noting in full: "At stake is the old problem of how the rational project of a just society, in abstract contrast to obtuse reality, can be realized after confidence in the dialectic of reason and revolution, played out by Hegel and Marx as a philosophy of history, has been exhausted—and only the reformist path of trial and error remains both practically available and morally permissible" (57). This quotation occurs in the context of discussing how the issue of the possibility of a just society returns in the thought of John Rawls.

With such a claim about reformism, I have several problems. Why would the "failures" of Marx and Hegel and their forms of revolutionary theory and practice imply the necessary failure of all such attempts? Even if one does not, as I do not, accept the idea of a teleologically ordered philosophy said by Habermas to be present in the philosophies of Marx and Hegel, why could one not separate out Marx's critique of capitalism as unjust and irrational and his argument for full economic, political, and cultural democracy—communism in Marx's terms or democratic socialism in ours—as I and others do? If, as Habermas probably has in mind, the failure of socialism and communism in Eastern Europe is salutary, why does that failure imply the failure of socialism and communism as such?

Indeed, if the eastern European model of socialism is flawed in many different ways, why does the failure of this version imply the invalidity of socialism and communism as such? And does Habermas even have a suspicion that such a version is not even close to the version Marx defended in his works early and late? Indeed, Marx probably turned over in his grave at what was done in his name, at the technocratic, totalitarian, oppressive interpretation of what he intended to be an egalitarian democracy, indeed leading to the elimination of the state. Moreover, is not a decentralized, democratic market socialism possible, overcoming capitalism in principle but respecting and incorporating the system–life-world distinction? Finally, if capitalism is genuinely unjust, as I think it is, then reformism is a moral cop-out, as problematic as a white person saying in the slave-ridden South that a democratic slavery is the best we can do and we must simply beat back or ameliorate the unsettling side effects of the system of slavery. Would any self-respecting black accept such a claim? Is not a revolutionary stance in such a situation the more ethically and politically adequate stance? And if it is indeed clear that revolution now is not on the agenda, is not "practically available," then is not the appropriately moral thing to do to create conditions for revolution, reforms in the short run that point toward revolution and transformation in the long run? And if, as I am, Habermas is worried about the violent, terroristic nature of some revolutions, why is that nature inevitable or necessary? Why cannot revolutions be all or mostly nonviolent, rooted in popular consensus? And if they are violent, why can the violence not be kept under moral and communicative control? Examples that come to mind are the fall of the regimes in Eastern Europe, the Nicaraguan revolution in 1979–80, and, further back, the American Revolution, which was much more democratic, communicative, and consensual than the terror-ridden French Revolution.

Even Marx was not in favor of violent, terroristic revolutions. Terror and violence for Marx are manifestations of the failure of a revolution, because it has become nondemocratic and nonconsensual. For Marx, the motto was "nonviolent if possible, violent if necessary." But violence was always to be kept under the control and limits of democratically rooted consensus.[4]

In the third chapter, "A Reconstructive Approach to Law I," Habermas's basic concern is to show why private and public autonomy, human rights and popular sovereignty, mutually presuppose one another (84). He attempts in this chapter, with a fair amount of success, to reconcile private and public law at a conceptual level. There is a tension between human rights and popular sovereignty because of premises inherited from the philosophy of consciousness, rooted in the isolated Cartesian human subject as a basis of philosophy, jurisprudence, and social contract theory.

PRIVATE AND PUBLIC AUTONOMY:
HISTORICAL CONSIDERATIONS

Habermas often elucidates his own position in the light of a dialectic between opposed positions. We have seen him do this already in his first chapter with the tension of facticity and validity and with the system–life-world opposition. His own position often emerges as a dialectical resolution of the tension between opposites. Thus a communicatively grounded concept of law emerges as the resolution of the facticity-validity tension, and law as a mediator between system and life-world as a resolution of that tension. In the third chapter, the genesis of rights grounded in communicative action will resolve the tension that has emerged historically in the theory and practice of democracies between private and public autonomy.

Habermas begins to get at this issue by talking about the way the paradoxical emergence of legitimacy out of legality must be explained by means of the rights that secure for citizens the exercise of their political autonomy. Why paradoxical? Subjective rights, individual freedom of action for citizens, manifests the same structure as all rights that grant spheres of free choice to the individual. Political rights, too, are subjective liberties making lawful behavior a duty and leaving open the motives for conforming to norms. Yet, the procedure of democratic legislation confronts participants with the normative expectation of behavior oriented to the common good. Subjective liberty is not merely subjective and private but is socially and democratically mediated. The procedure of democratic legislation has its legitimating force only from a process in which citizens reach an understanding about the rules for their living together. In modern societies, law can stabilize behavioral expectations only if it preserves an internal connection with the socially integrating force of communicative action. Habermas aims to elucidate the puzzling connections between private liberties and public autonomy with the help of the discourse concept of law; the meaning of this concept will emerge in this chapter. This connection illumines and resolves a stubborn problem arising in two different contexts, jurisprudence and social contract theory (82–84).

In German civil law jurisprudence, the theory of subjective right was initially influenced by the idealist philosophy of right. According to Savigny, a legal relation secures the power justly pertaining to the individual person, an area over which his own will rules with our consent. Here the connection between individual liberty and intersubjective recognition by legal consociates is operative. As analysis proceeds, however, an intrinsic value begins to pertain to private law, independently of its authorization by a democratic legislature. For George Friedrich Puchta, too, law was essentially subjective or private law, the recognition belonging to all human beings as subjects with power of will. Rights are negative rights, the right against unpermitted intervention by the state into the freedom, life, and property of the individual. Private autonomy is secured in such legally protected spheres mostly through contract and property rights (84–85).

In the later nineteenth century, awareness grew that private law could be legitimated only by private autonomy having a foundation in the moral autonomy of the person. Once law lost its idealist grounding in such a conception, rooted mostly in Kant's moral philosophy, the individual power to rule could not ground itself in the moral autonomy of the person. After this bond was severed, individual rights were seen as refluxes of an established legal order that transferred to individuals the power of will objectively incorporated into law. Idealistic normative grounding in the individual gave way to the positivistic, legal grounding in the legal order of the state (85).

Such an objective grounding of right runs a certain course from von Ihering's utilitarian interpretation, in which utility and not will makes up the substance of right; to Kelsen, who characterizes individual rights as interests objectively protected by law and detaches the legal concept of the person not only from the moral but also from the natural person; to the nadir of a systems theory such as Luhmann's that rids itself by methodological fiats of all normative considerations. After fascism in World War II, there was a reaction to the dethronement of the legally and morally entitled individual and a rebirth of natural law, which attempted to restore the connection between private and moral autonomy. Such a rebirth, however, proved not to be convincing, because it ended up rehabilitating the individualistically truncated understanding of rights, which in turn invited a functionalist interpretation of private law as the framework for capitalist social relations (86–87).

In opposition to this teaching, Raiser drew on social law to correct the individualistic approach and to restore to private law its moral, social content. Subjective right needs to be augmented by social right, so that the individual is integrated by law into an ordered network of relationships surrounding him and binding him to others. Raiser's reinterpretation of private law through a shift from early bourgeois formal law, stressing the private rights of the individual against the state, to the materialized law of the welfare state is insufficiently abstract. His reinterpretation cannot and should not be confused with a revision of the basic concepts and principles, which have remained the same and have simply been interpreted differently in different contexts (87–88).

Habermas notes that Raiser reminds us of the intersubjective nature of rights, which the individualistic reading had rendered unrecognizable. Taken by themselves, rights do not imply the atomism that Raiser wants to correct, but rather flow from the citizens who mutually grant one another equal rights and at the same time as private persons use rights strategically and encounter one another competitively as potential opponents. At a conceptual level, civil rights presuppose collaboration among subjects who recognize one another as free and equal citizens in reciprocally related rights and duties. In such mutual recognition, subjective rights emerge co-originally with objective law. A statist understanding of objective law is also misleading, because this first issues from rights that individuals mutually acknowledge (88–89).

Both the idealistic concept of private law and legal positivism conceal the real problem connected with the issue of private rights; the source from which enacted law may draw its legitimacy is not explained. This source is the democratic lawmaking process, which calls on the principle of popular sovereignty. Legal positivism does not introduce this principle in such a way as to preserve the intrinsic moral content of classical liberties. "In one way or another, the intersubjective meaning of legally defined liberties is overlooked, and with it the relation between private and civic autonomy in which both moments receive their full due" (89).

Human rights and the principle of popular sovereignty, as this brief reflection on the history of jurisprudence shows, are the sole means that can justify modern law. They are the precipitate left behind once the normative substance of an ethos embedded in metaphysical and religious traditions has been subject to postmetaphysical criticism and justification. To the extent that moral and ethical questions are distinguished from one another (the moral being the universal prescription of a communicative praxis that is self-reflexive and the ethical being the set of norms, principles, and values expressed in particular traditions), they find expression in the dimensions of self-determination and self-realization. Although we cannot simply align these dimensions with human rights and popular sovereignty, affinities exist between the two pairs of concepts. Borrowing from discussions in the United States, we could say that "liberal" traditions conceive human rights as the expression of moral self-determination, and "civic republicanism" interprets popular sovereignty as the expression of ethical self-realization. From both perspectives, human rights and popular sovereignty do not so much complement one another as compete with one another. And from Habermas's dialectical perspective, they should complement one another. To show how they do is one of the aims of the rest of this chapter (99).

Frank Michelman, a legal theorist, sees in the American constitutional tradition a tension between the impersonal rule of law founded on innate human rights and the spontaneous self-organization of a community that makes its law through the sovereign will of the people. Such a tension can be resolved from one side or the other. Liberals, on the one hand, fear the danger of the tyrannical majority and postulate the priority of human rights guaranteeing the prepolitical liberty of the individual and setting limits to the sovereign will of the political legislator. The proponents of civic republicanism, on the other hand, stress the intrinsic noninstrumentable value of civic self-organization, and human rights are seen to be binding on a community only to the extent that they are elements of its own consciously appropriated tradition.

On the liberal view, rights impose themselves on our moral insight as something given in a prepolitical state of nature; according to republicanism, the ethical-political will of a self-actualizing collectivity is forbidden to recognize any right not corresponding to its own authentic life project. In one instance, the moral-cognitive predominates, in the other, the ethical-volitional. Kant and Rousseau, by way of contrast, conceive autonomy as unifying practical reason and sovereign will in such a way that human rights and popular sovereignty mutually interpret one another. Nonetheless, neither of these authors succeeds in fully integrating these concepts. Kant's is more of a liberal, Rousseau's more of a republican, reading (100).

Kant obtains the universal principle of law by applying the moral principle to external relations. He begins his *Elements of Justice* with one right owed to each human being by virtue of his humanity, the right to equal individual liberties backed up by authorized coercion. This primordial right regulating "internal property," when applied to external property, yields just the private right of the individual. This system of natural rights belongs inalienably to each human being as a human being and is legitimate prior to its expression in the shape of positive law. Such a system is conceived on the basis of moral principle and hence independently of that political autonomy of citizens first constituted in the social contract. Hence, private rights as moral rights are as such in a state of nature prior to any government or social contract. Political autonomy must be explained on the basis of the internal connection, accomplished in the social contract, between popular sovereignty and human rights. Because the path Kant follows is from morality to law, he must deny to the social contract the central position it has in the thought of Rousseau (100–101).

Rousseau starts with the constitution of civic autonomy as an internal link between popular sovereignty and human rights. Because the sovereign will of the people can express itself only in the language of general and abstract laws, the right of each person to equal liberties is necessarily present. Rather than being prepolitical as they are in Kant, human rights emerge in the constitution of the state. The united will of the citizens is bound, through such abstract laws, to a legislative procedure that in principle excludes all nongeneralizable interests and admits only regulations guaranteeing equal liberties for all. Rousseau, however, does not consistently follow through on this idea, because he owes more to the republican tradition than does Kant.

Rousseau gives the idea of self-legislation more of an ethical than a moral interpretation to the extent that he conceives political autonomy as the realization of the consciously apprehended form of life of a particular people. He counts on political virtues that are anchored in the ethos of a small, homogeneous community. If, however, the practice of self-legislation must feed off the ethical substance of a people who already agree on their value orientations, Rousseau cannot explain how the postulated orientation of the citizens toward the common good can be mediated with the rights of private persons. How can the normatively construed common will be mediated, without coercion, with the free choice of individuals? Where is the universalistic perspective of human rights that makes it impossible for a majority to oppress a minority in the name of a common good and a common, particular set of values? The ethical version of popular sovereignty must lose sight of the universalistic meaning of Kant's principle of law (101–2).

Rousseau's mistake is to think that the normative content of original right can be captured by a grammar of general and abstract laws alone. Yet it is clear that substantive legal equality cannot be explained by the semantic properties of general laws, because the form of universal normative propositions says nothing about their general validity. The claim that a norm lies equally in the interest of everyone is rationally acceptable because all of those possibly affected should be able to accept the norm on the basis of good reasons. Such acceptability can become clear only under pragmatic conditions of rational discourse in which the only thing that counts is the compelling force of the better argument based on the relevant information. The internal connection between popular sovereignty and human rights lies in the normative content of the very mode of exercising political autonomy, which is not secured simply through the grammatical form of general laws but only through the communicative process of opinion-and-will-formation (102–3).

Both Kant and Rousseau miss this internal connection. Kant misses it because he thinks the capacity for self-determination bringing reason and will together can only be found in a subject originally present prepolitically. Rousseau misses it because he ascribes such autonomy to the macrosubject of a people or nation, in which the human rights of individuals can only be protected by the nondiscriminatory form of general laws. "Both conceptions miss the legitimating force of a discursive process of opinion-and-will-formation, in which the illocutionary binding forces of a use of language oriented to mutual understanding serve to bring reason and will together—and lead to convincing positions to which all individuals can agree without coercion" (103).

Because the sought-for internal relation between popular sovereignty and human rights consists in the fact that the system of rights states precisely the conditions under which the forms of communication necessary for the genesis of legitimate law can be legally institutionalized, the system of rights can be reduced neither to a moral reading of human rights nor to an ethical reading of popular sovereignty. The reason is that the private autonomy of citizens can be neither set above, nor made subordinate to, their political autonomy. Rather, they emerge co-originally when we decipher, in discourse theoretic terms, the motif of self-legislation according to which the addressees of law are simultaneously the authors of their rights (104).

An implication of the above analysis is that positive law is not subordinated to moral law as Kant and others are wont to do. Rather, in a postmetaphysical level of justification, legal and moral rules are simultaneously differentiated from traditional ethical life and appear side-by-side as two different but complementary kinds of action norms. Correspondingly, then, the concept of practical reason must be understood so abstractly that it can assume a different meaning depending on which kind of norm is in question, a moral principle or the legal meaning of democracy (105).

Kant proceeds differently. He starts with the concept of the moral law and obtains juridical laws from it by way of limitation. Moral theory supplies the overarching concepts such as free will and free choice; law and legislation serve in the first place to characterize moral judgment and action. In legal theory, these basic moral concepts undergo limitations in three dimensions: in not referring primarily to free will but to the free choice of the addressees, in pertaining to the external relations of one person to another, and finally in being furnished with coercive power. Moral legislation is reflected in juridical legislation, morality in legality, and duties of virtue in legal duties (105–6).

This construction of Kant's is guided by the Platonic insight that the legal order imitates the noumenal order of the "kingdom of ends" and embodies it in the phenomenal world. This intuition is not entirely false, for a legal order can be legitimate only if it does not contradict basic moral principles, and, because of the legitimating components of legal validity, positive law has a reference to morality inscribed within it. But this reference should not mislead us into ranking morality above law, as though there were a hierarchy of norms. Rather, morality and law stand in a complementary relationship (106).

From a normative point of view, that moral and civic autonomy are co-original can be explained by recourse to a parsimonious discourse principle that merely expresses the meaning of postconventional requirements of justification. This discourse principle, D, takes the following form: Just those action norms are valid to which all possibly affected persons could agree as participants in rational discourses. "Valid" pertains to action norms and all general normative propositions following from them. Normative validity is understood in a nonspecific sense that is indifferent to the distinction between morality and legitimacy. "Action norms" are temporally, socially, and substantively generalized behavior expectations. By "those affected," we are to understand anyone whose interests are touched by foreseeable consequences of a general practice regulated by the norms at issue. "Rational discourse" includes any attempt to reach an understanding over problematic validity claims insofar as this attempt takes place under conditions of communication enabling the free processing of topics, contributions, information, and reasons in the public constituted by illocutionary obligations. The expression refers indirectly to bargaining processes to the extent that these are regulated by discursively grounded procedures (107–8).

The moral principle and the legal principle differ first of all in their reference. The moral principle first results when one specifies the general principle for those norms that can be justified if and only if equal consideration is given to all the interests of all who are possibly involved. Its reference system is the republic of world citizens. The principle of democracy results from a corresponding specification for those action norms that appear in legal form. Such norms can be justified by calling on pragmatic, ethical-political, and moral reasons, and the form of a particular political community is the reference system. Legal norms express the authentic self-understanding of this community, which includes the totality of social or subcultural groups that are indirectly involved in reaching agreements. All groups, rich or poor; Protestant, Catholic, Jewish, or atheist; women, men, gays, or lesbians; and black, white, brown, or yellow, are actual or possible participants in such self-understanding, which can take the form of agreement of principle or a compromise reached under fair bargaining positions and rational balancing of interests (108).

Legal norms are distinguished by their artificial character from moral principles and other action norms. They are a recent product of social evolution. In contrast to natural or quasi-natural rules, whose validity is to be judged solely from a moral point of view, legal norms are an intentionally produced layer of norms that are reflexive, or applicable to themselves. Hence the principle of democracy must not only specify a procedure of legitimate lawmaking, but it must also steer the production of the legal medium itself. There are thus two tasks a system of rights must accomplish: it must institutionalize the communicative framework for rational political will-formation, and it must ensure the very medium in which alone this will-formation can express itself as the common will of freely associated moral persons (111).

The formal characteristics of the medium of law can be unfolded by means of the complementary relation between law and morality. Following Kant, Habermas describes the legal medium through three abstractions referring to the addressees of a law. Law abstracts, first, from the capacity of the addressees to bind their will morally of their own accord, because it assumes that free choice is a sufficient source of law-abiding behavior. Such behavior can be based not only on moral reasons but also on strategic reasons such as fear and reluctance to get caught breaking the law. Second, the law abstracts from the complexities that action plans owe to their life-world contexts, restricting itself to the external relations that take place between social actors. Third, law abstracts from the kind of motivation; it is sufficient that action conform to rules (112).

Because the movement from knowledge to action is uncertain on a merely moral level, on account of the moral action's highly abstract system of self-control and the vicissitudes of socialization processes promoting such demanding moral competencies, law engages the actor's motives in a way other than internalization. If one breaks the law, she will be punished. There are external sanctions operative that regulate external behavior, and these thus complement the system of morality. Law makes up for the indeterminacy of morality because it spells out precise rules. Law also provides a way for morality to extend to all spheres of action, including those media-steered interactions in which participants are unburdened of all moral expectations other than general obedience to law (114–16).

THE GENESIS OF RIGHTS

As Habermas understands it, the principle of democracy emerges from the linking of the discourse principle and legal form. Neither by itself is sufficient. One begins by applying the discourse principle to the general right to liberties, a right constitutive for the legal form as such, and ends up legally institutionalizing the conditions for a discursive exercise of political autonomy. By means of this political autonomy, the private autonomy that was first abstractly posited can retroactively assume an elaborated legal shape. The principle of democracy, it is clear, can only appear within the heart of a system of rights. The genesis of these rights is a circular procedure in which the legal code and the democratic process for producing legitimate law are co-originally posited (121–22).

The presentation of rights moves from abstract to concrete:

1. Basic rights that result from the politically autonomous elaboration of the right to the greatest possible measure of equal individual liberties.

These rights have the following necessary corollaries:

2. Basic rights that result from the politically autonomous elaboration of the status of a member in a voluntary association of consociates under law.
3. Basic rights that result immediately from the actionability of right and from the politically autonomous elaboration of individual legal protestation (122).

These three rights generate and define the legal code as such. They result from the application of the discourse principle to the medium of law as such. They are not to be understood as liberal rights against the state, because the state has not been constituted yet. Rather those rights regulate the relationships among freely associated citizens prior to any legally organized state authority. Such a state authority will come later and presumes the already constituted legal medium, discourse principle, and democratic principle. The state, we can say, in Habermas's argument is derivative from, and dependent on, these principles and serves them and helps to realize them and render them concrete in a way that was not fully clear in the social contract theory that moves from Machiavelli and Hobbes through Locke and Kant to Rousseau (122).

4. Basic rights to equal opportunities to participate in processes of opinion-and-will-formation and in which citizens exercise their political autonomy and through which they generate legitimate law.
5. Basic rights to the provision of living conditions that are socially, technologically, and ecologically safeguarded, insofar as the current circumstances make this necessary if citizens are to have equal opportunities to utilize the civil rights listed in 1 through 4 (123).

Habermas makes some further comments that elucidate this system of rights. First, unlike most rules, legal rules govern the interaction of subjects in a concrete, particular society. The discourse principle implies that no one can be unilaterally deprived of membership rights but must be guaranteed the freedom to renounce the status of a member. Second, institutionalization of the legal code requires guaranteed legal remedies through which any person, feeling her rights have been infringed upon, can assert her claims. In the light of the discourse principle, one can justify basic rights of due process providing all persons with equal legal protection, an equal claim to a legal hearing, equality in application of law, and thus equal treatment before the law.

Third, the general right to equal liberties, along with the correlative membership rights and guaranteed legal remedies, establishes the legal code as such. There is no legitimate law without these rights. Nonetheless, we still do not have the familiar liberal basic rights, because we do not yet have a state and because the legal code at this point is unsaturated, indeterminate, and unspecified. On the one hand, basic rights must be given concrete shape by a political legislature in response to changing circumstances. On the other hand, particular rights such as personal dignity or life, liberty, and bodily integrity function to establish a legal code only if they can be seen as explicating the legal categories listed above. More particularly, rights derived specify and render concrete the legal code; that legal code, however, grounds and legitimates these more particular rights.

Fourth, the system of rights is not given to the framing of a particular constitution in advance as natural law; rather, rights are constituted in particular constitutional interpretations. Finally, by securing private and public autonomy in a balanced manner, the system of rights operationalizes the tension between facticity and validity. Both moments combine in the mutual penetration of legal form and discourse principle, positivity and legitimacy, coerciveness and appeal to good reasons flowing from the exercise of democracy (124–29).

What are we to make critically of Habermas's argument so far? At first glance, his argument has much to recommend it. I am persuaded by his argument for the importance—indeed, the necessity—of law for the constitution of modern democratic societies. Habermas's argument here presents a powerful challenge to any leftist, anarchist arguments against the law or against the state. The entwining of the discourse principle, democracy, and law is necessary: No adequate law without democracy, no full democracy without law.

Habermas has gone a long way in principle toward overcoming the dichotomy between private right and public right, liberalism and republicanism, private autonomy and public autonomy. That human reason in communicative praxis constitutes itself as both individual and social, private and public, in creating, sustaining, and living in a constitutional democracy is undoubtedly true.

I am less convinced that principles 4 and 5 adequately extend, express, and articulate fully consistently principles 1, 2, and 3. Both principles ultimately, implicitly or explicitly, take a bourgeois form that endangers the synthesis and balance between private and public freedom, individual rights and social solidarity. Because capitalism is essentially anticommunal, as money becomes the real mind and community of social interaction, finally in Habermas's theory the balance between private and public achieved abstractly and theoretically in principle tips over into subordination of the latter to the former. Such an abstract synthesis points beyond the present to a fully democratic society, which late capitalism is not and cannot be.

Let us look at principle 4: basic rights to equal opportunities to participate in processes of opinion-and-will-formation in which the citizens exercise their political autonomy and through which they generate legitimate law. Here one key word is "political," a term that seems to (and as further pages make clear, does) exclude socioeconomic and sociocultural autonomy and democracy. What is being secured here is that political rights must guarantee participation in all deliberative and decisional processes relevant to legislation (127). What is excluded here is a similar right to participate in the decisions made by an economic firm or sociocultural institution such as an art museum. Why does Habermas do this? Would a city, state, or nation constituting itself democratically similarly restrict the meaning of democracy, putatively universal, to just one possible political form? Has not Habermas tacitly "capitalized" the participation principle here in a way that belies the full, principled openness of communicative action to all possibilities offered, all arguments advanced, and all viewpoints expressed? If we are fully open, then why not consider the democratic socialist possibility, argument, and viewpoint?[5]

One might argue in his defense, of course, that this reflection on economic or sociocultural democracy would, or should, come later in the working out of the details of constitutional state. But the question is, then, why privilege the political over the economic and sociocultural? Does that privileging reflect a capitalist liberal bias? Would a community constituting itself similarly privilege the political, or would it see political participation as complementing, and being complemented by, economic and sociocultural participation? In fact, the issue of economic and sociocultural democracy does not come up later in *Between Facts and Norms*.

So the question remains, Would not the appropriate fourth principle be one that respected democracy in its full scope rather than limiting it in an arbitrary way to the political? If one wants to limit it in this way, should not a reason or argument be given, in the light of a communicative orientation to the better argument? Or, slightly less desirable, one could leave democracy unspecified, open to various political, economic, and social embodiments, and what those are would come out in further debates on the constitution. Nor is it a defense of Habermas to say that he is simply *realistically* respecting what is being done now in western democracies, because his own communicative ethic warns us about the danger of false consensus. Is the realistic consensus that liberal democracy is the best we can do a true or false consensus? The only way to find that out would be to consider all possibilities, capitalist, anticapitalist, and socialist, in the context of the ideal speech situation. Is bourgeois realism rational, or is it, as Marcuse many years ago argued, simply one-dimensional thought reflecting and legitimating an irrational, unjust society? Because of the utopian character of Habermas's communicative praxis, he has no right to invoke realism at this point. Any so-called realistic consensus, in one capitalist country or in them all, has to be brought before the bar of communicative reason.[6]

Now one could say, in defending Habermas, that he has not adequately argued for this position here, but there may be other books in which he does or from which arguments could be drawn that would make his case more plausible. This recourse to other books is double-edged. I have already pointed how other books, in which the accumulation-legitimation conflict is discussed, seem to be in flat contradiction to the capitalist position endorsed here. And what could these other books and other arguments be? One might be the system–life-world distinction, in which the economy at first glance seems to be simply a matter of the medium of money, with little or no human interaction. But I have argued, and Habermas has elsewhere conceded, that reading "system" in this way is

to misinterpret it and that human interaction between workers and customers, workers and bosses, does go on. If that is so, why could not this
interaction take a democratic form? Is Habermas worried about the
necessity for technical expertise in economic firms, thereby eliminating
the desirability or feasibility of total, immediate, direct democracy? If so,
such democracy would legitimately be excluded, but not the mediated
and representative democracy that I and others have defended within
the firm, in which expertise is employed but always in such a way that it
is subject to the democratic decision making of the firm as a whole. The
expert proposes, but the workers as a whole in the firm dispose.[7]

No matter how we twist and turn it, therefore, Habermas's argument
seems either deficient or arbitrary or both. The immediate text that we are
considering and *Between Facts and Norms* as a whole seem to assume a liberal, bourgeois, capitalist meaning to freedom and democracy, giving
political freedom a priority over other kinds. And although there may be
a basis for arguing against worker democracy, Habermas does not unfold
it here or in other books. He just seems to assume without argument that
such worker democracy is not "realistic," but such realism does not
cohere with his commitment to communicative praxis in which all possibilities and viewpoints should have a hearing. Habermas defends capitalism here at the price of a performative contradiction with his theory and
recommended practice. Such realism is appropriate to Reinhold Niebuhr,
and we have come to expect it from him and his disciples, but not from
Habermas.

Let us turn to principle 5: basic rights to the provision of living conditions that are socially, technologically, and ecologically safeguarded, insofar as the current circumstances make this necessary if citizens are to have
equal opportunities to exercise the civil rights listed in principles 1
through 4. Here the problem is somewhat different. The principle as stated is a fully universal material principle of provision that does not seem
to imply or require the welfare capitalist form of that principle or the welfare capitalist form as the most adequate form. The principle, as stated,
seems open to both a democratic socialist and a welfare capitalist version
or embodiment. But here and in the rest of the book it is clear that Habermas intends a welfare capitalist version of the principle. This is not
argued for and is assumed arbitrarily in a way that belies the practice and
goal of communicative action.

Yet the welfare state version is clearly inadequate. Not only is there still
the accumulation-legitimation tension already mentioned, but there is
also a contradiction between the requirement of formal equal opportunity and the significantly unequal material provision that capitalism makes

possible, likely, and necessary. The CEO, for example, has enormous resources of time, energy, money, opportunity, and access to power that the average worker does not even come close to approximating. Formal equal opportunity, if it is to mean anything, requires roughly equal material provision; otherwise opportunity for most of us is just on paper; a formal equal opportunity is in contradiction with lack of real opportunity, formal liberty with the absence of the worth of liberty, the capacity to practice liberty effectively and realize purposes. Principle 5, therefore, as articulated by Habermas needs to be further specified to assure roughly equal, sufficient material provision and real opportunity. I will deal with this issue further in the last chapter.

Capitalism, however, because its overriding goal is to maximize the profits of the capitalist over against the worker, is set up both in and outside the workplace to make such equality of provision impossible. In the workplace the ideal is as much profit as possible and as little wages as possible. Outside the workplace the idea is to limit what goes out to welfare, lest it cut into profits and into forms of state spending that disproportionately benefit the capitalist class. Moreover, rough equality of provision could be institutionally secured only by rough equality of power. But because there is neither equality of power nor economic or social democracy, there is, and can be in principle, no equality in provision and, therefore, no equal full participation. Equality of provision is in contradiction with the principle that unequal profits go to one class of society, the class that owns and controls and derives the benefit from the means of production. Principle 4 is in contradiction with principle 5, as that is interpreted by Habermas. Principle 5 cannot be realized in any even roughly adequate way so long as it is just political autonomy that is secured, and even this political autonomy is compromised by the unequal material provision of the welfare state.

Why would a community setting itself up as a community able in a fully communicative way to choose between democratic socialism and welfare state capitalism choose the latter? Not only is there a greater share in wealth and income for everyone in a democratic socialist society, but there is also a greater share in power for everyone and a greater happiness in participating in a community that is fully democratic, economically, politically, and socioculturally. Would capitalism even be in the running in such a fully open communicative situation? Who would or should choose a pinchpenny welfare state, a merely or mostly formal opportunity to participate, and economic and social institutions that operate over and against oneself as alien? Moreover, because disproportionate economic power flows over into the political institutions, even those are flawed. Why would a citizenry choose less private and public happiness over more?[8]

To sum up my objections to principle 5, first of all, I argue that Habermas restricts its meaning and application to the capitalist welfare state in a way that is arbitrary and fails to live up to the unlimited questioning of the ideal speech situation. Second, both as stated and as applied to the capitalistic welfare state, it is too indeterminate and thus leaves room for huge gaps in wealth and income that work against equal opportunity. If it is to be realized, formal equal opportunity requires a roughly equal material opportunity. Third, if one interprets and instantiates the principle in this latter way, roughly equal material opportunity is undermined by the narrow political meaning of democracy in principle 4, because that principle involves private ownership and control of the means of production in a way that militates against equal material opportunity. Fully equal formal and material equality implies equal access to means of economic, political, and cultural self-development, which private ownership and control of the means of production directly contradict. Fourth, principle 5, even in its possible welfare state instantiation, is in contradiction with principle 4, because even Habermas's political democracy requires roughly equal material resources, and a person with hundreds of times more income and wealth than the average person in the population can wield enormously disproportionate political power and influence. Finally, the result is a contradiction in Habermas's own limited terms between merely legal formal opportunity and real opportunity, between a formal equal opportunity and a real, material unequal opportunity or lack of opportunity.[9]

What would Habermas say to such questions and objections? In a book of essays on the public sphere, Nancy Fraser raises cogently the question about the roughly equal material provision that should underlie political participation. Habermas's answer seems dismissive, arbitrary, and arrogant. Let us consider Fraser's question first: "Isn't economic equality—the end of class structure and the end of gender inequality—the condition for the possibility of a public sphere, if we are really talking about what makes it possible for people to participate? Is capitalism compatible with this?"

Habermas's answer is:

> I'll have to get over the shock to answer such a question. . . . As I understand you, you are saying let's try to be early socialists and utopian socialists and then say what we think the design should be. . . . I do think that I have been a reformist all my life, and maybe have become a bit more so in recent years. I think that there is a need . . . to contain, from the system perspective, those

side effects that not only make us suffer but almost destroy core areas of class and racially specific subcultures. . . . I don't think that there can be any kind of revolution in societies that have such a degree of complexity; we can't go back anyway, in spite of all the romanticist anti-movements. For academics revolution is a notion of the nineteenth century.[10]

This response, while good-humored and humorous, is not adequate at all, but it does make clear Habermas's position, which remains unchanged in *Between Facts and Norms*. He is reformist, antirevolutionary, convinced that revolution is a nineteenth-century concept in light of the complexity of late-twentieth-century societies. Tell that to the people of Eastern Europe, to those of Nicaragua, Cuba, Haiti, to all those Third World people for whom revolution was on the agenda, but which the United States, Europe, and Japan forcibly suppressed over and over again. Why is "complexity" any more an obstacle in the economic or sociocultural sphere than in the political realm in western capitalist societies where democracy is, according to Habermas, alive and well, or at least alive and kicking?

CONCLUSION

In spite of Habermas's undoubted insights and achievements, there are many contradictions in his work: between a communicative praxis in principle open to considering all possibilities and one that restricts and limits possibilities; between a fully universal concept of democracy and one that restricts it arbitrarily to the political realm; between a sense of democracy and communicative praxis that points beyond the capitalist status quo in a legitimately utopian way and one that restricts itself to such a status quo in an obscurantist, uncritically realistic manner; between formal equal opportunity and lack of real, equal opportunity; between liberty and the worth of liberty.

We have also noted conflicts and tensions between and among the principles. Principles 1 through 3, which assert an abstract balance between private and public, are in tension with principles 4 and 5, which tilt the balance in a privatistic, individualistic direction. The first three principles establish the legal form for democracy; the last two implicitly deny it by denying the necessary reciprocity between freedom and equality, making democracy possible. The overwhelming character of private capitalist power makes impossible a full exercise of participative freedom by all, and restricting democratic freedom to the political domain ensures massive socioeconomic inequality. Freedom and equality go together or not at all, and if not at all, then there is no effective full participatory democracy for all.

Moreover, principles 4 and 5 are at odds with one another. Because there is no equality of economic and socioeconomic power enshrined in principle 4, there is and can be no equality of material resources and consequently no effective equal opportunity. If there is no equality of material resources, then this deficiency is at odds with the political democracy intended in principle 4. If there is no equality of material resources, there is no effective, full political participation.

Finally, we have discovered that a community constituting itself as a community legally would not and should not choose the bourgeois form that Habermas advocates without argument. Rather, because of the greater freedom and equality in the democratic socialist version, such a community would and should choose the democratic socialist version of human rights over the late capitalist version. Capitalism, because of its essentially antidemocratic and antiegalitarian ethics, undermines the conditions for effective communicative praxis. The very values that a community would and should value, according to Habermas—democracy, legality, equality, and freedom—are more fully, more effectively, and more consistently and universally realized in the democratic socialist version. Habermas does not, therefore, live up to the implications of his best insights, and a contradiction emerges between the full, effective expression of communicative praxis and Habermas's stunted bourgeois version, undermining democracy and communication at their roots.

Because Habermas's scheme of human rights is conceptually flawed and incoherent, his version of legal democratic capitalism cannot work even in principle. This point will be developed more fully in the next chapter. Further chapters show why and how empirically the conception is not working in the practice of western democratic states. "Everybody's working for America, but America is not working for anyone."[11] The full dialectical truth manifests itself most fully at the end of the book in the interplay between principle and fact, the conceptual story and the empirical story.

NOTES

1. Jürgen Habermas, *The Theory of Communicative Action*, vol. 2, *Lifeworld and System: The Critique of Functionalist Reason*, trans. Thomas McCarthy (Boston: Beacon Press, 1987), 113–99.

2. Jürgen Habermas, *Between Facts and Norms*, trans. William Rehg (Cam-

bridge: MIT Press, 1996), 42–66. Page numbers in parentheses throughout this chapter refer to this book.

3. Habermas, *Theory of Communicative Action,* vol. 2.

4. For Marx's basically nonviolent, nonterroristic, democratic approach to social change and revolution, see Shlomo Avineri, *The Social and Political Thought of Karl Marx* (Cambridge: Cambridge University Press, 1970). On the contrast between the American and French Revolutions, see Hannah Arendt, *On Revolution* (New York: Viking Press, 1965).

5. For my more fully developed argument that such a community would not choose capitalism in any form and would choose democratic socialism, see *Critique, Action, and Liberation* (Albany: State University of New York Press, 1995), 160–61, 166–72.

6. Herbert Marcuse, *One-Dimensional Man* (Boston: Beacon Press, 1964), 1–55, 123–99.

7. Marsh, *Critique, Action, and Liberation,* 238–42. Axel Honneth and Hans Joas, eds., *Communicative Action,* trans. Jeremy Gaines and Doris L. Jones (Cambridge: MIT Press, 1991), 250–64. Habermas in a few places in other works explicitly discusses the issue of workplace democracy. In *Habermas: Autonomy and Solidarity,* ed. Peter Dews (London: Verso, 1986), 187, he says that "I no longer believe that a differentiated economic system can be transformed from within in accordance with simple recipes of workers' self-management. The problem seems rather one of how capacities for self-organization can be sufficiently developed in autonomous public spheres." He does not say why he rejects self-management and thus leaves unanswered the objection, which I put forth in my book, that such forms of self-management are possible in modern, complex societies and firms and have actually been practiced with great success.

In a later book, *A Berlin Republic: Writings on Germany,* trans. Steven Rendell (Lincoln: University of Nebraska Press, 1997), 141–42, Habermas affirms the "renewed relevance of purely normatively based models for a 'market socialism.' These pick up the correct idea of retaining the market economy's effective steering effects and impulses to innovation without at the same time accepting the negative consequences of a systematically reproduced unequal distribution of 'bads' and goods.'"

This latter quotation shows a growing openness to the idea of market socialism that I and David Ingram and others defend, but the implications of this admission are not worked out systematically by Habermas. Rather, the admission seems to be just one more example of the contradictory opening up to perspectives beyond a capitalist framework and yet wishing to stay within that framework that I find throughout *Between Facts and Norms.* This is the way Ingram interprets Habermas in "Individual Freedom and Social Inequality: Habermas's Democratic Revolution in the Social Contractarian Justification of Law," in *Perspectives on Habermas,* ed. Lewis Edwin Hahn (Chicago: Open Court, 2000), 289–307.

See Ingram's useful, extended argument for workplace democracy, against Habermas, in *Reason, History, and Politics* (Albany: State University of New York Press, 1995), 236–40.

8. Marsh, *Critique, Action, and Liberation,* 160–61, 166–72.

9. For a fuller development of this argument concerning formal opportunity, material opportunity, and equal access to means of self-development, see Marsh, *Critique, Action, and Liberation*, 139–67.

10. Greg Calhoun, ed., *Habermas and the Public Sphere* (Cambridge: MIT Press, 1992), 468–70.

11. Daniel Berrigan, *Ten Commandments for the Long Haul* (Nashville: Abingdon, 1981), 69.

4

The Genesis of the State

Up to this point we have seen Habermas reflecting on the horizontal genesis of basic rights within a community of citizens; such a genesis focuses on the relationship between communicative praxis and law. This relationship, however, remains tenuous and incomplete unless and until it can stabilize itself vertically in a constitutional state. If the system of rights is to be more than metaphorical, it must stabilize itself in a system of political power that is already presupposed in the medium of law. Such law in its genesis and infancy owes its binding character to the communicative praxis of citizens. But this political power must become fully expressed in a constitutional state. Habermas's focus shifts from the link between communicative praxis and law to that between law, resting on and deriving from communicative praxis, and political power. Law is the middle term between the communicative praxis of citizens and the state. As law is essential to the unfolding of communicative praxis, so also is political power in the form of the state. Habermas gives scant comfort to those liberal theorists such as Locke who see the state as a necessary evil, or to those anarchists or Marxists who see the state as essentially withering away in the face of immediate community. Communicative praxis in the modern era essentially unfolds and comes to be and fulfills itself through the mediation and representation of law and the state.[1]

This chapter discusses the three main sections of chapter 4 of *Between Facts and Norms* on the genesis of the state, the internal relation between law and politics, the generation of communicative power, and the use of administrative power bound to communicative power. Again, this chapter presents a mixture of very true, compelling insights and confusions, contradictions, and anomalies. Since the vertical genesis of rights flows from, and is based on, the horizontal genesis, if the latter is problematic, so also will be the former. Habermas's account of the state, while it brilliantly captures and partially reconstructs the intelligibility and meaning of the modern welfare state, misses its contradictory nature as a capitalist state. Habermas ends up with an account of the state that presents it as too consistent, benign, and unproblematic. The problems present in the previous chapter haunt this chapter, and new ones arise.

THE INTERNAL RELATION BETWEEN LAW AND POLITICS

We begin by noting Habermas's claim that law presents itself as a system of rights only if it can stabilize behavioral expectations. Such rights can take effect and be enforced only by organizations able to make collectively binding decisions. These decisions owe their collective bindingness to the legal form in which they are clad. Because rights require the political state, and the state requires law for its legitimacy, we see the internal connection between law and politics in the state (133).

Because the right to equal liberties assumes concrete shape in basic rights, these, as positive law, are backed by the threat of sanction and can be enforced against norm violations and opposing interests. The right to membership in a voluntary association of equals presupposes a spatio-empirically limited community, to which members can belong and which can constitute itself as a legal community only if it possesses a centered authority acting on behalf of its citizens and able to protect itself from both internal enemies and internal disorder. The equal right to individual legal protection takes shape in concrete rights that ground claims to an independent and impartial judiciary. The equal right to political self-determination grounds equal claims to participation in democratic legislative processes, established with governmental power. The political will-formation of the legislature depends on an executive power that can implement adopted programs in a bureaucratic exercise of political power. The scale of this apparatus varies with the degree to which a society makes use of law to influence its reproductive processes. But the necessity of such an apparatus is accelerated by social entitlements to the social, cultural, and ecological preconditions for the equal opportunity to utilize private liberties and participatory political rights (133–34).

In Habermas's words, "the state becomes necessary as a sanctioning, organizing, and executive power because rights must be enforced, because the legal community has need of both a collective self-maintenance and an organized judiciary, and because political will-formation issues in programs that must be implemented" (134). Habermas insists that the state is not just a factual necessity for the system of rights but is implicit in it.

Political power of the state is not externally juxtaposed to law but is pre-supposed by law and established in the form of law. It is not the legal form as such that legitimates the exercise of state power, a mistake that some earlier theorists made, but only the bond with legitimately enacted law, which is rationally accepted by all citizens in a discursive process of opin-ion-and-will-formation (135). If the state is constituted in legitimate, democratically enacted law, then the state must be and is inherently demo-cratic. If it is not, or if it is only in a contradictory way as in late capitalism, this legitimacy is lacking, and Habermas at his best and most consistent requires the full meaning of democracy, not just the partial, political one described in the last chapter. Political democracy without economic and social democracy remains unrealized, partial, contradictory, and merely or mostly formal. Minus the full meaning of democracy, the state cannot *in principle* be legitimate (134–35).

An implication, of course, of this analysis is that democracy as the civic exercise of autonomy has to be incorporated in the state in the form of a legislature. The practice of self-determination is institutionalized in a number of ways: informal discussion of opinion in the public sphere, participation inside and outside of political practices, participation in general elections, deliberations and decision making in parliamentary bodies, and so on. A popular sovereignty linked to individual liberties is embodied again in governmental power in such a way that the principle requiring that all governmental authority be derived from the people is realized through communicative presuppositions and procedures of an institutionally differentiated opinion-and-will-formation. According to the discourse-theoretic presuppositions of government by law, popular sovereignty no longer is embodied in a visibly identified or tangible gath-ering of citizens, but rather in "subjectless" forms of communication cir-culating through forums and legislative bodies. Only these anonymous forms of communicatively fluid power can bind the administrative power of the state apparatus to the will of citizens. Such relinquishing of any dream of fully direct, unmediated sovereignty or visible, collective people should not be interpreted to mean that popular sovereignty is divested of its "radical democratic" content. But Habermas so waters down the meaning of radical that it becomes almost identical with "con-servative" or "liberal" or "new liberal." How can these be radical? Per-haps only in the sense that Habermas's democratic ideal of the rational, constitutional state is in principle unable to be realized in modern capi-talist forms of the state, and thus points beyond that state. "Radical" can only be defended by going to a meaning that Habermas does not intend, but which is implied in his articulation of the democratic constitution. In saying that this radical ideal shoots beyond the present status quo, I am also recognizing a good deal of validity in that ideal (135–36).

The conceptual framework of modern natural law developed in the philosophy of the subject, who is conceived as an isolated, rugged individual confronting other individuals in a state of nature. This conception blocks an adequate sociological understanding of the cohesion of kinship societies in prepolitical institutions and the way the complex of law and political power was for a long time able to join forces with the prepolitical substratum. The phenomena that first appeared in modernity—the conglomerate of administrative power, the emergence of positive law, and the emergence of legal authority—conceal the beginning of a kind of political authority initially developed in the context of traditional societies. In tribal societies, prestige-based social power of chieftains, priests, members of privileged families, and so forth was linked with recognized behavioral norms whose obligatory force stemmed from mythic powers and a sacred background. They form a syndrome that made institutions of conflict resolution and collective will-formation possible before the step to organized state power was taken. This state power could arise on an archaic foundation of social integration that modern forms of natural law do not consider (138–39).

To begin with, Habermas constructs two types of conflict resolution and collective will-formation, making use neither of state-sanctioned law nor of legally formed political power, but present as elements from which law and political power can be mutually constituted. With Parsons, he assumes that social interaction in space and time is subject to a double contingency; each actor expects the other to act one way or another. Thus every social order must rely on a mechanism of action coordination. Coordination problems take one of two forms. There is a conflict either of individual action orientations or with the choice and realization of collective goals. In the first case, the question arises, According to what rules should we live together? In the second, the question is, Which goals do we want to achieve and in what ways? Conflict realization refers to stabilization of behavioral expectations in the case of disagreement, which Habermas, following Parsons, names "pattern maintenance." *Collective will-formation* refers to the choice and effective realization of goals, which Parsons names "goal attainment" (139).

Sample interactions in both kinds of situations fall along a continuum defined by the pure types of value-oriented and interest-governed action. In one case, coordination of interpersonal action takes place through value consensus; in the other, through a balance of interests achieved by means of an arbitrator. The categories of "authority" and "compromise" stand for two principles of will-formation in the light of which disagreements about goal attainment can be resolved. Either the people involved have recourse to persons or families enjoying sufficient prestige to render decisions based on shared value commitments, or the disputing parties reach a tolerable compromise, based on their factual power (140).

These four problem-solving strategies can be illustrated in tribal institutions. Arbitration and compromise depend on a kind of social power that has emerged either from prestige differentials among stratified family groups or from differentiation, whether for war or peace, of the roles of elders, priests, and chiefs. The other two techniques of conflict resolution, through consensus or an authoritatively guided collective will-formation, depend directly on a normative complex in which custom, morality, and law still symbiotically interpenetrate (141).

The co-original constitution of binding law and political power can be represented in a two-stage model. The first stage is characterized by the position of a chieftain or king who takes the role of a royal judge and monopolizes the function of conflict resolution. The second stage is the legal institutionalization of an administrative staff, making collective will-formation possible in the organized form of the state. When a leader who at first enjoys just a superior reputation can concentrate in his hands the hitherto dispersed function of conflict resolution, normative authority accrues to him, and social law becomes binding law. Two simultaneous processes go hand-in-hand: authorization of power by sacred law and sanctioning of law by social power. In such a way, political power and binding law emerge as the two components constituting a legally organized political order (142).

In the second stage, the co-original components of binding law and political power join up in the institutionalization of offices that provides the political authority with an administrative staff, making possible state-organized authority. Not only does law legitimate political power, but also political power can make use of law to organize political rule. The ruler can make legally binding decisions as a means of realizing collective goals, and at the same time an organized penal system provides the acts of the judiciary with a coercive character. Power contributes to realization of collective goals, and law stabilizes behavioral expectations in society as a whole. At the same time, power institutionalizes law politically, and law organizes the exercise of political power. Power and law perform functions for each other as well as for society as a whole (142–44).

As modernity emerges, however, and comes into full flower in the seventeenth and eighteenth centuries, law loses its sacredness and hence the legitimating power that was rooted in that sacredness. As a result, the legitimacy problem previously covered over, or resolved by, the sacred character of law, that of a normatively justified privileging of powerful interests, becomes manifest again. A gap opens up between instrumentally conceived power and instrumentalized law, which the natural law of that period tried to close with its recourse to practical reason. Such an approach, however, did not succeed (144–46).

Enter the discourse-theoretic conception of political autonomy, which explains why the legitimation of law requires that the communicative freedom of citizens be brought into play. Drawing on Arendt, Habermas argues that legislation depends on generating another kind of power that no one individually is able to possess. Rather, such power springs up between people when they act together in public and vanishes when they disperse. Both law and communicative action have their co-original source in the opinions about which many publicly are in agreement. If the sources of justice from which law draws its legitimacy are not to run dry, then communicative power must underlie the administrative power of the government. This point is something that early modern theorists of natural law, like Hobbes and Locke, missed (146–47).

In contrast to such natural law theorists, Arendt distinguishes between power and violence, and essentially nonviolent communicative power is allied from the beginning with legitimate law. The freedom-founding acts of such power emerge most clearly when "revolutionaries seize the power scattered through the streets, when a population committed to passive resistance opposes foreign tanks with their bare hands, when convinced minorities dispute the legitimacy of existing laws and engage in civil disobedience, when the sheer 'joy of action' breaks forth in protest movements" (148). Habermas, still drawing on Arendt and quoting her here, articulates the revolutionary possibilities of communicative action in a way that belies his own merely reformist theory. If revolutionary acts were possible and legitimate in the past, why are they not in the present and future? Also, we may ask whether he is not overly idealizing modern capitalistic societies. Would it not be truer to say that communicative action in its orientation to legitimate law is contradicted in practice and institutionally by any state and economy in which there is a legitimation gap between what they claim to be ideally and what they are in fact and operation, functioning on behalf of special, powerful interests, often violently and coercively in a way that harms the true interests of much of the rest of the population? In this sense, modern natural law theories, although inadequate theoretically, are correct empirically. If so, are there not revolutionary implications in communicative action, which Arendt enthusiastically endorses and from which Habermas backs away (147–50)?

The concept of communicative politics in the full sense, in Habermas's view, includes communicative practice articulated in public opinion-and-will-formation and the issuing of law, as well as administrative power and competition for access to that political system. At this point, we note one of the most important statements in the book: "This leads me to propose that we view law as the medium through which communicative power is translated into administrative power" (150). The transformation of communicative power into administrative power has the character of an empowerment within the framework of statutory organization. The idea of the constitutional state in general requires that administrative systems be tied to lawmaking communicative power and "kept free of illegitimate interventions of social power (i.e., of the factual strength of privileged interests to assert themselves)" (150). In this way, the idea of government by law illumines the political task of balancing the three main forces of macrosocial integration: money, administrative power, and solidarity (150).

There is much here that recommends itself. But what if, because of problems already mentioned in the horizontal genesis of rights, the operation of communicative praxis is limited, compromised, and contradicted by powerful interests? What if it is impossible, both factually and in principle, to eliminate, or even come close to eliminating, the further intrusion of such interests into not only the legislative but also the administrative arena? What if the competition for power takes the form of "selling the president" or member of Congress or senator? What if we have the best Congress money can buy? If these are problems in principle and not merely in fact, then consistency demands a revolutionary extension and application of communicative action. If such action is intrinsically oriented to justice and is undermined by a social system that is intrinsically unjust, then communicative action must become revolutionary. Mere reformist adaptation is a cop-out. Justice is the middle term linking communicative praxis and revolutionary transformation. The problem with Habermas is not that he is unfaithful to the insights of others but that he is not faithful to, or consistent with, his own best insights; he cops out on himself.

COMMUNICATIVE POWER AND THE GENESIS OF LAW

The rights of political participation refer to the legal institutionalization of a public opinion-and-will-formation terminating in decisions about politics and laws. Such a communicative process instantiates the discourse principle in a double sense. There is, first, a cognitive sense of filtering reasons, information, topics, and contributions in such a way that the outcome of a discourse enjoys the presumption of rational, democratic accountability. There should be no dominance by one class, race, or sex in such a way that its reasons, arguments, and programs are privileged over those of other groups. Second, there is the practical sense of establishing relations of mutual understanding that are violence free. Police violence in the streets enforcing racist capitalist power and protecting the "haves" from the "have-nots" and imperial violence in defense of capitalist interests is, it would seem or should seem, excluded; yet Habermas does not draw these conclusions. Penetration of discursive lawmaking and communicative power formation is necessary because a political community is not simply a moral community. Political questions, because they involve strategic, ethical, and technical questions as well as moral ones, differ from moral questions (151–52).

A community confronted with questions of what it ought to do is confronted with different kinds of questions, each with its own kind of logic. Pragmatic questions pose themselves from the perspective of an actor seeking suitable means to realize goals that are already given. Such questions are pursued using arguments that relate empirical knowledge to given preferences or ends and that assess the consequences of alternative choices according to previously accepted maxims or decision rules (159–60).

The question What ought we to do? can, of course, take us beyond the horizon of strategic or purposive-rational action. Ethical-political questions arise when members of a society, in the face of important life issues, wish to gain clarity about their shared form of life. Such questions are answered with clinical advice based on a reconstruction of the form of life that has been brought to awareness while being interrogated. This advice combines descriptive and normative components, in that what should be is related to what we are as a community. Ethical discourses are arguments based on hermeneutical explication of the self-understanding of a nation's historically distinctive form of life. Such arguments weigh value decisions in this context with a view toward an authentic conduct of life, a goal absolute for us as a community. Western capitalist societies, for example, at one point in their history decided it was more authentic to become welfare states and thus move away from a laissez-faire economy (160–61).

Even on the ethical level, Habermas underestimates how much western capitalist societies are at odds with themselves, contradictory, and divided. Michael Walzer, a communitarian using this kind of ethical reflection, argues that the self-understanding of these societies as *capital-*

istic conflicts with their sense of themselves as *democratic,* and that the way to gain a more consistent authentic self-understanding is to move to democratic socialism. Such an argument can be taken by itself as another objection on the ethical level to Habermas's defense of the status quo, or it can be linked to our reflections already carried out on the basis of the universalistic rights contained in precepts 1 through 5, which flow from the discourse principle and communicative praxis. The ethical argument concretizes and particularizes the universalistic argument, and the universalistic argument buttresses the ethical argument. Because we are already committed to democracy on a universalistic and ethical level, we should reject a socioeconomic system that does democracy in and should put in place an economic system that sustains and enhances democracy. The universalistic argument also helps us to choose which way to go when two principles, here capitalism and democracy, are in conflict on the ethical level. A strict communitarianism such a Walzer's, in deciding which way to go, has to be either arbitrary or tacitly universalistic.[2]

In moral questions, as we have already seen, the goal-oriented or teleological point of view under which we view pragmatic questions and the ethical point of view under which we consider issues of communicative self-understanding give way to the normative point of view under which we consider how we can regulate common life in the equal interest of all. A norm is just only in that all involved can will what is obeyed by each in all comparable situations. Moral norms have the character of unconditional, categorical imperatives, detached both from teleological ends and the particular, ethnocentric understanding of a particular community. We can, for example, build or use a weapon, but is such building or use just? We can invade a certain nation and enhance our economic well-being, but is such invasion just (161–62)?

All such discourse can occur in a legislative process of making laws. As one moves from purposive-rational to ethical and moral questions, issues may arise that are not resolvable completely under any of these perspectives, taken individually or together. Then the legislature must have recourse to bargaining to arrive at an agreement that is acceptable under three conditions: the arrangement is more advantageous to all than no arrangement at all, free riders who withdraw from communication are excluded, and those who might contribute more to the arrangement than they gain from it are excluded (165–66).

The discourse principle is brought to bear on such agreements indirectly insofar as it regulates bargaining from the standpoint of fairness. There should be equal distribution among the parties, and procedures should be followed that provide all parties with an equal opportunity to apply pressure to influence each other through bargaining so that all interests come into play and all have an equal chance of prevailing. Moreover, no generalized or universal interest should be the object of a compromise or bargain, only those interests that are not generalizable.

Such compromise formation, therefore, does not and cannot exclude moral discourse. Here is a very strong reason why, against a fashionable pragmatism especially prevalent in the United States, political will-formation cannot be reduced to achieving a compromise. Such a claim also applies to ethical-political discourse, which at least must be compatible with moral principles. A fundamentalist understanding, for example, that subordinates individual rights to collective goals and gives rise to nonegalitarian arrangements and regulations is not compatible with moral principles. Implicitly or explicitly racist, sexist, or heterosexist arrangements are not compatible with the morally discursive character of western democracies. That they are still deeply racist, sexist, and heterosexist, perhaps, is incompatible with Habermas's reformist arguments and proposals here. What is called for is deep reform, not radical transformation.

Because racism, sexism, and heterosexism, however, are aspects of the capitalist system taken as a whole—taken as a process of self-expanding value, which the system picks up and uses to divide and fragment resistance or to sell products, such as occurs when a beautiful, sexy supermodel is in an advertisement for underwear; to ideologically legitimize social or political policy and decisions—they will not be overcome fully until capitalism is overcome. I am not saying that racism, sexism, and heterosexism are deducible from capitalism as origin, cause, logic, or motivation, only that capitalism picks them up and uses them for its own ends when it encounters them in a society. Thus racism can be used as a rationalization for cutting welfare for the poor, many of whom happen to be black or Hispanic, in a way that favors capitalist priorities; sexism can be used to go after women receiving food stamps or unmarried mothers on welfare. Racism can be used in foreign policy adventures to demonize a leader like Saddam Hussein of Iraq or Daniel Ortega of Nicaragua, who led the Sandinistas in the 1980s.[3]

Other issues, however, point to radical transformation in a way that takes us beyond Habermas's reformism. We may ask whether in capitalist societies compromise between putatively universalizable interests such as a clean, safe, and beautiful environment or a genuinely pluralistic system of public communication and capitalist imperatives does not occur regularly and as a matter of course. And is such a situation avoidable in such societies, in fact and in principle? We may ask whether fair bargaining can occur in legislatures where the overwhelming power of money regularly intervenes to elect, influence, and, if necessary, punish legislatures if they do not go along with the imperatives of capital. How is there equal power to influence outcomes when the rich and capital have so much more money and time and access to the legislature than other groups, such as labor or the poor or consumer groups? And even though reform (e.g., campaign spending reform) is possible, can it ever be fully successful in a society with such enormous differentiation in class power? Would not and could not capital, if we closed off one avenue of influence, simply develop others? If we limit contributions by individuals, as we did in the early 1970s in the United States, then individuals in a wealthy firm can join together to make a hefty contribution and to form organizations not covered by the law regulating individual contributions. If that is limited, then political action committees are formed outside the firm. If unlimited class power is the problem, then do we not need to take that on in principle and in itself, rather than just dealing with its permutations and manifestations, which in principle are infinite? As long as such class power is in principle legitimate, it will find a way around any limited law or regulation (164–66).

PRINCIPLES OF THE CONSTITUTIONAL STATE AND THE SEPARATION OF POWERS

Up to this point, we have been concerned with preparatory reflections. Now we are prepared to justify the principles of government by law from a discourse-theoretic point of view. Binding law and political power form a complex in which each complements the other. Political, administrative power regenerates itself from legitimately enacted law, and law is made concrete and effective through administration. To counter the danger that law will be instrumentalized for the strategic employment of power, the idea of government by law requires that the state apparatus be organized in such a way that any use of publicly authorized power must be legitimated in terms of legitimately enacted law. If that turns out not to be the case, if racial or sexual or heterosexual or class power cannot in principle be prevented from illegitimately influencing the administrative and legislative process, then the model of Habermas's constitutional state is flawed. While I believe the first three—racism, sexism, and heterosexism—can be dealt with in principle, although not currently in fact, the fourth cannot. Is the legitimation of administrative power, as influenced by capitalist power on the administrative level as well as in many different ways on the legislative level, compatible with Habermas's constitutional state (168–69)?

The discursively structured opinion-and-will-formation of the political legislature should proceed in forms that allow the question What ought we to do? to be asked and answered under various aspects. In light of this premise, Habermas develops the principles of the constitutional state from the perspective of the legal institutionalization of the network of discourse and negotiation that we have just considered, describing the movement from the purposively rational to the ethical to the moral to bargaining and compromise.

The principle of popular sovereignty states that all government authority derives from the people. The individual's right to an equal opportunity to participate in democratic will-formation is combined with the legally institutionalized practice of civic self-determination. This principle is a hinge between the system of rights and the construction of constitutional democracy. Starting with discourse theory, we arrive at, first, a special interpretation of the principle of popular sovereignty. This interpretation yields, second, the principle of comprehensive legal protection for individuals, guaranteed by an independent judiciary; third, the principle requiring that administration be subject to law and to judicial review and parliamentary oversight; and, fourth, the principle of separation between state and civil society, which intends to prevent social power from being translated directly into administrative power without passing through the sluices of communicative power (169–70).

Habermas's model of the sluice remarkably resembles the modern capitalist welfare state, with paradoxical and mixed results blending positive insight and negative error and confusion. He shows the limited intelligibility of the state, and, unintentionally, its contradictory character. Habermas's argument for the constitutional state unintentionally shows the nonidentity between his constitution and the actual welfare state. I agree in outline with his argument but would argue that his version of the constitutional state has never been tried, nor could it be, in really existing capitalist societies. Contrary to his realistic intentions, his constitutional state remains utopian and calls for realization in a qualitatively different kind of society.

In discourse-theoretic terms, the principle of popular sovereignty states that all political power derives from the communicative power of citizens. If the exercise of public authority is oriented and legitimated by the law that citizens give themselves in a discursively structured opinion-and-will-formation, then such a practice owes its legitimating force to a democratic procedure intended to guarantee a rational treatment of political questions. Interlinked forms of communication ensure that all relevant questions, issues, viewpoints, and contributions are brought up and processed in discourses and negotiations on the basis of the best available information and arguments. The legal communications make possible the effective utilization of equal communicative freedom and enjoin the pragmatic, ethical, and moral use of practical reason and, when necessary, fair bargaining and compromise (170).

But what if an undemocratically constituted class power (remember that there is no economic or social democracy) makes such openness to all viewpoints impossible? What if elections and influence brought to bear upon legislators are so dominated by money that all other competing interests, for example, labor or the poor, cannot get an equal or fair hearing in the legislature? Citizens and legislators are dealing with, and opposed by, a source of power that has not been consented to democratically, the power of capital, which stands over and above and against them as an alien power and foreign body. How is full, adequate democracy even remotely possible in such a situation?

Going on, Habermas suggests that we consider popular sovereignty in terms of power. Legislative power must be transferred to the totality of citizens and must be able to generate communicative power in their midst. Justified and binding decisions about policies and laws demand, on the one hand, that deliberation and decision making take place face-to-face. On the other hand, because not all citizens in big democracies are able to participate face-to-face, we have the parliamentary principle. According to this principle, representatives are chosen democratically, modes of decision making such as majority rule operate in ways that are fair and effective, and committees are chosen in such a way that special interests are not favored or privileged (170–71).

Also the logic of discourse yields the principle of political pluralism, inside and outside of representative bodies. Especially crucial is the way parliamentary bodies must be anchored in, and linked to, informal streams of communication emerging from public spheres open to all political parties, associations, citizens, and points of view. Together, the principles of guaranteed autonomy of public spheres and competition among different political parties and the parliamentary principle exhaust the principle of popular sovereignty. I would add a fourth principle, that of extending democracy to economic and social domains. Otherwise we have a foreign body—capital—in these processes of opinion-and-will-formation; legislators are elected and influenced by capitalist firms that are not constituted democratically and are not really run in a democratic manner. Such firms must try to influence these processes undemocratically because popular sovereignty, in which all of the people have a genuine voice, threatens the rule of capital. A country actually "of, by, and for capital," in which the common good of the people is subordinated or sacrificed to the good of capital, might actually become "of, by, and for the people." Capital cannot tolerate this possible state of affairs. Popular sovereignty is anticapitalistic, and capital is inherently undemocratic (171).[4]

Comprehensive legal protection, according to Habermas, presumes parliamentary bodies that justify and adapt laws in accordance with democratic procedures. Laws form the foundation for application of legal statutes to individual cases. From the actionability of legal claims follows the guarantee of legal remedies and the principle of comprehensive legal protection for each individual. Dividing the authority to make and apply law into different branches of government, legislative and judicial, is not only pragmatic and efficient because of the academic institutionalization of jurisprudence and the doctrinal refinement of law but also is based on normative and systematic reasons. One is that justification and application of norms are two different but related forms of discourse. In application, a decision must be reached about which norms are applicable and what the relevant aspects of the situation are, and this requires a constitution of roles in which the parties present their case before a judge representing the community. In justification, in contrast, there are only participants, and no one is above them with the power to monitor and censure what they do and say. The second reason is that, because the judiciary enlists means of repression provided by the state apparatus, the judiciary must be separated from the legislature and prevented from programming itself. Here we see the point of binding the judiciary to existing law (171–73).

The principle of the legality of administration brings out the central meaning of the separation and balancing of powers. Beyond the different logics of argumentation characterizing the justification and application of norms, institutional differentiation between different branches of government such as the legislature and administration has the purpose of binding administrative power to law in such a way that the administration regenerates itself solely from a communicative power that citizens engender in common. Such a binding implies that regulations, ordinances, and other administrative acts can be nullified if they can be shown not to be in accordance with law and that administrative power may not be used to intervene in, or substitute for, processes of legislation and adjudication. Also the constitution of an executive authority has the effect that liberties resulting from the right to equal freedom acquire the additional meaning of liberal rights against the state enjoyed by private legal subjects. The rights that citizens reciprocally accord one another in the horizontal dimension of citizen-citizen interaction extend to citizen-state interaction. Because the state is derivative from, and founded on, communicative praxis functioning horizontally, the state has to respect the conditions of its genesis. Because the state emerges as a further, vertical institutionalization of individual and public freedom, we cannot negate in a contradictory way that freedom or the conditions for its unfolding (173–74).

Habermas points out that in German constitutional law, the separation between state and civil society has been too much and too often interpreted along liberal lines of rights against the state. In more general terms, however, the principle refers to the legal guarantee of a social autonomy guaranteeing each person equal opportunity to make use of his right to political participation and communication. According to the liberal model, however, the state should limit itself to supplying internal and external security; all other functions are left to a self-regulating economic society largely freed from government regulation in the expectation that just living conditions will spontaneously result from the free play of the ends and preferences of individuals.

Even more generally, however, the principle of separation of state and society requires a civil society, that is, "a network of voluntary associations and a political culture that are sufficiently detached from class structures" (175). Habermas admits here that the relation between social power and democracy in modern democracies is problematic and says that he will return to the point in a future chapter. Civil society is expected to absorb and neutralize the unequal distribution of social positions and power differentials, so that power comes into play only insofar as it facilitates the exercise of civil autonomy and does not restrict it. A question here would be whether such an expectation is even plausible, given the fact that the dominant players inside the public sphere are corporations like NBC and CBS, which are there to make money and to sell and defend moneymaking as a way of life. For this reason, because we are dealing with players inside the public sphere, and therefore legitimate by the standards of capitalist modernity, injustice is not simply a matter of colonization from outside that sphere, which is the one problem Habermas has with capitalist modernity.

If such an expectation is not plausible, then I would suggest a third constitutional way to embody the separation between state and civil society, the democratic socialist, in addition to the early capitalist and welfare state models. This model has the advantage of removing class power in principle, because it overcomes the separation between worker and capitalist in principle in democratic ownership and control of the means of production.

Note, nonetheless, Habermas's empirical honesty here, in contrast to its deficit elsewhere. Notice also his emphasis on the public sphere as crucial to his conception of democracy. Much will depend on his later argument defending that sphere to see if it can bear the burden of saving democracy from the vicissitudes of unequal class power. I wish to end this part of the discussion by quoting Habermas in full on the inhibition of democracy:

> As restrictive, the disposition over social power provides some parties with a privileged opportunity to influence the political process in such a way that their interests acquire a priority not in accord with equal civil rights. Businesses, organizations, and pressure groups can, for example, transform their social power into political power by way of interventions, whether they do so directly by influencing the administration or indirectly by manipulating public opinion. (175)

Habermas recognizes as possibility and actuality what I also think is true in principle in democratic capitalist societies. Can the public sphere, operating as it now does, liberate us from such inhibiting effects?

More directly, how is justice in the legislative, administrative, judicial, and public arenas possible in a sea of injustice, which in Habermas's scheme hardly comes into question? A capitalist system that is exploitative, dominating, tyrannizing, colonizing (Habermas does try to deal with this issue), and marginalizing is already in many respects unfree, unequal, and unfair in the context in which legislative, administrative, judicial, and public justice emerge. A contradiction between the unjust context and the putatively just political system comes into play. Genuine political justice, which is all Habermas is interested in, is as implausible in this context as a gnat bringing an elephant to its knees or a small dog taming a tiger or a grasshopper a lion.

The possibilities are the complete flooding of the political state by the unjust context, a scenario that approaches being fascistic in the First or Third Worlds; a contradictory welfare state; or citizens mobilizing themselves, using the possible resources of the state, to transform the context. But Habermas has given up on this last scenario. It is "unrealistic" and "revolutionary" in a way that he does not want to be; and he does not find this context, except for its colonizing tendencies, problematic. And yet this third scenario is the one that is consistent with the imperatives of communicative action.

Habermas further admits that thinking about the state as a neutral power rising above the pluralism of civil society was always ideological. But, in the face of the huge potential of political power in deep-seated social structures, even a political process emerging from civil society must gain the autonomy necessary to prevent the administration, whether as executive authority or as sanctioning power, from sinking into being one party among others and favoring capitalistic priorities over those of other groups. But has Habermas given us any reason for thinking that his claim here is not equally ideological? He has already admitted that the modern state as a capitalistic state suffers a tension between accumulation and legitimation rooted in class structures. How plausible is it to hope that a process of democratic decision making emerging from civil society can prevent administration from becoming one party among others? Would it not be more plausible to think about removing the class divisions that give rise to the imbalance in the first place? Or, to keep to the contours of Habermas's thought experiment, would it not be better not to allow such class structures to arise in the first place in the light of a community constituting itself in a fully democratic way, socially, economically, and politically? Once again in the passage under discussion, Habermas admits empirically what I am saying is a problem in principle, a problem that he admitted in his own earlier work (175–76).

Habermas sums up this part of the discussion by saying that the principle of the constitutional state developed so far fits into an architectonics resting on a single idea, that the state should serve the politically autonomous self-organization of a community that has constituted itself with a system of rights as an association of free and equal consociates under law. The institution of the state must accomplish two things. On the one hand, communicative power must emerge and find binding expression in political and legal programs. On the other hand, communicative power must be able to apply and implement laws and programs in such a way that social integration is fostered through stabilization of expectations and realization of collective goals. He spends the rest of the chapter going more into detail on both of these issues (176).

In the context of this discussion, a further issue arises. What about the situation that has come up in modern welfare states in which administration must make value choices and implement or create materialized versions of law? Law is not merely applied in conformity to its form as it emerges in the legislature, but in some sense it is newly interpreted and made as administrative agencies try to implement statutes like the Water Quality Act, the Air Quality Act, or the Consumer Product Safety Act. Does not this development undermine the traditional distinction among legislative, executive, and judicial branches of government and Habermas's own idea of political constitution (189–90)?

Habermas has two answers to such a question. The first is that one must distinguish between the principles of the constitutional state and the form those might take in any concrete, national state. The principles, therefore, could be, and were, institutionalized differently in the early liberal state, in which the distinction is much more clear-cut between and among government functions that more or less correspond to principles, and the modern welfare state, in which there is not such a clear correspondence. His second answer is that the objection is against the early liberal interpretation of the state, which one can assert is not argued for here, but not against the principles themselves, which are instantiated differently in the modern welfare state. One response to the greater leeway of welfare state bureaucracies was to build into the decision-making process of the administration itself new forms and arenas for deliberation in order to avoid improper self-programming. Another was to introduce the quasi-judicial hearing. All of these techniques tend to broaden, intensify, or refine the participation of affected parties in the administrative process (190–91).

CONCLUSION

In this chapter we have raised a number of issues about Habermas's articulation of the constitutional state: the presence of capitalism as an undemocratic foreign body hostile to democracy, the influx of capitalist power into the legislative and administrative arenas, and the impact of capitalist class power on the all-important public sphere. These difficulties in principle lead to the conclusion that a contradiction exists between the principles of the constitutional state and capitalism. Not only on the horizontal level but also on the vertical level, capitalist class power adversely affects the generation and operation of the legislative, judicial, and administrative powers, as well as the public sphere that is supposed to keep them honest when all else fails.

Since the vertical constitution depends on, and flows from, the horizontal constitution of a community of citizens, the former will be as good as the latter. The inconsistencies and contradictions in the horizontal constitution that were noted in the preceding chapter also affect the vertical constitution. The specific difficulties noted in this chapter are the entirely understandable effects of the inadequate horizontal level. Like it, the vertical is flawed, self-contradictory, incoherent, and implausible. Is it plausible that a community fully open in freedom to all possibilities would create a contradictory welfare state with the imbalance of power that that implies: inequality, lack of real opportunity, the injustice of the warfare-welfare bureaucracy and the prison-industrial complex, our impoverished inner cities, and our greater and greater willingness to give welfare to the rich and cut welfare for the poor? These are problems on the vertical level itself. But if the community constituting itself as a democratic community would and should choose full economic, social, and political democracy and full, real material equality as a condition for full, equal political participation, then such a community would and should choose a democratic socialist state, a fully democratic state, not a democratic capitalist state that is being eroded by international capitalist class power manifest in such organizations as the World Trade Organization.[5]

To be more specific, if merely political democracy and the lack of effective material equality are the two main problems in horizontal constitution, we would expect these problems to be present in the state at each level, the legislative, the judicial, the administrative, and, surrounding and underlying and influencing them, the public sphere itself. If disproportionate economic power implies and leads to disproportionate political power and influence, we would expect that to be manifest in the legislature in terms of who runs for office, who has the financial support to run for office, who is elected, what issues come up for discussion, what laws are passed and not passed, and which people and groups have access to the legislature. Moreover, we would expect such power to influence unequally and unfairly who is considered or chosen for administrative and judiciary office, how administration and justice are implemented, which laws are deemed worthy of being enforced and which are not, which victims of injustice are worthy of administrative and judicial redress and which are not. Because such unequal power is dominant both within and outside the public sphere, there is no possible way in principle that all viewpoints will receive a fair hearing and discussion, even though there are laws on the books that require fairness and openness. This conceptual argument does not require an empirical supplement. It has its own independent validity and stands or falls on its own. Unequal economic power linked to corporations as undemocratic foreign bodies in modern democratic, capitalist societies and states leads inevitably to unequal social and political power, which makes a shambles in principle of any approximation to democracy that would even remotely satisfy Habermas's principles.

The many kinds of contradiction on the horizontal level translate into contradictions on the vertical level. We have a legislature that is unrepresentative and, therefore, passes laws that are not just and representative, that favor the rich and corporations over against other legitimate interests and groups. Because administration must apply the law that is passed, it can only be as just as the laws. In addition to difficulties arising on the administrative level itself, such as choice of personnel, it is impossible to administrate fairly, equally, and impartially laws that are unfair, unequal, and partial. Instead of the administration of justice, therefore, we have the administration of injustice, or a contradictory administration of justice and injustice, by Habermas's own standards.

Because the judiciary must apply laws that are partially or totally unfair, it cannot fairly apply such laws, again not just because the laws are problematic but also because of dynamics at the level of the judiciary itself, such as who is chosen and so on. Finally, a public sphere that should be open to all viewpoints and groups in principle is necessarily dominated by the rich and corporations inside and outside the public sphere. Consequently, what should be in Habermas's eyes a final guarantor of justice and a way of keeping the legislative, administrative, and judicial spheres honest becomes a final guarantor and legitimator of injustice and dishonesty. The public sphere becomes largely a plaything of propaganda and manipulation rooted in strategic rather than communicative action; it does anything but appeal to the better argument. The public sphere becomes a tool of private interests and thus denies itself as public sphere. Propaganda that unfairly reinforces the agendas of the dominant class, race, and sex competes with communicative praxis ordered to the better argument and shoves it to the side. As a result, truth, the aim of the public sphere, is subordinated and sacrificed to falsehood.[6]

Even though the argument from principle against capitalism and the capitalist sphere has its own distinct logic and validity, it can also function in a second way as an empirical hypothesis. Similarly, the empirical analysis to be developed more fully in the following chapters can lead us to ask, What is the best ultimate explanation for these widespread, frequently recurring phenomena? Is it plausible to see them, as one must who adopts conservative or liberal reformist accounts of capitalism, as basically benevolent, as accidental results of this system? Why then do we have not the lessening of poverty but its intensification; not the lessening of repression but its increase and the development of new forms such as the prison-industrial complex; not increased democracy and open, public discussion but their eclipse as late capitalism goes on its way? Under a merely reformist analysis that sees capitalism as basically beneficent and unproblematic, as Habermas does, do we not have to see these as anomalous, coincidental, unexplained, or inadequately explained? Are not such phenomena better explained as appearances of an essentially flawed, contradictory, irrational, and unjust social system called capitalism or the capitalist state? Thus, the principled analysis of structure leads to empirical inquiry, and this leads back to structural explanation.

NOTES

1. Jürgen Habermas, *Between Facts and Norms*, trans. William Rehg (Cambridge: MIT Press, 1996), 132–33. Page numbers in parentheses throughout this chapter refer to this book. See my discussion and defense of such a democratic socialist state in *Critique, Action, and Liberation* (Albany: State University of New York Press, 1995), 133–30.

2. See Marsh, *Critique, Action, and Liberation*, 67–76. Michael Walzer, *Spheres of Justice* (New York: Basic Books, 1983), 295–303.

3. For a fuller discussion of this issue, see my discussion in *Critique, Action, and Liberation*, 282–88, 343–50.

4. See Marsh, *Critique, Action, and Liberation*, 162–76, for a fuller development of this argument concerning the incompatibility of capitalism and democracy.

5. Dennis Moynihan, "Anti-WTO Activist Jamboree"; Robin Hahnel, "Going to Greet the WTO in Seattle"; and Michael Albert, "Seize the Day," all in *Z Magazine*, November 1999, 5–14.

6. Noam Chomsky and Edward Herman, *Manufacturing Consent: The Political Economy of the Mass Media* (New York: Pantheon, 1988), 1–35.

5

Law and Jurisprudence

In the two preceding chapters, I have interpreted and criticized Habermas's philosophy of law as laid out in his normative genesis of the legal community and the state. In Habermas's next two chapters, which I treat in this chapter, he turns to legal theory in order to test his philosophical analysis against specific legal theories that are and have been influential in Germany and the United States. Here further dimensions of the internal tension between facticity and validity emerge, dimensions that are rooted in the legal decision-making process and the role of the Federal Constitutional Court in Germany and the Supreme Court in the United States.

In the fifth chapter of Habermas's *Between Facts and Norms*, the main issue is the jurisprudential tension between the need for judicial decisions to conform to existing statutes and precedents and the demand that decisions be right or just in light of moral standards. Here Habermas surveys legal realism, legal hermeneutics, and positivism before considering in great detail Ronald Dworkin's theory of judicial decision making as a possibly more adequate alternative, retaining valid aspects of the other two theories but rejecting other aspects and integrating everything into a higher, more comprehensive viewpoint. Habermas finds much that is valid and persuasive in Dworkin's theory, but he also finds it wanting in certain respects. In chapter 6, Habermas treats the separation of powers and the role of constitutional courts by inquiring into the apparent competition between legislature and judiciary in the welfare state, the so-called value jurisprudence of the German high court, and the American debate over the nature of constitutional review. In this last discussion Habermas treats John Hart Ely's proceduralism, Frank Michelman's and Cass Sunstein's civic republican proposals, and Bruce Ackerman's distinction between "normal politics" and "higher" constitutional lawmaking. In the discussion of these issues in chapters 5 and 6, features of a new kind of proceduralist understanding of law and decision making emerge (in relation to previous legal paradigms). These features include the intersubjective, dialogical aspect of judicial decision making; basic rights as deontological in relation to other values; a nonpaternalistic conception of the Supreme Court as safeguarding the discursive qualities of judicial decision making; and a nuanced, balancing integration, critique, and overcoming of liberal and republican theories of decision making, incorporated now into the higher viewpoint of Habermas's proceduralist conception.

This chapter is divided into five parts: a brief consideration of legal realism, legal hermeneutics, and positivism; Dworkin's theory of law; competition between legislature and judiciary in the welfare state; the limits of value jurisprudence, which tends to dissolve the difference between collective goals and constitutional rights; and judicial review. What Habermas comes up with here has much to recommend it, especially in his dialectical overcoming of such dichotomies as liberal and republican, coherence with the legal tradition and moral rightness, and legislature versus judiciary. What also emerges, however, is a further specification and concretion of the problems discussed in previous chapters. Normative issues springing from the tension between capitalism and democracy come home to roost jurisprudentially in an empirical manner. Legal theory itself, in a way that Habermas does not fully realize, is caught up in the same contradiction. His dialectic, it turns out, is not radical enough. It stops short of where it needs to go and thus leaves issues mystified.

LEGAL REALISM, HERMENEUTICS, AND POSITIVISM

Habermas begins his discussion in chapter 5 by arguing that different modern legal orders not only represent different ways of realizing the same rights and principles discussed in earlier chapters but also can reflect different legal paradigms. By the latter he means the exemplary views of a legal community regarding the way a system of rights and constitutional principles can be actualized in the particular context of a given society. The two most successful paradigms in the history of modern law, still competing today, are those of bourgeois formal law and the welfare state, "paternalized" law. The perspective of discourse theory suggests that a third legal paradigm, the proceduralist, should displace and sublate those earlier paradigms. He begins with the assumption, to be proven and developed throughout the rest of the book, that mass welfare state democracies are most appropriately understood in proceduralist terms. Again, I ask how and why such a stance is possible or valid, given that the capitalism underlying and grounding both paradigms obtains today more viciously and universally than ever. Would not a proceduralist model require for its adequate, concrete embodiment a qualitatively different society, one that is democratic not only politically but also socially and economically and realizing fully the ideal of community present in Habermas's paradigm. Is not Habermas here practicing a crypto-utopianism that belies his intended neo-Hegelian realism, in which the rational is actualized and the actual is rational? Habermas's proceduralist paradigm gives us a more adequate picture of late capitalist society than the other two paradigms only if one gives a radical version of that paradigm, rather than Habermas's liberal, reformist version. A radical version of discourse theory stresses the contradictions in late capitalist society pointing toward a qualitatively different society.[1]

In any event, Habermas is going to make his approach plausible from the perspective of legal theory proper, that is, in view of the legal system in the narrow sense. Taken as an action system, law includes the totality of interactions regulated by legal norms; all social communities fall under law. The legal system in the narrow sense includes not only all interactions oriented to law but also those geared to produce new laws and to reproduce law as law. Institutionalizing the legal system in this sense requires the self-application of secondary rules that constitute and confer the official power to make, apply, and implement law. "Legislative, judicial, and administrative powers of government differ analytically according to these functions" (195). Habermas reminds us that not only legislatures but also courts make law insofar as they interpret and develop it, and so do administrative agencies, insofar as they exercise a rather broad discretion. Law is applied not only by the courts but also indirectly by the administration. Finally, law is implemented not only by the administration but also directly by courts (195–96).

A discourse theory of law must prove itself at the level of the legal system in the narrow sense and legal theory. Unlike a philosophical theory of justice, legal theory moves within the domain of particular legal orders. Unlike philosophy, legal theory cannot afford to ignore those aspects that result from the connection between law and political power. Like jurisprudence, legal theory privileges the judge's perspective, because of the function of the judiciary within the legal system in the narrow sense. Because all legal communications refer to actionable claims, court decisions provide a perspective from which the legal system can be analyzed. This choice of perspective implies only a methodological commitment, which does not restrict analysis to processes of adjudication. Legal theory extends to the legislative and administrative domains, hence to all of the subsystems reflexively concerned with the production and reproduction of law, as well as the legal system in the broad sense. Consequently, legal theory, in contrast to the doctrinal work of jurisprudence, claims to achieve a theory of the legal order as a whole. Nevertheless, first of all, legal theory remains a theory of adjudication and legal discourse. Within the sphere of adjudication, the tension between facticity and validity manifests itself as a tension between the principle of legal certainty and the claim to a legitimate application of law, rendering right or correct decisions. Is it enough for a legal decision to be consistent and coherent with the established body of past decisions, or must it also be right? Or is being right the essential point, with the consequence that we can jettison or downplay the decision's relation to legal precedent (196–97)?

Not surprisingly, Habermas's conviction is that both perspectives are necessary. The principle of legal certainty demands, on the one hand, that decisions be consistently rendered within the framework of the existing legal order, an opaque web of past legislative and judicial decisions, possibly including customary law as well. On the other hand, the claim to legitimacy of a decision requires that it not only be consistent with similar decisions in the past and in accord with the current legal system but also rationally grounded so that all participants can accept it as rational and fair. Judges decide present cases within the horizon of a present future, and their opinion can claim validity in the light of rules and principles accepted as legitimate. A decision can be consistent with legal traditions and not accepted as fair by the community. Such was the case with the separate but equal provision concerning black and white schoolchildren in the United States immediately before 1954 (198–99).

But does such a theoretical account integrating facticity and validity obtain in the real, social, legal world? In considering this question, Habermas reflects on three different approaches: legal hermeneutics, legal realism, and legal positivism. Legal hermeneutics revives the Aristotelian principle that no rule is able to regulate its own application. If a legal case is a state of affairs falling under a rule, such a case is constituted as such only by being described in terms of the norm applied to it. At the same time, this norm acquires a more concrete meaning by virtue of being applicable to this state of affairs. A norm always takes in a complex lifeworld situation only in a selective manner, and the single case constituted by the norm never exhausts its meaning. Hermeneutics proposes a process model as a way of understanding how to arrive at a "fit" between norm and particular case. Interpretation begins with a vague preunderstanding of a prior relation between norm and case that gradually becomes more articulate to the extent that norm and circumstances specify one another and constitute the case by making the norm more concrete. According to hermeneutics, the rationality problem of adjudication is solved by contextualizing reason in the historical nexus of a received tradition. As should be obvious, legal hermeneutics one-sidedly opts for certainty over rightness or, more exactly, reduces rightness to certainty (199–200).

The realist theory of law responds to a factual pluralism in which various belief systems compete with one another, and recourse to a prevailing ethos developed through interpretation does not offer a convincing basis for legal discourse. What counts for one person as a historically valid principle is for another mere ideology or prejudice. Interest positions of the participants rooted in psychological, historical, or economic grounds determine the selectivity of judicial decisions. Because of this claim, legal realism engenders a skepticism about legal decisions. One can no longer distinguish between law and politics. Moreover, the very stabilizing function of law, based on the conviction of those affected that a legal decision is legitimate, is undermined by such skepticism. The observer's point of view in legal realism is incompatible with the first-person, idealistic expectations of participants that all cases can be decided consistently and rightly. The realist thus cannot explain how this functionally necessary accomplishment of the legal system is compatible with such skepticism (200–201).

Legal positivism tries to avoid such skepticism by seeing the legal system as a closed system that facilitates the consistency of rule-bound decisions and renders the law largely independent of politics. A "basic norm" or "rule of recognition" enables one to determine unambiguously which norms belong to valid law at any given point in time and which do not. The validity of legal regulations is measured solely by the observance of a legally stipulated procedure of lawmaking. Such legislation privileges the correct process of enactment over the rational justification of a norm's content.

The legitimating of the legal order as a whole shifts to its historical origin, to a basic norm or rule of recognition that legitimates everything without itself being capable of rational justification or grounding. It is a part of a historical form of life that must be accepted as settled custom. Such an approach subordinates validity to certainty, as hard cases where a selectivity has operated on the basis of class or race or sex become difficult for the positivist to explain or justify. Why should we accept such decisions, especially if our understanding of justice has advanced? But to change such decisions requires a criterion of rightness that the positivist cannot supply (201–2).

DWORKIN'S THEORY OF LAW

Enter Ronald Dworkin. His theory of law can be seen as an attempt to overcome difficulties and blind spots of the hermeneutical, realist, and positivist positions. In opposition to hermeneutics, Dworkin argues for a deontological theory of rights to explain how a legal decision can be both certain and right. In opposition to realism, Dworkin holds to both the possibility and the necessity of consistent, rule-bound decisions guaranteeing legal certainty. In opposition to positivism, he maintains the possibility and necessity of "single right" decisions that are legitimate with respect to their context in light of recognized principles. The hermeneutical role of preunderstanding does not leave the judge totally at the mercy of historical authority. Rather, he has the obligation to investigate critically the way the history of law reveals the traces both of reason and of unreason. When courts correctly decide who has political rights and what these rights are, these rights enjoy positive validity in light of consistency with the legal tradition and are also right in light of the standards of justice.

It is Dworkin's position, as it is Habermas's, that rights exist because of a historically embodied, articulated, and developed sense of practical reason. This reason is articulated as the principle of equal concern and respect for each person. The basic norm tallies with Kant's principle of right and Rawls's first principle of justice, according to which each has a right to equal liberties. This right cannot be grounded in further principles and thus enjoys the stature of a natural right of all men and women that they have simply as human beings, and it confers a moment of unconditionality on legal claims. Such a right cannot be trumped by collective goals (203–4).

When Dworkin speaks of arguments of principle justifying judicial decisions externally, in most cases he has legal principles in mind—that is, standards that result from the application of the discourse principle to the legal code. Those are distinct from policy arguments; such are laws tied to policies such as redistributive taxation or resource allocation, which are addressed in a morally neutral way to addressees but may become morally relevant to the extent that they proceed from morally justified policies. Political policies are justified in the list of principles and existing rights, but only arguments of principle can preserve the internal connection between the decision about an individual case and the normative substance of the whole legal order (204–8).

Dworkin develops the distinction between a rule and a principle to explain the inadequacy of the positivist conception of law. Rules are concrete norms sufficiently specified for application to typical cases, like stipulations for drawing up a will, whereas principles are general legal standards in need of interpretation, like human rights and equal treatment. Both rules and principles are norms with deontological validity, and both are distinguished from policies, which are teleological. Rules contain an antecedent "if" clause that specifies the typical situational features constituting conditions of application, whereas principles either appear with an unspecified validity claim or are restricted in their applicability only by general conditions requiring interpretation. A conflict between rules can be resolved either by introducing an exception clause or by declaring one of the rules to be invalid. When principles conflict, such an all-or-nothing decision is not necessary. If one principle is deemed more contextually appropriate to a situation than another, the latter does not lose its validity but only retreats into the background. I may decide, for example, that in a certain situation my obligation to visit a sick friend has a priority over my promise to go to a party. That promise does not lose its validity but only its contextual relevance to the situation. What is true of this moral conflict is true also of a conflict between legal principles (208–9).

Because positivists see all legal conflicts as conflicts between rules requiring an all-or-nothing decision, they arrive at a false notion of autonomy. Positivists are forced to reach decisionistic conclusions because they start from a one-dimensional conception of law as a system of rules without principles. As soon as principles are admitted, both the closed character of the rule system and the irresolvability of conflicts disappear (209).

Through analyzing the distinction among principle, rule, and policy and the different roles they play, Dworkin begins to grasp the posttraditional level of justification required by positive law. Contrary to what positivists think, emancipation from traditional religious-metaphysical contexts does not leave law totally contingent. Contrary to what legal realism argues, law does not lack an internal structure of its own and thus is not totally at the mercy of politics. Contrary to legal hermeneutics, deontologically based principles are not simply drawn from the history of an ethical community. Rather, the institutionalized history of a legal system can be criticized and reconstructed (209–10).

According to Dworkin, legal principles and the political policies compatible with them provide the arguments for reconstructing the bulk of existing law. He calls for the construction of a theory of law, not a theory of justice. This task consists in discovering valid principles and policies in the light of which a given legal order can be justified in its essential elements such that all individual decisions fit into it as aspects of a concrete whole. Dworkin imagines such a task to be performed by a judge whose intellectual capacities would compare to the physical strength of Hercules. Judge Hercules has two components of knowledge at his disposal: he knows all the principles and policies necessary for justification, and he has a complete overview of the body of existing law.

Hercules must expand his theory to include the idea that a part of institutional history may be mistaken as a part of an ongoing historical process. Also, not all elements of the legal tradition bind the judge in the same sense; precedents may receive quite different weights for different decisions. A reconstructive legal theory should be sufficiently selective to allow one right decision stating which claim may be honored in the existing legal order. The theory of Judge Hercules reconciles the rationally reconstructed decisions of the past with the claim to rational acceptability of the present. It reconciles history and justice, certainty and validity, institutional history and judicial originality. A judge must make fresh judgments about the rights of parties who come before him, but these political rights reflect, rather than oppose, decisions of the past (212–13).

So far, so good. What is to be said critically about the validity of Dworkin's approach? Clearly it marks an improvement over legal hermeneutics, legal realism, and positivism. Habermas is clearly sympathetic with Dworkin's theory, to the extent that it lends itself to a dialectical approach to law, reconciling such opposites as certainty and validity. However, Habermas finds the theory monological as it stands, relying on the competence and knowledge of a single judge, presuming the superiority of the judge to the citizens. Habermas's recommended corrective flows from his discourse model of intersubjective, democratic community, of which the judge would be a part and which he would represent. The standpoint of integrity in law implies that law is a means of social integration achieved dialogically among persons. The ideal demands of legal theory are best expressed in the political ideal of an open society of interpreters of the constitution rather than the ideal personality of an extremely virtuous and knowledgeable judge (223–24).

Critical legal studies (CLS) has a critique to which Dworkin and Habermas are more vulnerable and which Habermas does not fully, satisfactorily answer. CLS again takes up issues of legal realism, which initially shook the assumptions of legal theory that rights exist, that actual cases can be consistently decided in agreement with a body of existing law, and that court decisions are, as a rule, rational. Dworkin's theory, as we have seen, gives these assumptions a less vulnerable constructionist reading. From the perspective of CLS, however, Dworkin's defense of these assumptions by having recourse to a very idealized theory of law exposes him to new objections.

Because, according to CLS, flesh-and-blood judges fall very much short of the ideal Hercules, the recommendation that one orient oneself in everyday work by this figure would make possible a desire to endorse legal decisions that are in fact determined by interest positions, ideological biases of various kinds, and political attitudes. Judges select principles and policies and construct their own legal theories from them in order to rationalize decisions and thus to conceal the real prejudices underlying the decisions.

Dworkin could respond to this objection by saying that if some court decisions are better explained by extralegal factors than by legal situation, the facts speak against the validity of the legal decisions. Such decisions are examples of the bad decisions that Hercules would resist and throw out in his reconstruction. Indeterminacy and bad decisions do not flow from law as such but from the individual judge's failure to develop and use the best theory possible and from the institutional history of a legal order that to some extent resists rational reconstruction. Even if one does not share Dworkin's optimism about the consistency and rightness of American law, one need not renounce Hercules as long as existing law offers some historical basis for rational reconstruction. As radical as I am, therefore, in that I am inclined to be more critical than Dworkin of American legal practice, I agree with this point. As contradictory, the history of American law does have some rectitude and validity in it, but not nearly as much as Dworkin claims (213–15).

In a next round of criticism, critics attempt to prove that Dworkin expects his Hercules to carry out an unrealizable program. Duncan Kennedy tries to show that the development of American private law and judicial practice revolves around two incompatible principles. On the one hand, there is a freedom of contract in a liberal society regulated by competition carried on in a purposive-rational manner. On the other hand, there is the good-faith principle underlying a reciprocally obligating contract relationship flowing from an association based on mutual concern and solidarity. CLS generalizes the results of this and other studies to show that existing law in general is shot through with contradictory principles and policies and hence every attempt at rational reconstruction is going to fail. The contradictions form a structure that yields no, even idealized, decision practice guaranteeing equal treatment and justice. What we have here is not a rule system but chaos (215–16).

Habermas answers this objection by making a number of points. First of all, if we assume that cases typical for present-day adjudication involve not only application-specific rules but also principles, it is quite clear why collisions occur and yet do not betray a deeper incoherence. Except for those norms with "if" clauses specifying detailed application conditions, all norms are inherently indeterminate. The coherence of a legal system is endangered if in fact principles of this latter sort are inherently contradictory, each claiming equal validity for the same class of cases. All norms of this kind, however, are indeterminate and need additional specifications in the individual case. They require a distinct discourse of application, which aims to comprehend all the relevant circumstances of a situation and to determine the most appropriate norm for the situation. When a norm proves to be appropriate, then that norm can ground a single judgment claiming to be right. That a norm is prima facie valid means merely that it has been rationally justified. Only its impartial application leads to a valid decision about a case (217).

What are we to think of this apparently ingenious reply, an example of Habermas functioning at his best and worst as a theorist? His answer certainly covers some instances of adjudication, but does it cover all? Is there more to be said for CLS's argument that bourgeois society is inherently conflictual on the level of principle itself? I think there is. Indeed, we have been arguing that in our discussion in the preceding two chapters, in which we argued for an inherent conflict between capitalism and democracy, equality and freedom, the fourth principle concerning political autonomy and the fifth principle concerning equal opportunity. If such claims are true of Habermas's system of rights, then they are certainly true of the democratic capitalist system on which he draws for his theory and which, he, like Dworkin, claims embodies a high level of progressive reason.

In the late nineteenth and twentieth centuries, for example, there was a political and legal movement to enshrine big corporations and make them legal persons. This in fact did happen, over the protest of small capitalists and entrepreneurs who represented an earlier stage of capitalism, as well as others who saw democracy itself as threatened. Not only reflection on principle but also over a hundred years of hindsight as we see the destruction wrought by, and the antidemocratic character of, corporations, suggest that these critics were right.[2] Does this enshrining of the corporation amount to a contradiction with Habermas's fourth and fifth principles, the freedom principle and the equality principle?

If there is an internal conflict in the legal system itself that expresses the structural contradiction between capitalism and democracy, then we would expect it to manifest itself massively in an empirical way in the history of capitalist countries, and indeed that has happened. We have already mentioned the white, upper-class background of the judiciary from the beginning of the U.S. Republic, its identification with the interests of capital rather than those of the poor and labor, a double standard for costly white-collar crime versus the much less costly blue-collar crime, and the prison-industrial complex.

We can add to those observations: White collar crime is not a rarity but a regularity, and many companies are repeat offenders. The Justice Department discovered that 60 percent of the 582 largest U.S. companies were guilty of one or more criminal actions such as tax evasion, price fixing, illegal kickbacks, bribes to public officials, consumer fraud, and violations of labor codes, workplace safety, and environmental laws. In recent years General Electric was convicted of 282 counts of contract fraud and fined $8 million; C.T.E., Boeing, RCA, and Hughes Aircraft pleaded guilty to felony charges of trafficking in stolen Pentagon budget records; and Dale Electronics was fined $3.7 million for deliberately concealing flaws in military electronic equipment. Yet not one of the executives involved in these crimes went to jail.[3]

Corporate executives are almost never incarcerated for the felonies they commit, and penalties often go uncollected. Protex Industries was fined $75 million for endangering workers at a hazardous industrial site, but the fine was later suspended. The General Accounting Office discovered that the Justice Department has not collected $7 billion in fines and restitutions from corporations and individuals convicted of felonies. Contrast with this the sentences of a Norfolk, Virginia, man who received ten years for stealing 87 cents, a youth in Louisiana who received fifty years in jail for selling a few ounces of marijuana, and a Houston youth who was sentenced to fifty years for robbing people of $1 as they left a restaurant. These instances give some plausibility to the claim by Justice Hugo Black that there can be no equal justice "where the kind of trial a man gets depends on the amount of money he has." Legal services in this society best serve those who can buy them. Yet Habermas's and Dworkin's model of legal adjudication does not account adequately for such phenomena.[4]

The so-called war on drugs in the United States manifests the same kind of problem. The growing prison population consists mainly of petty drug offenders, not violent felons and mobsters from organized crime. Since 1980, the federal prison population has almost quadrupled. Three-quarters of the new arrivals are drug offenders, who face harsh mandatory sentencing. A California teenager on his way to a rock concert was sentenced to fifteen years without parole for possession of three grams of LSD. In Texas, a young man with less than a gram of LSD received twenty years in prison without parole. Most of those arrested and convicted are blacks, Hispanics, and poor whites; yet most of the drug use in the United States is carried on by upper- and middle-class whites. Little has been done to prosecute the big drug cartels or those who launder drug money through established financial institutions. Profits from the drug trade were used to finance a right-wing mercenary war against a progressive government in Nicaragua, and both the Central Intelligence Agency and the Drug Enforcement Administration supported and helped to cover up this effort in various ways.[5]

The problem is not just inconsistency between and among laws but frequent and far-reaching inconsistent enforcement of laws already on the books. One can question, therefore, Habermas's distinction between an "internal" logic of learning embodied in the law and an "external" interference by class or racial bias. Rather, such bias, which is built into the structure of law itself, makes possible and likely such frequently recurring phenomena as these. Class, race, and sexual background and bias influence the formation of the constitution and of particular laws and applications of law flowing from it, and the internal structure of lawmaking and legal decision making makes possible and likely the flourishing of corporations, the wealthy, and whites. The internal intersects with the external dialectically and reciprocally.[6]

I do not wish to deny Habermas's argument entirely. There is a valid internal logic of lawmaking and decision making that can be argued for in the democratic capitalist constitution, but that is contradicted by other principles and decisions that have been made over the course of centuries and continue to be made. Contra Habermas and Dworkin, then, what would be required is a radical Hercules who would do a far more drastic surgery on the legal tradition, finding much more that is problematic, wrong, inconsistent, and unjust. What name should be given to this radical judge who has knowledge of a consistent system of rights and legal history and is animated by profound sympathy for those many victims of the legal process over the course of history: women, gays, lesbians, blacks, Hispanics, the poor, labor, the homeless, and the unemployed? I propose that we name this judge Karl Marx.[7]

THE COMPETITION BETWEEN LEGISLATURE AND JUDICIARY

In chapter 6 of *Between Facts and Norms*, Habermas continues the discussion begun by focusing on Dworkin's theory through reflecting on the apparent conflict between judiciary and legislature in making and applying law. Because judicial decision making is linked to law and legal statutes, the rationality of adjudication depends on the legitimacy of existing law. This legitimacy depends upon the rationality of a legislative process that is not at the disposal of agencies responsible for the administration of justice. The constitutional aspects of politics and legislative practice are important topics in jurisprudence, but from the perspective of legal theory, both of these areas open up from the perspective of adjudication, which is most fruitfully studied by reflecting on the role of the constitutional courts. Here the issue is that theoretically quite distinct functions are combined in single institutions.

There are three issues to be considered in this discussion. The first considers the critique of adjudication from the perspective of separation of powers. Here we move into a discussion of legal paradigms, liberal versus welfare state. The second continues the discussion of Habermas's previous chapter by reflecting on "value jurisprudence" as it occurs in the Federal Constitutional Court of Germany. Habermas's critique here is directed against a methodological self-understanding of the court, according to which the orientation by principles is seen to be equivalent to the weighing of goals, values, and collective goods. The third discussion leads into the question of how we should understand the political process, conceived by Habermas as a process of will-and-opinion-formation interpreted from the point of view of a discourse theory of law. Here the role of the Supreme Court in the United States will be seen to be that of protecting the democratic, legislative procedure; at stake here is the renewal of a republican, noninstrumental understanding of politics (238–40).

The Dissolution of the Liberal Paradigm of Law

Constitutional courts normally carry out several functions at once. Taking the Federal Constitutional Court as an example, we see three tasks: settling intragovernmental disputes, reviewing the constitutionality of norms, and considering constitutional complaints. Each of these, Habermas thinks, is defensible, legitimate, and necessary. Least problematic from the perspective of separation of powers is responsibility for constitutional complaints and concrete judicial review; that is, the higher constitutional court reviews cases that have been decided by a lower court. That the court settles cases of intragovernmental dispute can seem more problematic, because of its possibly infringing on separation of powers, but can be justified by the requirement to settle conflicts between governmental agencies that depend on collaboration. The principle of separation of powers cannot be violated by a court that lacks the means to enforce its decisions on parliament and administration (240–41).

The competition between the constitutional court and the democratically legitimated legislature becomes more acute in abstract judicial review, in which the court is asked to decide whether a statute passed by parliament is constitutional. Because, prior to adoption, this is a question that parliament must decide, it makes sense also to institutionalize such review inside parliament after a law is passed, perhaps by a parliamentary committee staffed by legal experts. Such a procedure also has the advantage of motivating within the legislature a reflection on the normative content of constitutions, which tends to get lost in the crush of parliamentary business. Such a procedure recommends itself even if we assume that the separation of powers is primarily concerned with keeping the administration from becoming independent in relationship to communicatively produced power (241).

There is a necessary asymmetry between the legislature and the court, on the one hand, and the administration, on the other, because the administration does not have control over the normative grounds of legislation and adjudication and is, therefore, subject to parliamentary oversight and judicial review. Because of this relationship, supervision of the other two branches by the executive is excluded. Anyone wishing to replace the constitutional court by appointing the head of the executive branch as the guardian of the law, as Carl Schmitt once wanted to do, is misguided. If we interpret the logic of separation of powers in terms of argumentative theory, then it makes sense to construe the legislature self-reflexively, as able to review its own activity. Beyond question, such abstract judicial review belongs in the legislature, and it might not be entirely misguided to reserve this function, even at a second level of appeal, to a legislative self-review developed into a quasi-judicial procedure. The transfer of this power to a constitutional court requires argument (241–42).

The constitutional court will in any case enter into a discourse of basic rights when it is a matter not of reviewing parliamentary statutes after their adoption but of hard cases when basic rights collide or when, in the light of one basic right, two or more statutes collide. That in such cases the right interpretation has to be formed and that this is in a certain way creative does not have to endanger the logic of the separation of powers. Interpretation operates in both legislation and adjudication, but in one according to a logic of justification and in the other according to a logic of application to hard cases (243–44).

Some of the strongest criticism of the relationships between legislature and court, however, are rooted not in methodological but in historical perspectives. Critics note a contrast between ideal types: the liberal paradigm, in which state and society are separate, and the welfare state paradigm, which no longer merely guarantees comprehensive legal protection but also provides its citizens a safety net for socially conditioned risks and losses. It would be a basic mistake, from Habermas's point of view, to evaluate the welfare state from the perspective of an outdated liberal paradigm, which stresses the rights of the individual against the state and misses or deemphasizes the prior horizontal relationship between and among citizens. What comes out more explicitly in the welfare state paradigm is the structure of basic rights as a whole, which can no longer be guaranteed merely by an unfettered economic society spontaneously reproducing itself but "must be realized through the benefits and services of an interventionist state that provides infrastructures and wards off risks—a government that at once regulates, facilitates, and compensates" (247). Moreover, the horizontal relation of citizen to citizen, such as the necessity to maintain basic dignity or the necessary minimal material provision to make possible political participation, comes more clearly and explicitly to the fore in the welfare state paradigm (244–53).

Although all of this sounds wonderful, it makes the welfare state sound too coherent, consistent, and benign. What needs to be stressed again is the accumulation-legitimation tension, in which the welfare state is torn between two contradictory imperatives, that of securing the particular need of capital and that of securing the needs of the population as a whole. To the extent that the former predominates, as it does for the most part, then the democratic imperative and horizontal and vertical genesis of the rights of the citizen are subordinated to that goal. One can agree with this point and nonetheless concede that the welfare state paradigm is a forward move from the liberal paradigm. But it is a contradictory forward move. It is an imperfect next step toward liberation, not the parousia.

Habermas recognizes this point on the level of legal theory; thus he argues for a proceduralistic paradigm of law. But what is the concrete socioeconomic embodiment and instantiation of such a paradigm? Such a question becomes especially crucial when we note that on a concrete socioeconomic level, societies in the West are moving away from the welfare state as it obtained from 1930 to 1970 toward a version that is much crueler to the poor, that grants much of the population much less political participation and material provision. The tension between accumulation and legitimation is being resolved in favor of accumulation, a backward move in the light of Habermas's own theory and one that can hardly give him comfort. Yet, curiously, he does not address this trend in *Between Facts and Norms* and thus leaves the following syllogism strongly appealing. The choices are liberal capitalism; welfare state capitalism; some unhappy mixture of the two, using the rhetoric of liberal capitalism (what we are moving toward now); or democratic socialism. The first three are not defensible by the tenets of Habermas's own theory. Therefore democratic socialism must emerge as the socioeconomic context and ground of the proceduralist paradigm of law.[8]

Value Jurisprudence

Habermas begins his discussion of value jurisprudence by noting that doubts about the legitimacy of the Federal Constitutional Court in Germany are based not only on the issue of the paradigm shift but also on methodological assumptions. In Germany, justified criticism is directed against the doctrine of values that expresses a methodological understanding of judges and leads to problematic effects in important precedent-setting cases. Often, however, the criticism is unmediated and does not make clear that the disturbing constitutional consequences are only the effects of a certain methodological self-understanding of the court. Critics like Böckenförde miss the possibility of a correct understanding of constructive interpretation that does not assimilate rights to value (253–54).

The distinction between principles and values is conceptual. Principles are higher-level norms, in the light of which other norms can be justified, and have a deontological sense; values are teleological. Norms of action obligate the addressee equally and without exception, whereas values are intersubjectively shared preferences that are worth striving for. Norms are binary in that they are either valid or invalid; values express preferences that can be satisfied more or less in relation to other values. Norms are absolute and unconditional, expressing what one is to do and binding all equally. Values are relative, expressing what is good for me or us or some group over the long run. Norms must not contradict one another if they claim validity for the same circle of addressees. Values compete for priority from case to case and can contradict one another (255).

Because the logical properties of values and norms differ, there are differences in application also. The question of what I should do in a situation is posed and answered differently in the two cases. Norms help me to decide which action is commanded; values help me to decide which action is recommended. Norms tell us that this action is right, equally good for all. Values come out of a particular culture or form of life and help me to discover what is best for us, for our particular community. Values, of course, enter into law, but they are domesticated by a system of rights that has priority. One who equates the constitution with a particular order of values is making a huge mistake (256).

This integration and sublation of liberalism and republicanism is impressive and has much to recommend it. Nonetheless, I think deontology trumps teleology too much in an unjustified way. In *Critique, Action, and Liberation,* I argued for a reciprocity between right and good, deontology and teleology, duty and happiness on three levels: right, morality, and justice (see the preface for a summary of that argument). It seems to me that such a reciprocity is present and implied, although unacknowledged, in Habermas's theory in at least the following ways: First, consensus seems to be the good or goal aimed at in the practice of communicative action, and the practice of such action is a value or a good. All other things being equal, it is preferred over strategic action or purposive-rational action as a way for human beings to interact together. Second, a democratic society ruled by law is a good in a normative, universalistic sense to be striven for, preserved, and protected against threat. Could we not say that such a good is the common good of such a democratic society and thus is not merely particularistic in the way that Habermas ascribes to ethical theories?

Third, the participation defended by principle 4 in the system of rights is a right and a good to be striven for, and material goods as necessary for participation in principle 5 are both rights and goods. Fourth, the just administration of just laws and the just application of such laws are also goals and goods to be striven for. Otherwise the laws remain merely abstract, and justice and well-being as aspects of the common good are not concretely achieved. Fifth, the free play of difference and opinion in the public sphere interacting with and influencing formal political processes is a good; indeed, it is important for the public happiness in a flourishing democratic society in which citizens find it worthwhile to live. Finally, liberation from the shamelessness of unjust systemic power rooted in administration and economy, to the extent that that imposes itself on the public sphere or legislature, is a good.

With such qualifications, we can still accept Habermas's distinction between a universal system of rights, morality, and democracy and particular ethical traditions. Present on this universal level, however, is an interaction between right and good that is a more adequate dialectical sublation of liberalism and republicanism. Good is not just something aimed at in a strategic or purposive-rational manner; it is also a universalistic component of morality, democracy, communicative action, and the system of rights. Such a qualification allows us, as one consequence, more positive motivation on a universal level than Habermas allows. I do not have to resort primarily to the ethical level for motivation to be a good citizen, participant, or activist, because motivating goods are also present on a universal level. Such participation is motivated not simply by justice in a deontological sense but also by liberation.

In the discussion among American constitutional scholars, the distinction is between approaches that see basic rights as legal principles and those that see them as values or goals. Both Paul Brest and John Hart Ely make this distinction, as does Michael J. Perry, a neo-Aristotelian. Perry sees the text of the Constitution as manifesting the ethical self-understanding of the ethical community. Like a sacred text, the Constitution founds new ideas, in the light of which the community in an ongoing discussion is more able to achieve insight into what its real, deeper interests are. Perry sees the constitutional judge in the role of a prophetic teacher, whose interpretation of the divine text of the Founding Fathers secures the continuity of a tradition that is constitutive of the community's life. According to this perspective, the Supreme Court must interpret and concretize norms in a manner equivalent to implicit lawmaking. The Court is transformed into an authoritarian agency that competes with the legislature (257).

Because in cases of collision between values, all reasons can assume the character of policy arguments, the barrier erected in legal discourse by deontological understanding of legal norms and principles collapses. When values conflict, there is no clear logical or rational way of arguing for one over the other. On one hand, the danger of irrational rulings increases because functionalist or teleological perspectives win out over normative ones. On the other hand, as soon as the deontological character of basic rights is taken seriously, they can be withdrawn from cost-benefit analysis (259–60).

Here, as in the case of the discussion about the German court, such methodological considerations issue in a critique of false self-understanding but do not deny the possibility of rationally deciding constitutional questions in general. Here the distinction in kind between justification and application is pertinent. Just as the interpretation of basic norms and principles is no different from the interpretation of ordinary norms, the application of principles is no different from the application of norms and thus does not have to generate rationality gaps. Rulings on constitutional complaints and concrete constitutional review are limited to application of constitutional norms presupposed as valid. An adjudication guided by principles does not have to violate the hierarchical structure intended to ensure that reasons available for decision making at any level are given in advance by a higher-ranking authority (261).

As soon as a norm does not allow a coherent application in conformity with the constitution, the necessity for abstract judicial review arises. Although this is a process that must be undertaken from the legislator's point of view, it does not have to be institutionalized in the legislature. As long as the review is exercised by an independent judiciary that does not impose its mandates on the legislature but only overturns norms, pragmatic and legal-political considerations seem to support the institutional locus of authority being in the judiciary, as it is currently in the Federal Republic of Germany and the United States. However one answers the question concerning the correct institutionalization of powers, it is neither necessary nor possible to return to the liberal view of government, which holds that basic rights are subjective rights or liberties only in relation to the state and do not also constitute an objective order binding on all spheres. One main reason for Habermas's claim here is that we need to hold on to democracy in a late-welfare-state context. "Economic power and social pressure need to be tamed by the rule of law no less than does administrative power" (263). In this light, the function of the court in a context of separation of powers and the welfare state is to make citizens' private and public autonomy equally possible (262–63).

I am sympathetic to Habermas's reasoning here. We certainly cannot and do not want to return to a liberal model. One can ask, however, whether the taming of economic power performed by the capitalist welfare state is sufficient. Would not a democratic socialist model eliminating capitalism in principle, and therefore fully institutionalizing democracy in economic, social, and political spheres, be a more effective approach? And would that not represent a further extension, application, and concretion of the system of rights and democracy, now only imperfectly secured and expressed in a contradictory way under the welfare state model? Is the purpose of the welfare state to contain capitalism, or is it to make capitalism's rule more effective and legitimate, to bring about a context where more and more money can be made by the people and the firms that matter? Merely pushing back colonization while leaving untouched the nondemocracy of the economic sphere seems curiously halfhearted and incomplete on Habermas's part, especially since he has already rejected the liberal claim that the economy is sacrosanct in relation to state intervention. Could there be here on Habermas's part a tacit adherence to the liberal model—push back colonization but do not interfere with the sacred rights of corporations to behave nondemocratically and, for the most part, autonomously within the economic sphere—that is in serious tension with this quite laudable and serious commitment to democracy? Could not full economic, political, and social democracy be the fully rational, consistent, communicative expression of the system of rights, especially since, as we have already argued, Habermas's commitment to capitalism undermines that system in his formulation of it, rendering it inconsistent and incoherent?

John Ely, another American theorist, is on the right track when he insists on the form as well as the content of legislation. The principle of equal treatment is violated not only by the content of laws that discriminate against ethnic and religious minorities, the handicapped, and gays and lesbians but also by inadequate democratic procedural conditions for the genesis of law. Ely, however, is inconsistent when he directs his mistrust not only against legal paternalism or value jurisprudence but also against principles as such. His own commitment to democratic procedure is just such a principle (265–66).

The Role of the Supreme Court

In the United States, constitutional scholars argue about constitutional adjudication more from the standpoint of political science than from that of legal methodology. The debate turns upon the division of labor between the Supreme Court and the democratic legislature, and reflection focuses on the rationality of the legislative process: how the process in fact occurs and, primarily, what it should be. In such critical reflection, the difference between liberal and republican perspectives again becomes pertinent.

Frank Michelman approaches the task posed by abstract judicial review in a manner similar to Ely in that he, Michelman, claims only a derivative authority for the Court based upon the people's right to self-determination. Unlike Ely, however, Michelman looks at the issue from a neo-Aristotelian and republican perspective, relying on a tradition of political theory that moves from Aristotle through Roman philosophy and the Italian Renaissance to Rousseau and Harrington. The republican concept of politics refers not to rights of life, liberty, and property possessed by private citizens and guaranteed by the state but mainly to the practice of self-determination by citizens oriented to the common good and understanding themselves as free and equal members of a cooperative, self-governing community.

The main difference lies in how the democratic process is understood. Is it, as liberals would say, a matter of organizing private interests against an administration specialized in using political power for collective goals? Or is it, as republicans see it, a reflexive form of substantial ethical life, in which communities become aware of their dependence on one another and develop relations of reciprocal recognition in an association of free and equal citizens? If so, solidarity as a third source of social integration emerges, in addition to the market and the state.

Does the citizen possess merely negative rights against the state, or does the citizen have positive political liberties of political participation? Is law primarily a matter of negative rights protecting the individual against state encroachment, or is it a matter of rights rooted in an objective legal order based on mutual respect? Habermas argues that these dichotomies miss the intersubjective meaning of a system of rights founded mutually by citizens. From the standpoint of discourse theory, reciprocal observance of rights and duties is grounded in symmetrical relations of recognition. Republicanism, because it binds the legitimacy of laws to their democratic genesis, comes closer to the discourse concept of law, which puts the integrity of the individuals and their liberties on par with the integrity of the community in which individuals are first able to mutually recognize one another both as individuals and as members of a community (268–71).

A similar kind of contrast emerges in debate over the nature of the political process. Liberals see this process as a struggle for positions of administrative power, republicans as rooted in a structure of communicative action oriented to mutual understanding. Politics as a practice of civic self-legislation finds its paradigm not in the market but in dialogue. Liberals and republicans also differ in the nature of the procedural conditions legitimating opinion-and-will-formation. Liberals see these as nonnormative and strategic, republicans as normative and communicative. Prepolitical self-understandings can come into question and change in an insightful way. Once again, rather than presenting an either/or choice, the discourse model of public discussion and legislation indicates that both strategic and communicative imperatives can, do, and should come into play. Habermas attempts to occupy a middle ground both descriptively and normatively between the excessively pessimistic liberal model and the impossibly demanding, idealistic republican one (272–74).

Because the republican standard of democratic procedure is so high, it inevitably leads to seeing politics as practiced in welfare state societies as failed politics. For this reason, republicanism is tempted to argue for an activist Supreme Court, one that intervenes as a guardian in legislative decision making and procedure, keeping it on the right track. In Habermas's opinion, "It is the exceptionalistic description of political practice—how it ought to be—that suggests the necessity of pedagogical guardian or regent" (278). The point would be to occupy a middle ground between republican and liberal positions. The Court can stay within its ability to apply the law, "provided that the democratic process over which it is supposed to keep watch is not described as a state of exception" (279). According to Ely, it is only in moments of constitutional excitement when history overheats that the people step forward from their normal civil privatism and act communicatively in a participatory manner. Such an event happened in the New Deal era. Otherwise, there are long intervals when the people sleep and the Court has to step forth as guardian. It is the Court that bridges the gap between real and ideal (274–79).

Habermas here is rejecting Ely's account of actual democratic practice both descriptively and normatively, in stark contrast to Habermas's stance later in the book when he admits, in the context of discussing the public sphere, that Ely's description is basically correct (374–79). In such a situation, we perceive a dilemma. Not agreeing with Ely seems to put Habermas on shaky empirical ground, which he later leaves. Agreeing with Ely commits Habermas to saying that, for the most part and most of the time, democratic capitalist societies function undemocratically and unjustly in the light of his own system of rights, and the gap between real and ideal appears. Maybe he should here, in the name of realism, be more sympathetic to Ely's guardian judge, but such a move wreaks havoc with the discourse theory of argumentation, which distinguishes between justification and application and argues for a separation of powers between legislative and judicial realms.

The inconsistency is plausible and perhaps inevitable, given Habermas's liberal commitment to the status quo. The explanation for the gap is not anything in the legal or legislative or communicative process as such but the capitalist infusion into, and influence on, that process, ensuring that it will not and cannot function democratically or will do so only to the extent that it does not interfere with capitalist self-interest. Many empirical and historical studies suggest that Americans' interest in politics has decreased dramatically since 1900. As statistics about voter turnout show, this comes from an awareness that their interests are not adequately represented, all questions are not aired or heard, and effective power is not brought to bear in order to pass laws, issue administrative decrees, and ensure judicial decisions respecting the interests of all. Citizens are thus exercising in a lived way the tenets of the ideal speech situation. In the last twenty to thirty years in the United States, the situation has worsened considerably, as both major parties have become more and more wings of the business party and people have become more and more disillusioned, discouraged, and cynical about the electoral process. Participation in major and many minor elections drops to 50 percent or less of the eligible electorate, and Reagan, Bush, Clinton, and yet another

Bush (with a still weaker claim), who have received only a fraction of that inadequate percentage, claim a mandate. No wonder voters, rather than wasting their time in a charade, simply stay home. Under the circumstances, it is, or might be, a sensible choice. They are just being good Habermasians.[9]

Habermas can legitimately criticize these abuses of the democratic process from the perspective of his discourse theory, theory of rights, and democratic theory putting a high premium on participation. Going all the way with the theory and the criticism growing out of it would and should lead him to argue for the radical democratic transformation of the capitalist system and the institutionalization of full democracy. Such a move would fill the gap between real and ideal. Short of that, he remains in an inconsistent, contradictory halfway state. Or he can accept the democratic, capitalist status quo as inevitable, and here he veers away from the ideal and normative toward an uncritical realism and empiricism. But then the question becomes, How do we fill the gap between real and ideal? At this point judicial activism and guardianship become plausible, one reasonable inference from Habermasian realism linked in a contradictory way to idealism. Another contradiction emerges insofar as he can only preserve democracy by resorting to an undemocratic judicial activism, which violates his own logic of argumentation to the extent that it moves from applying the law to legislating it or overseeing such legislating. The only way to be rational, consistent, and communicative in the light of Habermas's own persuasive theory is to move to radical social transformation. This, too, is utopian, but it is a consistent and realistic utopianism, based upon emerging social movements and contradictions in the social order, whereas Habermas's utopianism is inconsistent in several ways and supremely unrealistic. Western capitalist societies are moving further away from it, not closer to it.

Of course, we should realize that judicial activism and guardianship will not solve the problem either. For, as we have already seen, the judiciary itself is rooted in the capitalistic order, depends on it, serves it, and draws most of its membership from its top professional and economic echelons. The result, at best, is a judicial activism that reins in and hides the worst excesses of capitalistic injustice, making it more mediated and less direct. The result, at worst, is a Supreme Court that, in service of the capitalistic system, presides over the erosion of the system of rights, the rollback of many of the lauded elements of the welfare state, "ending welfare as we know it," removing more and more of the barriers against state intrusion on subjective rights, weakening environmental laws and their application. The Court does not mitigate injustice; it enhances it and makes it legal. This, I would argue, has been the tendency in the last twenty to thirty years in the United States. The very welfare state that emerged painfully is eroding before our very eyes.

The real referent of Habermas's theory, the welfare state, is being transformed into something quite different, much less morally and legally adequate to his own standards. As western capitalistic democracies become more and more like the Third World; as repression grows with the prison-industrial complex; as we move from a warfare-welfare state to a warfare-carceral state; as poverty, unemployment, homelessness, and hunger grow and are not addressed because of cutbacks in programs; as there is regress and not progress according to the best lights of his own theory, even his realistic cop-out ceases to be realistic. Bourgeois realism is unrealistic. At this point he has another choice: either to give up on this communicative ideal entirely and become merely a defender of the status quo or to cling to the ideal in a way that is increasingly implausible. Ideal and real split apart in a way that does violence to the integrated descriptive and normative exigencies of his theory. And they come apart in spite of his very impressive, almost heroic strategies to keep real and ideal together. He becomes realistic in a vulgar, one-dimensional way or naïvely utopian in spite of the best tendencies and intentions of his own theory.[10]

NOTES

1. Jürgen Habermas, *Between Facts and Norms,* trans. William Rehg (Cambridge: MIT Press, 1996), 194–95. Page numbers in parentheses throughout this chapter refer to this book.

2. Martin J. Sklar, *The Corporate Reconstruction of American Capitalism, 1890–1916* (Cambridge: Cambridge University Press, 1988).

3. Michael Parenti, *Democracy for the Few,* 2d ed. (New York: St. Martin's Press, 1995), 121.

4. Parenti, *Democracy for the Few,* 12–23. Holly Sklar, *Chaos or Community* (Boston: South End Press, 1995), 133–40. Alexander Cockburn and Jeffrey St. Clair, *White Out: The CIA, Drugs, and the Press* (New York: Versol, 1998), 1–62. Gary Webb, *Dark Alliance* (New York: Seven Stories Press, 1998).

5. Parenti, *Democracy for the Few,* 133. Mark Lewis Taylor, *The Executed God: The Way of the Cross in Lockdown America* (Minneapolis: Fortress Press, 2001), 20.

6. Howard Zinn, *A People's History of the United States: 1492–Present,* 2d ed. (New York: Harper Perennial, 1995). In this book Zinn presents a view of U.S. history seen from the point of view of its victims rather than, as it mostly is written, from the point of view of its victors. See James L. Marsh, *Critique, Action, and Liberation* (Albany: State University of New York Press, 1995), 174–76, for my argument that commitment to a radical stance of justice implies identification with the poor.

7. Parenti, *Democracy for the Few,* 127–29.

8. I argue in *Critique, Action, and Liberation* that this retrenching or rollback on the part of the welfare state is a part of a new regime in capitalism called flexible accumulation. "This manifests itself in an attack on and lowering of wages, a greater reliance on sub-contracting and small business, smaller inventories, weakening of labor unions, a greater reliance on the strength of financial capital in relation to industrial capital, and a post-modern aesthetic in which everyone is a celebrity for fifteen minutes" (301–6). A further aspect of flexible accumulation is the full internationalization or globalization of capital, which I interpret and criticize in *Process, Praxis, and Transcendence* (Albany: State University of New York Press, 1999), 264–97, and the prison-industrial complex, which I have discussed in this book.

This new regime emerges from and replaces Fordism, which characterized both U.S. and European capitalism from 1930 to 1970: increased management of consumption based on higher wages, positive state intervention in the economy and care for the victims of this economy, big corporations, big labor unions, economy of scale, dominance of industrial capital, and a stable, modernist aesthetic.

I owe the term "flexible accumulation" and much of the analysis to David Harvey, *The Condition of Post-Modernity* (London: Basil Blackwell, 1989). It may be accounted a major theoretical failure of Habermas that he does not take into account this changed physiognomy of late capitalism. See also Sklar, *Chaos or Community*.

9. Alan Wolfe, *The Limits of Legitimacy* (New York: Free Press, 1977), 292–94; Walter Dean Burnham, *Critical Elections and the Mainsprings of Politics* (New York: Norton, 1970); Sklar, *Chaos or Community*, 141–60.

10. Herbert Marcuse, *One-Dimensional Man* (Boston: Beacon Press, 1991), has an early critique of bourgeois realism as one-dimensional thought manifesting and justifying a one-dimensional society. See my own critique of bourgeois realism in *Critique, Action, and Liberation*, 331–36.

6

Deliberative Politics
and Administrative Social Power

In chapters 5 and 6 Habermas dealt with the tension between facticity and legitimacy within the law itself. In chapter 7, he addresses the external relation between facticity and validity, that is, the tension between the normative self-understanding of the constitutional state expressed in discourse-theoretic terms and the social facticity of political processes that run their course along more or less constitutional lines. Habermas here links his normative model of democracy to sociological theories of democracy. Up to this point, we have considered political power from the point of view of how it ought to be related to administrative and social power. In this chapter, we will consider how in fact, empirically, this relationship obtains.

The facticity-validity tension arises in a different way within social theory itself, but not in such a way as to imply an opposition between "real" and "ideal," because the normative content already laid out has been politically inscribed in the social facticity of observable political processes. Consequently, a constructive sociology of democracy must choose its basic concepts in such a way that "particles" of existing reason can already be found in political practices, even though these may be distorted and contradictory. This approach does not require a philosophy of history, such as occurs in Marx or Hegel, to support its efforts. Its only premise is that one cannot adequately describe the operation of a constitutionally organized political system at an empirical level without referring to the validity dimension of law and the democratic genesis of law. To leave this dimension out of one's empirical description is to risk a less-than-adequate, less comprehensive account of the political system.

In chapter 7, Habermas goes about his reflection in three stages. First, he considers and rejects a reductionist concept of democracy that attempts to eliminate democratic legitimacy from power and law. Then, after considering substantive models of democracy, he develops a proceduralist conception of democracy. Finally, he considers Robert Dahl's attempt at a sociological translation and empirical testing of the proceduralist account of democracy. Here the goal is to confront critically the ideal of the self-organization of freely associated citizens with the reality of highly complex societies. Aspects of social systems emerge that are anonymous, institutionalized, and unconscious, running along without the full conscious control, intention, and direction of a citizen or group of citizens or the citizenry as a whole. Here Habermas attempts to save the idea of democracy by unburdening it of excessively idealistic claims and expectations, so that it will no longer be possible or legitimate to talk about immediate, nonrepresentational democracy permeating the social system as a whole consciously and intentionally. Modern societies are simply too complex for that to occur.

Again, my response to Habermas, as is his to other thinkers, is a dialectical yes and no. These claims about the limits of democracy in modern societies are helpful and true up to a point, but I still ask whether he does not limit democracy too much. Does Habermas wrongly equate an unavoidable system of complexity with processes within the capitalist state and economy that are avoidable and can be overcome? Is there not within administrative and economic systems an interaction of different kinds of reason—communicative, strategic, purposive-rational, and compromising—that plays off against anonymous aspects of the system? Are these administrative and economic realities simply or mostly to be described as "systemic," in opposition to various conscious uses of reason, or are they not more adequately described as an interaction between and among conscious and unconscious aspects? Finally, if such realities do admit of such conscious rationality, is there not the possibility of a further democratizing of these spheres, leading perhaps to full economic, political, and social democracy? Here I understand democracy in a mediated sense, having recourse to representation, expertise, and unconscious systemic aspects but nonetheless extending to the whole of society. Does Habermas uncritically equate immediate democracy with universal democracy? Is it unavoidable systems complexity that blocks full democracy, or is it capitalist self-interest and injustice inscribed into system and life-world that are avoidable and that can and should be overcome?

Habermas's distinction between system and life-world and the inevitability and desirability of administration and markets is correct. He rightly objects to overly idealized, earlier versions of popular democracy, whether Rousseauist, Marxist, or anarchist. But as I have argued in other books, mediated democratic socialism is possible and desirable.[1] Here my earlier objection on a normative level to his purely political concept of democracy has its empirical, social-scientific correlate. This limiting of democracy to political democracy is as arbitrary and wrongheaded on an empirical level as it is on a normative level. And as earlier, mistakes on the normative level flow from and lead into empirical, social-scientific error. Habermas rightly says in this chapter that the political system is only one subsystem among others, but that implies a limitation of democracy only if it is mistakenly equated with political democracy. We have shown above that it is a normative error. In this chapter, we will show that it is an empirical error. A contradictory normative essence leads to a contradictory empirical appearance. Normative and empirical become here aspects of the contradictory Habermasian whole.[2]

REDUCTIONIST MODELS OF DEMOCRACY

Habermas begins by noting his own assumption that the conceptual relation between political power and law is empirically relevant through the conceptually unavoidable pragmatic presupposition of legitimate lawmaking and through the institutionalizing of a corresponding practice of democratic self-governance by citizens. Such an assumption might seem question-begging against empiricist concepts of power that remove that normative component from the beginning and subject the normative self-understanding of modernity to a quite illuminating critique. Habermas will treat this empiricism in the next chapter. Here he is concerned with a cryptonormative approach that merely borrows the empiricist premises from the social sciences and tries to demonstrate that democratic practices can be legitimated from the perspective of the participants themselves in terms of descriptive, empirical categories. One example of such an approach is that of Werner Becker (289–90).

He begins with the assumption that normative validity claims in politics and law lack a cognitive meaning, but he tries to explain why elites and citizens could have good reasons for participation in mass democracies. Just as power in general manifests itself in the empirical superiority of the stronger interest or will, so also political power is displayed in the stability of a political order. Legitimacy is expressed in the de facto recognition on the part of those governed, and it can range from mere toleration to free consent. The consent based on legitimacy is based on subjective reasons claiming to be valid within a particular ideology and frame of reference, but these reasons are "subjective" in that they resist cognitive assessment. So long as order is maintained, one reason is as good as another. From this point of view, even a dictatorship is legitimate if it is stable and remains in power (290).

Becker introduces the concept of democracy through the rules governing equal universal suffrage, party competition, and majority rule. These are justified as norms that are connected with effective sanctions. His argument has three steps, of which each has two parts, the first giving an objective explanation and the second translating that into the "good reasons" the participants have for consenting. In the first stage, Becker argues, in a pluralist democracy, legitimacy comes from a majority vote reached in elections that are free, equal, and secret. This idea acquires its plausibility from a modern worldview guided by what Becker calls "ethical subjectivism," which secularizes the Judeo-Christian understanding of "each individual before God" and assumes the fundamental equality of all individuals. Such subjectivism, however, replaces the transcendent origin of obligatory commands with an immanent validity reached in the subject's own will. Individuals produce normative validity through free consent. This voluntaristic understanding corresponds to a positivist sense of law, which says that the law includes all that a duly appointed lawgiver posits as law.

If participating citizens want to make this explanation their own, they are first tempted to look for ways of grounding ethical subjectivism—for example, in human rights or a deontological perspective. Empiricism, however, teaches them that such attempts ignore the irreducible contingency and arbitrariness of what is normatively valid. According to Habermas, this occurrence of contingency renders the proffered objective explanation unsatisfactory for the participants in the democratic process. They need at least good purposive-rational reasons for why norms proposed by the majority should be accepted as valid by the minority. If such reasons are merely subjective and have no objective warrant, as Becker says, then they cannot legitimate the political order (291–92).

In a second stage of argumentation, Becker tries to account for the consent of the minority. He explains the acceptance of majority rule in terms of a domesticated struggle for power. Because the majority has more numerical strength, it can threaten to renounce the agreement not to use violence when things do not go according to its will. Habermas responds that such an interpretation of majority rule is plausible if avoiding violent disputes is a goal for all. The explanation, however, remains unsatisfactory for the participants as long as it remains unclear how minorities can be protected from the hegemony of the majority, exercised violently or peacefully. In addition, what guarantee is there that the disputing parties will submit to majority rule (292–93)?

In a third stage of argumentation, Becker, in order to protect minorities, has recourse to basic liberties. Guarantees of minorities' interests are best explained by the majority's fear of becoming a minority and losing some or all of these liberties. The majority, anxious over possible loss of its power, and minorities, seeing a possibility of a change in power, will go along with the rules of the game. Competing elites split the electorate into several camps according to ideological standpoints, and each tries to convince the other by programmatic means, mostly with social rewards promised to those who go along.

The problem with this analysis, Habermas argues, is that what elites consider plausible may not be plausible for citizens. Why should citizens, whether a majority or a minority, adopt one viewpoint over another while there is no objectively valid viewpoint, because political arguments merely have rhetorical functions? Why do citizens see through the political advertising and nonetheless accept it? What seems plausible from an objective, third-person perspective is not plausible from a first-person, participant perspective. Indeed, why should we accept Becker's argument in his whole book, since that account on his terms is just an ideological advertisement for liberal democracies? Moreover, the assumption here is that citizens are aware of the role of compromise in modern democratic societies. But why accept a compromise as fair? Here Becker can continue to seem plausible only by talking about the "fairness" of compromise. But this claim contradicts his argument that political arguments are merely rhetorical; that something is called "fair" can only be a political advertisement (293–95).

Becker's argument can easily be seen as self-contradictory and self-defeating both textually and performatively. At this point, Habermas turns to liberal and republican conceptions of democracy in an attempt to give a better account of how norms and reality are related. Do their implicit conceptions of society offer a better point of contact with current sociological analyses (295–96)?

Liberal and republican models represent an improvement over empiricist models but are still not adequate. Prior reflection in other chapters has shown that the central element of the democratic process lies in the procedure of deliberative politics. This ideal of democracy has implications for the concept of society in those other models of democracy that view society as centered around the state. The procedural model differs both from the liberal conception of the state as guardian of economic society and from the republican ideal of ethical community expressing itself in the state (296).

According to the liberal view, the democratic process occurs exclusively in the form of compromises among interests, and the fairness of compromises is rooted in universal and equal suffrage, the representative composition of parliamentary bodies, the mode of decision making, rules of order, and so on. Such rules are grounded in liberal basic rights. According to the republican view, democratic will-formation takes the form of ethicopolitical self-understanding that relies on the substantive support of a culturally established background consensus. Discourse theory takes elements from both sides and integrates these in the concept of an ideal procedure for deliberation, decision making, and lawmaking. As he has done many times before, Habermas is being dialectical here, giving a nuanced yes and no to two other positions and arguing that his own viewpoint is superior, a higher viewpoint (296).

Democratic proceduralism as practical reason no longer resides in universal human rights nor in the ethical substance of a specific community but in the rules of discourse and forms of argumentation borrowing their normative content from the structure of communicative praxis. This description should set the stage for a normative conceptualization of state and society. The only presupposition is the type of public administration that emerged in the early modern period with the European nation-state and that developed ties with the capitalist economy.

In the republican view, citizens' opinion-and-will-formation forms the medium through which society constitutes itself as a political whole. Because democracy becomes equivalent to the political self-understanding of society as a whole, the republican view leads to an understanding of politics as directed against the state apparatus. Society has been revitalized to the point where it can appropriate bureaucratically alienated state power. Liberals, on the other hand, do not try to eliminate the gap between the citizenry and state power but only to bridge it. The constitution should curb the administration through normative provisions such as basic rights, separation of powers, and statutory controls. The constitution should motivate the state through competition among political parties and between incumbents and opposition to adequately consider societal interests and value orientations. Such a state-centered understanding of politics forgoes the unrealistic republican concept of a citizenry capable of collective action. This liberal understanding is oriented not toward the input of a radical political will-formation but toward the output of government activities successful on balance. It argues against an administration that interferes too much in the spontaneous private social commerce of private persons (297–98).

Discourse theory invests democratic procedure with normative orientations that are weaker than those in the republican model but stronger than those in the liberal model. In agreement with republicanism, it emphasizes opinion-and-will-formation, but it does not make the constitution secondary. Rather, the constitution is essential for institutionalizing democratic, communicative forms of democratic opinion-and-will-formation. In agreement with liberal theory, discourse theory has some positive role for the market and the state and for purposive-rational and strategic action, but it drops the individualistic assumptions of liberal theory and insists on the positive, essential role of participatory democracy. Discourse theory emphasizes the citizens' input into the democratic process as well as the output of government activities. According to discourse theory, the success of deliberative politics depends not on a collectively acting citizenry but on the institutionalization of the corresponding procedures and conditions of communication, as well as on the interplay of institutionalized deliberative processes with informally developed public opinions. Proceduralized popular sovereignty and a political system linked to the peripheral networks of the public sphere go together with the image of a decentered society (298).

Discourse theory frees itself from the philosophy of the subject, whether conceived as the macrosubject of republican theory or the individualistic subject of liberal theory, and has recourse to higher-level subjectless forms of communication functioning as the arenas and means of opinion-and-will-formation. The flow of communication among public opinion formation, institutionalized elections, and legislative decisions guarantees that influence and communicative power are transformed through legislation into administrative power. Discourse theory retains from liberal theory the distinction between state and society, but it distinguishes the public sphere, as the social basis of autonomous public spheres, from both the economic and administrative systems. "The socially integrating force of solidarity, which can no longer be drawn solely from sources of communicative action, must develop through widely diversified and more or less autonomous public spheres, as well as through procedures of democratic opinion-and-will-formation institutionalized within a constitutional framework" (299).

Such an institutionalized network, moreover, should be able to hold its own against the two other sources of social integration, money and administrative power. In talking of subjectless forms of communication here, Habermas does not mean to deny the role of conscious subjects interacting intentionally, but he interprets them and popular sovereignty intersubjectively. Conscious subjects interact in a community within a network of institutionalized forms of communication. Communicative action is inevitably mediated by such institutionalized forms, over which subjects do not exercise total control or conscious awareness. These mediated forms, of course, link up with the further mediations of state and economy, administration and money. Any idea of totally immediate democracy exercised by the community in a totally or mostly immediate way on the community as a whole must be given up (299–301).

This line of argument is insightful and true up to a point and is a real advance over Habermas's earlier work, in which this idea of a network of institutionalized forms was not developed or was less developed. It is true as description both of what is going on and of what should go on. Even a democratic socialist society, as I conceive it, would have such a communicative network institutionalized constitutionally and interacting with a state administration and a market. Habermas goes on to say that such a notion of state and society has implications for how we view legislation and popular sovereignty. Liberals view democratic will-formation as legitimating the exercise of political power, and republicans see such formation as constituting society in a political community. Discourse theory brings in another notion, rationalization, which is more than mere legitimation but less than the constitution of power. Democratic opinion-and-will-formation functions as a sluice for rationalization of decisions made in the legislature and an administration bound by law and statute. Informal processes of communication interact democratically with the exercise of political power, not just monitoring it but programming it. Nonetheless, because the political system is alone specialized for coming to collectively binding decisions, it alone can act. It remains one subsystem within the total society (299–300).

The concept of popular sovereignty also changes. It is not the citizenry as a whole exercising its will in the practice of self-determination, as republicans would have it, nor is it the constitutionally delegated power of the state acting as a whole, but rather communicative praxis exercised within subjectless forms of communication influencing and monitoring and limiting the power of the state and money. We work here with a decentered idea of society, not one centered either in the people or in the state. The political system is just one subsystem among others, interacting with, and dependent on, other systems such as the economy and depending on the content of a rationalized life-world that meets it halfway. This is true for the formal procedures of an institutionalized opinion-and-will-formation and political discussion occurring informally in the public sphere. Life-world resources include liberal political culture, enlightened political socialization, and initiatives of opinion-building associations. We see how much is riding on the public sphere in Habermas's approach. We see also, or suspect, how difficult his argumentative task becomes if the public sphere turns out to be deeply flawed, dominated by systems of money and power within and without it (301–2).

Some caveats and cautions are in order here. As indicated in the introduction to this chapter, I worry that Habermas is conceiving the state, economy, and public sphere as separate, self-enclosed spheres. Do not and cannot employees and their foremen and bosses interact communicatively as well as purposive-rationally and strategically in the firm, and employees with the heads of departments in the state administration? In fighting for wages that are more just and fair and for administrative policies that respond to the poor, are not personnel, firms, and administrations acting communicatively? And, if so, then is it not claiming too little for communicative action and its possibilities to lock it up totally in such a way as to exclude the economy and the state? Why could not democratic practices of opinion-and-will-formation extend from the public and legislative spheres to the economy and the state? Indeed, if I am correct in my argument in preceding chapters, is this not what the full practice of communicative praxis calls for? Is Habermas claiming too little for it here? Is he too modest?

I worry, in other words, about a revived version of the reified system–life-world distinction rather than one that sees them as aspects of one social whole. Within the interplay of communicative praxis and institutionalized subjectless forms functioning as aspects in the public sphere, Habermas has admitted this point. Why could not communicative action and bureaucratic power, or communicative action and money, similarly function as aspects within the firm or state administration, which are as distinct and related spheres specialized for different tasks from the public sphere and legislature? Habermas has conceded this point, but his language here seems neither to have adhered to this concession nor to have realized its implications.[3] And once we give up the reified form of this distinction between system and life-world, what solid theoretical reason is there for not extending communicative action into the economic and administrative spheres? These would still be distinguishable, but now more by their function. The economy produces goods and services to be consumed, and the administration carries out legitimately enacted laws and policy. If Habermas were to follow my suggestion, communicative action and democracy would be more than lonely islands in a hostile sea of threatening systems. Democratized or communicatively influenced and informed, they would be able to meet the public sphere and legislature halfway in a manner that is blocked structurally by capitalism and by Habermas's own reifying tendencies.

Moreover, fact proves possibility. Different theorists have shown how democratically owned and controlled firms have worked and are working, even in a context that is dominantly capitalist. Firms as diverse as Plywood Mills in the Pacific Northwest in the United States, insurance firms in Washington, D.C., and the Mondragon Cooperative in Spain function as well as, or better than, their capitalist counterparts. Because they are organized democratically, they are far more just in sharing income and wealth among the workers and in allowing worker participation in making investment decisions and organizing the shop floor. For this reason, there is much more happiness in work.[4]

DEMOCRATIC PROCEDURE AND NEUTRALITY

Habermas begins the next section of his chapter by summarizing his conclusions. The discourse theory of democracy, in being thrown up against previously accepted notions of politically constituted society, is not obviously unacceptable or incompatible with functionally differentiated societies. I would add that, if my suggestions, emendations, and critique are correct, neither is a radical socialist conception of democracy. Deepening the question, we can ask how such democracy is possible under conditions for the reproduction of a complex society. A sociologically informed resolution of this question requires operationalizing the procedural core of democracy at the right level in a way that starts neither too high nor too low (302–3).

Norberto Bobbio starts at too low a level. His premise is that a meaningful discussion of democracy is possible only if one specifies a set of rules that establishes who is authorized to make collective decisions and which procedures are to be applied. A procedural minimum is present when there is political participation by as many citizens as possible; majority rule operates in political decisions; communication rights obtain, and thus there is a selection of opinions and policies from different programs and elites; and the private sphere is protected. The advantage of this minimalist definition lies in its describing the normative content of political systems as they already exist in western societies. Nonetheless, the normative core of democratic procedure is not exhausted by this operationalization when one has further recourse to discourse theory. Bobbio's definition does not touch the core of a genuinely proceduralist understanding of democracy that insists that democratic procedure is institutionalized in discourses and bargaining processes by employing forms of communication promising that all outcomes reached in conformity with the procedure are reasonable. Not only majority rule but also the discussion leading up to a majority's decision is important. In his denial or minimizing of this possibility, Bobbio is deemed too crude by Habermas. But what if Bobbio's procedural minimum is all that is possible in capitalist society and even that minimum is being worn away? What if Habermas's procedural core is in fact and principle incompatible with such societies, shooting beyond them in a way that is utopian? What if Habermas is not realistic even on his own terms? Here we note again how important the public sphere is for his theory. "Deliberative politics acquires its legitimating force from the discursive structure of an opinion-and-will-formation that can fulfill its socially integrative function only because citizens expect its results to have a *reasonable* quality. Hence the discursive level of public debates constitutes the most important variable" (304). Doubtless a public sphere permeated as much or more by propaganda, advertising, and manipulation as by communicative action would not satisfy Habermas's criteria. But what if under capitalism these unacceptable forms are prevalent and increasingly dominant? Would not a full understanding of fully discursive democracy imply getting rid of the source of the propaganda, advertising, and manipulation, namely, big corporations (303–4)?

Joshua Cohen, in contrast, aims too high for Habermas. Cohen has not seen through the idea of a society that is deliberately steered as a whole and thus is politically constituted. Habermas, however, wants democratic proceduralism as the core structure in a separate political system, but such proceduralism is not a model for all social institutions because it is embedded in contexts that it cannot regulate. I say yes and no to this claim: yes, to the extent that systems, institutions, and institutionalized forms of communication imply a mediation that is incompatible with direct, immediate democracy; no, to the extent that there is no reason in principle why communicative action cannot extend into corporations within and without the public sphere and into state administration in mediated fashion. Is Cohen as far off the mark as Habermas thinks (304–5)?

Is Habermas too silent about, and too accepting of, the current form of capitalist democracy, uncritically identifying with modern democracy or modern complex society as such? Capitalist democracy does limit proceduralism in the way that he describes and seems to accept as normative. Remember his own words: "All we need presuppose is a type of public administration that emerged in the early modern period with the European nation and *developed functional ties with the capitalist economy*" (297, italics mine). Yet if we adhere to this premise, is not Bobbio's minimalist definition of democracy the best we can do? Is not Habermas's dogmatism about this premise, his refusal to question it, at odds with the spirit and orientation of communicative action, which entitles us to subject everything to critical examination? And if we do this, does Habermas have any defense for his stance, other than the questionable reifying of the system–life-world distinction—a position that he has repudiated?

Cohen, according to Habermas, is also too silent about the relationship between the informal and formal modes of democracy. This "wild" public sphere functions more as a context of discovery that identifies a full range of problems and solutions; the formal decision-making power of legislatures has more to do with justification and less with discovery, with interest and decisions leading to the choice of a certain policy or law. In tension with the open, inclusive network of overlapping subcultural publics with fluid temporal, social, and substantive boundaries developing simultaneously and oriented to unrestricted communication is its vulnerability to "repressive and exclusionary effects of unequally distributed social power, structural violence, and systematically distorted communication" (337–38). The informal public sphere must enjoy the support of a society in which the equal rights of citizenship obtain. "Only in an egalitarian public of citizens that has emerged from the confines of class and thrown off the millennial shackles of social stratification and exploitation can the potential of an unleashed cultural pluralism develop" (306–8).

Is this a description or a prescription? If the former, is it verifiable? Does not Bobbio's minimalist definition of democracy have more empirical currency? If the former, how can it possibly come to be realized in a capitalist economy essentially oriented to class domination, inequality, and exploitation, which many think has become worse since 1980?[5] How can communication be unrestricted when democracy is restricted to the political sphere and questions about extending it are not allowed to come up in Habermas's own thought and in "really existing" capitalist society? Is this stunning sentence, which describes a situation only realizable in a postcapitalist, socialist society, compatible with the earlier historical premise about state administrations being linked to the capitalist economy? Here seems to be a tension between Habermas's normative theory and his unquestioned and unquestionable empirical, historical premises. How can citizens have socially effective equal rights when individuals enter the public sphere already unequal in resources, education, health, and ability to participate because of structures of class in the economy? And if this were possible, how is equality of participation possible in a society in which big corporations like CBS and NBC are the major players within the public sphere? Habermas's normative theory seems to be in tension with a class stratification, domination, and exploitation within and without the public sphere that he refuses to bring into question. And beating back colonization, Habermas's only solution to these problems, does not seem to throw off shackles of class exploitation and domination but only to tame and qualify them. How can class exploitation and its accompanying inequality be pushed back when they are already present within the public sphere in the big corporations?

Habermas completes the second section of the chapter by reflecting on the neutrality of procedurally regulated deliberation and communication. First, he asserts that regulated procedures must be supplemented with informal communication. Next, he rejects Ackerman's restriction of a discussion to such questions of justice and elimination of any discussion of the good life. If such ethical questions are bracketed out of discussion, then there will be no possibility of changing political attitudes, need interpretations, and value orientations. Discussion of ethical versions of the good life can be included as long as no decisions of the state are based upon a disputed view of the good life (308–9).

Even this tolerant version of the neutrality thesis is contested, however, from the opposite communitarian side. From this perspective, one hears the objection that no judgment of practical questions can be separated from the content of specific worldviews and life projects. Consequently, no presumptively neutral principle can be, in fact, neutral. Habermas answers this objection by arguing that neutrality is a necessary component of a practice that is without alternatives and in this sense unavoidable. Anyone, no matter what her specific ethical orientation, has to be committed to the practice of rational dialogue in order to persuade her opponents. The only alternative to such dialogue is manipulation and violence, and these are presumably less preferable to all participants in western democratic societies (310).

The communitarian objection, however, can be radicalized further. Even if the neutrality principle can be traced back to a universal rule of argumentation, the theoretical articulation and explanation of that rule can be infected with different conceptions of the good life. Habermas answers the objection by saying that at worst the articulation of antecedently acquired practical knowledge will exhibit perspectival distortions. The fallible or possibly false reconstruction does not touch the already functioning intuitive knowledge, present even when participants disagree about their articulations. Presumably, because such knowledge is accessible to us in our democratic practice, we can return to it to verify true, and invalidate false, reconstructions (311–12).

The nonrestrictive reading of the neutrality thesis provokes objections also from the liberal side. Here the objection is about opening up discourse to all questions and arguments brought forward by anyone. Feminists like Nancy Fraser, for example, insist that what counts as "private" and "public" can and should come up for discussion. Previously agreed-upon definitions should not be adhered to dogmatically in a way that contradicts the spirit and orientation of communicative praxis. But if so, liberals argue, does not such openness undermine legal protection of the private sphere (312–13)?

Habermas answers this objection by clarifying a confusion based upon two conceptual pairs, "private versus public" matters and "constrained versus unconstrained" discourses. In so doing, he makes a number of distinctions. Procedural constraint on public discourse, first of all, is not the same as the range of topics open for public discourse. Informal and formal opinion-and-will-formation are open to all ethically relevant questions of the good life, collective identity, and need interpretation. When legislators enact norms defining the crime of spousal abuse, for example, all the corresponding topics and contributions of all in the discussion can be included without detracting from the impartiality of legislative procedure. Making something previously a private matter a subject for public discourse does not yet imply an infringement of individual rights. Discussing something is different from deciding something, raising something as a hypothesis to be considered is different from deciding that a hypothesis is true or false, and understanding a possibility, possible law, or possible course of action is not the same as judgment or decision (313).[6]

We also must draw a distinction between private and public matters in two respects: accessibility and thematization, on the one hand, and the regulation of powers and responsibilities, on the other. Discussing something is not the same as meddling in another's affairs. The intimate sphere must be protected from intrusive forces, but not everything reserved to the decisions of private persons is excluded from public discussion. "Every affair in need of political regulation should be publicly discussed, though not every legitimate object of public discussion will in fact be politically regulated" (313). Thematization of boundary questions between private and public does not by itself imply any encroachment on existing powers and responsibilities. Such a point is easier to see if we realize that such decisions are often a day-to-day process moving from an informal level of struggle over the definition of needs to a formal level of law and enactment, as well as distinguishing between an informal public sphere that raises questions and thematizes issues and a formal, regulative sphere that passes and implements law (313–14).

These distinctions seem to the point and valid and answer to my satisfaction the objections of the liberal. My question to Habermas here is whether he is not more open to a feminist questioning of the private-versus-public distinction than to questions from a socialist or Marxist perspective as that applies to issues of class, private ownership of the means of production, and the privileged status of the corporation inside and outside the public sphere. From the perspective of the ideal speech situation, all questions are equal, but some questions seem more equal than others for Habermas. Why, we have been asking throughout this book, should democracy be confined to the political sphere so that, except for beating back colonization and intervention of the welfare state, the private economic status of corporations and private ownership and control of the means of production are left untouched and unthematized? Is this distinction any less problematic than that between private and public questioned by feminists? Would not a socialist feminism or feminist socialism that brings both into the light of day be more comprehensive both in respecting the unlimited exigency of communicative praxis toward raising, or at least being open to, all questions and in its orientation to total democracy, economic, social, and political? We note a tension here between Habermas's factual willingness to resist such questions and a principled openness of communicative action to all questions. The essentially utopian character of communicative praxis does not equate easily with a dogmatic, liberal adherence to the status quo.

Why is there such a dogmatism? In what is it rooted? One possibility is that Habermas is capitulating to a fashionable form of academic and political discourse on the left that screens out questions of class injustice and legitimizes issues of sexual injustice. But it is precisely about such screening out and adherence to fashion that one should be vigilant, especially in the light of communicative praxis. "Class issues are old hat and irrelevant; no responsible thinker on the left is concerned about them, especially after 1989–90 in Europe." We have heard such sentiments over and over again. Such a tacit orthodoxy makes Habermas and Habermasians more acceptable on the academic and political scene in the United States and Europe. They appear on curricula more easily than "that wild man Marx." Rawls, Dworkin, and others are part of the same safe, liberal community of discourse and take us, Habermas and Habermasians, seriously. Is that not marvelous?

Yet further questions arise. What if this screening out serves capitalism ideologically, not allowing questions to arise that should arise, that threaten the system and bring it into question? What if this left, liberal fashion is itself an ideological effect of late capitalism? Does Habermas have bourgeois blinkers on here, albeit of slightly insufficiently pinkish tinge?

THE SOCIOLOGICAL TRANSLATION
OF THE CONCEPT OF DELIBERATIVE POLITICS

In the last part of his chapter, Habermas draws on the thought of Robert Dahl to gain a more adequate understanding of democratic practice than Bobbio allows. According to Dahl, the common good of society lies in a democratic practice that includes all those affected; ensures equally distributed and effective opportunities to participate in the political process; provides an equal right to vote on decisions; guarantees an equal right to choose topics and to control the agenda; and creates a situation allowing all the participants to develop, in the light of sufficient information and good reasons, an articulated understanding of the contested interests and matters in need of regulation (315–16).

To date, Habermas admits, these criteria have not been sufficiently satisfied by an actual political order. Unavoidable social complexity makes it necessary to apply the criteria in a nuanced, differentiated fashion. What is required is representation, the delegation of decision-making powers, and sensitive modification of decision procedures to reduce their legal and organizational complexity. None of these adjustments presents any obstacle in principle to an approximate implementation of the procedure. Here again Habermasian reformism sees nothing in principle problematic about modern capitalistic societies. He misses the distinction between the modern complexity that is endemic to modern industrial society and the complexity rooted in the injustice of capitalist society, mixing the two in such a way as to make his reformism plausible. When we make that distinction, even admitting that there can be different degrees of democracy and communication in capitalism, there is a structural block in capitalist societies to appropriate implementation of procedure (316–17).

Reflection on Dahl leads to mixed results. On the one hand, deliberative politics loses much of its unrealistic appearance if one views it as an organized learning process that removes the burden on latent, life-worldly processes of social integration while continuing these processes within a legal system specialized for this kind of work. On the other hand, in complex societies, the gap between the need for coordination and the lack of social integration, a gap that politics and law are meant to close, seems to grow wider as the political administration system takes on more and more tasks that overburden decision making. A distinction is necessary between tasks essential to maintaining complex democratic societies as such and tasks that flow from the injustice of the capitalist system such as those falling on the welfare state, the Pentagon system, the prison-industrial complex, the imperial system abroad, and so on. In a fully democratic, just society, even one as geographically extended as the United States or Germany, would not such administrative tasks decrease both qualitatively and quantitatively? Taking care of the victims of capital, warehousing potential sources of resistance to its reign, and developing a vast military apparatus to sustain its reign at home and abroad would be unnecessary if we abolished capitalism. Bureaucracy, in the absence of the capitalist injustice in which so much of it is rooted, would be vastly reduced. Habermas's refusal to see this makes the problem harder for him to surmount than it needs to be.

In any event, Habermas says such complexity looks reified from the perspective of the communicative pure ideal speech situation. Here we need to be clear about the senses in which society can become independent and reified. Such a diagnosis need not refer to the ordinary resistance offered by everyday problems and by deficits in our attempts to resolve them. Nor can we contrast a society that has become second nature with the pure, communicative ideal mistakenly seen as realizable. Nor can we confuse conditions that enable communication, such as settled but intersubjectively recognized norms and laws, with contingent, arbitrary constraints (322–24).

Nor are unavoidable aspects of system complexity, revealed in the light of the communicative ideal, manifested in the unavoidable division of labor in the production and diffusion of knowledge, selectivity of the media in choosing topics, and asymmetry in the availability of information. Positive law tends to reduce such complexity. Another kind of complexity that Habermas does not consider as distinct in modern capitalist societies is commodity fetishism: advertising that persuades individuals to pursue false needs and to buy goods that they do not need; big corporations that exercise undue power in the marketplace, the public sphere, and all aspects of the state; big communications media that push money-making as a way of life over against much more marginal media; and elections so much influenced by the rule of money that there is little choice between candidates. As a result, the fetishism and alienation that Marx saw resident primarily in the economic sphere flow into the political and sociocultural realms such that relations between people take the form of relations between things. Just as the capitalist firm, money, and technology operate over and against workers and citizens as alien, so also do communications media and the state. They operate over and above and against citizens in a way that is avoidable in principle, even in complex, democratic societies (324–26).[7]

Habermas concludes this chapter by raising a further issue. How much does the social facticity of those unavoidable inertial features, even when they are taken into consideration by the formal structure of the constitutional state, provide a point where illegitimate power complexes independent of the democratic process can crystallize? How much does the unofficial circulation of such unlegitimated power encroach on the constitutionally mandated circulation of power (328)? We will consider this critical question in the next chapter.

CONCLUSION

We have seen here problems different from, and yet related to, those that arise in Habermas's development of normative theory. Just as the concept of democracy defined and defended normatively in the first few chapters is excessively narrow, leading to contradictions and anomalies, so here the sociological translation of that concept is especially problematic. It rests, or seems to rest, on a reified version of the system–life-world distinction that is not defensible. Moreover, concessions to feminism on the distinction between private and public allow us, in the spirit of communicative action, which puts no limit on questions, to question the status of the "private" corporation. Why should that be sacrosanct? Is Habermas tacitly adhering to a fashionable, whiggish, progressive version of critique in the light of which all questions are decidedly not equal?

Finally, we have seen how Habermas plays fast and loose with the distinction between unavoidable system complexity and avoidable, reified aspects of such complexity rooted in capitalist injustice. At the same time, he honestly raises the question about whether, and to what extent, illegitimate power complexes can arise in modern capitalist states. This vacillation between obfuscation and clarity, of course, has been with us from the beginning of the book and will stay with us until the end.

NOTES

1. James L. Marsh, *Critique, Action, and Liberation* (Albany: State University of New York Press, 1995), 315–55.

2. Jürgen Habermas, *Between Facts and Norms*, trans. William Rehg (Cam-

bridge: MIT Press, 1996), 132–33. Page numbers in parentheses throughout this chapter refer to this book.

3. See chap. 3, note 6.

4. Daniel Zwerdling, *Workplace Democracy* (New York: Harper Colophon, 1980). Martin Carnoy and Derek Shearer, *Economic Democracy: The Challenge of the 1980's* (Armonk, N.Y.: M. E. Sharpe, 1980).

5. Noam Chomsky, *Profit over People* (New York: Seven Stories Press, 1999). Holly Sklar, *Chaos or Community* (Boston: South End Press, 1995).

6. See Marsh, *Critique, Action, and Liberation*, 3–16, for my own articulation of the distinction among understanding, judgment, and decision.

7. Marsh, *Critique, Action, and Liberation*, 235–312. Karl Marx, *Capital*, vol. 1, trans. Ben Fowkes (New York: Vintage, 1977), 164–65. Karl Marx, *The Economic and Philosophic Manuscripts of 1844*, ed. Dirk J. Struick, trans. Martin Milligan (New York: International Publishers, 1964), 106–19.

7

✛

The Public Sphere, Civil Society, and the Rule of Capital

We come now to Habermas's all-important chapter 8, on civil society and the public sphere. In prior chapters, we have seen that the fate of his notion of democracy depends on these domains. The public sphere/civil society is the source of questions indicating social pathology and suffering in the life-world. It is the source of an immediate practice of democracy relative to more mediate, formal structures of the state. Unless this sphere operates vigorously and effectively, there is little or no centripetal movement from the people to centralized state structure and operations, and if there is little or no such movement, then we have democracy in name only. Finally, the public sphere and civil society ultimately validate or invalidate legislative, judicial, and administrative initiatives. If these cannot pass the test of public communication, then the state must return to the drawing board. The public sphere is the initial stage of a process of democratic participation and self-governance that then moves to legislative, judicial, and administrative levels within the formal state apparatus, and finally back to the public sphere. Ideally, modern democracies should operate within such a circle of opinion-and-will-formation, moving from question to answer; immediacy to mediation; understanding to judgment, decision, and validation.

The discussion in Habermas's chapter has three parts. The first part, after summarizing of theoretical developments, treats of Jon Elster's revision of the economic theory of democracy, which brings home the empirical relevance of the procedural concept of deliberative politics. Second, Habermas discusses Helmut Willke's concept of supervision, which intends to explain how a decentered, functionally differentiated society can cope with challenges to society as a whole. After criticizing

this proposal, Habermas, stimulated by Bernard Peters, develops a sociological model focusing on the empirical weight of constitutionally prescribed, official circulation of power. In the third part, Habermas asks
whether civil society, through the public sphere, develops impulses with
enough life to bring conflict from the periphery to the center of the political system.

Habermas's initial concern is to show how approaches to democracy
based on economic theory or systems theory lead to a sense of defeatism
and pessimism about the possibility of democracy not simply because of
empirical evidence but also because of misguided conceptual strategies,
which lose sight of what political power owes to its formal constitution in
legal terms. I will also argue against Habermas that his own pessimism
and timidity about democracy, and especially about the possibility of
socialist democracy, are due primarily not to empirical, social scientific
evidence but to misguided conceptual, empirical strategies and analyses.[1]

SOCIOLOGICAL THEORIES OF DEMOCRACY

Habermas begins by discussing the postwar theory of pluralism, which
relies on an empiricist concept of power. Pluralism understands politics
instrumentally, in that political and administrative power are just different manifestations of social power. Social power is measured in the ability of social interests to have their way. The sociological account of pluralism links up with the normative model of liberalism by means of simple
substitution of large organizations and organized interests for individual
citizens and individual interests. This account assumes that all politically
relevant collective actors have roughly the same opportunity to influence
political processes, that members of organizations determine the politics
of pressure groups and political parties, and that these are pushed by
members into willingness to compromise and to integrate interests
(330–31).

After these assumptions were proved false, pluralist theory was
revised along lines already pursued in the work of Schumpeter. Because
the composition of interest groups is indeed very selective and because
members are mostly inactive and exercise little influence on organizations, it was assumed that power struggles are conducted by elites.
Another assumption also proved untenable: that politicians and adminis-
trators depend on a variety of political actors having approximately equal
weight in the competition for political influence. A theory of political
elites emerged that reduced the role of the democratic process to

plebiscites between competitive leadership teams, the recruitment of personnel, and the selection of leaders. From a normative standpoint, the theory had to explain how a politics initiated and controlled by elites can satisfy nonelites. In this question, the burden of explanation shifts from the input to the output of the administrative system. Only the rationality of the elites themselves can guarantee that the administrative system functions in the interests of all. Can a self-programming political system assume on its own the tasks of detecting publicly relevant needs, latent conflicts, repressed problems, and nonorganizable interests (331–33)?

Since the late 1960s this theory has come into question. The administrative system can operate only within strict limits, and its operations seem to be reflexively oriented more to avoiding crisis than to steering. On the output side, large organizations and social systems are able to resist and deflect state interventions. On the input side, the unpredictability of independent voters limits the initiatives of the state (331–33).

As politics grows weaker, established parties have to fear withdrawal of legitimation, and steering deficits become more possible and actual. We come now to a fork in theoretical developments. Systems theory cuts the remaining link to normative models, limits itself to the self-referential problems of an autopoetic steering system, and takes up the organization problems of the modern state by translating them into steering problems. The economic theory of democracy, on the other hand, presupposes a methodology of individualism and focuses mainly on issues of legitimation. It is evident that both theories have reduced the normative component in social interaction too much. Problems arising in both theories have led to revisions that are suggestive but not consistently worked out (333).

The economic theory of democracy attempts to show how voter behavior expresses more or less enlightened self-interest, in relation to which politicians who wish to gain, or stay in, office respond to voter preference with specific policies. This account runs aground because of much empirical evidence to the contrary. Discussion of the "voter's paradox," for example, has shown that the level of voter turnout does not vary with voters' expectation that a single vote could decide a head-to-head race. Empirical evidence more and more speaks against all models premised on egocentric decision-making models that ignore how changes in interests and value orientations come into play also. Most recent revisions of the economic model consider how responsible political action takes into account simultaneously the perspectives of the expert, the generalized other (based on Mead's concept of the human other as making universal moral demands), and I myself (333–34).

Systems theory abandons the notion of individual and collective agency and conceives society as a network of autonomous subsystems, each encapsulated in its own semantics and having the other subsystems for its environment. The mode of operation internal to each system, and not the intentions or interests of participating actors, is what is essential. As a result, the political system, on the one hand, cannot hierarchically order all other systems. It is just one system among many. On the other hand, the state-centered understanding of politics already present in the liberal model comes into full play. The opinion-and-will-formation dominated by party competition is now cut off from all life-world roots in civil society, political culture, and socialization and incorporated into the political system. From Habermas's perspective, an already narrow understanding of the circulation of power in the economic model devolves into one that is totally systemic, anonymous, and devoid of human intentionality. A notion of circulation running counter to official circuits of power is set in motion: the administration steers the legislative process through its proposals of bills, extracts mass loyalty from its citizenry through parties that are political arms of the state, and makes direct contact with its clients. In such increased social complexity, the informal countercirculation of power is dominant, and the question of political responsibility is meaningless. A systems theory that has removed all normativity cannot be sensitive to the inhibiting normative constraints imposed on a constitutionally channeled circulation of power. Systems theory offers no framework for its own theory of democracy because politics and law are divided into two relatively enclosed systems and the political process is analyzed essentially from the perspective of a self-programming administration (334–35).

The realism gained by systems theory comes at a cost. Because all systems are self-enclosed and can only observe one another without being able to influence or communicate with one another, systems theory cannot explain how the political system is able to play even its minimal integrating role within society as a whole, rectifying disturbances and achieving a friendly coordination among systems otherwise drifting apart. How can coordination occur among many autonomous, self-referential systems (335–36)?

In summing up, we can see that "realistic" approaches lead to an economic theory of democracy that informs us about the instrumental self-interested features of democratic will-formation, on the one hand, and to a systems theory that informs us about the impotence of this will-formation, on the other hand. Both approaches, as we have just seen, run aground on various kinds of empirical and conceptual difficulties. Both approaches leave out, in a way that is fatal to their own projects, the full range of communicative action in the life-world and the way this accounts for the internal relation between law and political power. Such deficits stand behind the questions that both Elster and Willke instructively pursue. Elster's approach leads to an unexpected rebirth of deliberative politics (336).

Elster responds to a difficulty in rational choice theory still centered on the Hobbesian problem: How do strategic actors stabilize social relations solely on the basis of rational decisions? What interests Habermas is how Elster handles the difficulty of this theory when it is applied to political processes. First of all, Elster argues that it is unrealistic to start with a model that assumes that opportunities and preferences can be treated as given. Both of these change in the political process itself in a constructive opinion-and-will-formation. It is also unrealistic to assume that all social behavior is strategic and can be explained as the result of egocentric calculations. In the real social and political world there is not only strategic calculation but also a good deal of honesty and acting from duty. If people always and only engaged in opportunistic behavior, civilization as we know it would not and could not exist.

Elster, in developing the procedural aspects of rational will-formation, makes two revisions in the rational choice model. First, he adds an additional action type. Besides strategic or purposive-rational action oriented to consequences, there is norm-regulated action. No one could deal with or use norms strategically in a particular case if he could not count on the intersubjective validity of norms in general. I could not lie and hope to get away with it in a particular situation, for example, if I could not count on the general norm that everyone tells the truth holding sway. Elster, however, still clings to empirical premises in introducing the new action type, because he does not think that norm and value orientations can be rationally assessed or justified. The moral or ethical realm splits into two domains, one cognitive and rational, the other emotive and irrational. He either strips moral norms of their obligating character or admits them as binding with no rational character. A consequence of this stance, in which normativity and rationality exclude one another, is that rationally motivated agreement can only take the form of bargaining and compromise among strategically oriented actors. Norms take the form of empirical or irrational self-bindings, such that normatively regulated bargaining is a combination of rational calculation of success and social norms contingently steering from behind (337–38).

Such empiricism can explain neither how participants can change their preferences in the course of political will-formation nor how new options can open up. For this reason, Elster introduces argumentation as a further mechanism in addition to bargaining. Parties reach rational agreement with rational argument and with threats and promises. The former is subject to criteria of validity, the latter to criteria of credibility. With the criterion of validity a new kind of coordination of communication and action comes into play; the consensus brought about by argument must rest on identical reasons able to convince parties in the same way. This consensus-generating force derives from the ideal of impartiality governing practical discourse. Such a step requires, Habermas argues, a revision of the first revision concerning types of action. Since norms enter into the process of argumentation, they must be susceptible to rational grounds and evaluation. A rationality core is present in norms that Elster must, and does, acknowledge (338–39).

Elster uses these revisions to evaluate two constitutional assemblies, in Philadelphia (1776) and Paris (1789–91). By a comparative analysis of these conventions, Elster shows that parliamentary opinion-and-will-formation cannot be explained merely or primarily as resulting from a balance of strategically organized interests. Rather, argument and bargaining intertwine, but they often take place so spontaneously that they do not satisfy the fairness condition of regulated bargaining. According to Habermas, Elster's reconstruction can be read two ways, depending on whether one refers to their obvious message or to an analysis of the role played by certain kinds of arguments selected from the debates. From the first perspective, Elster constructs a piece of legal history such that we conclude that the will of the constitutional lawgiver was to enact a system that, under the perceived circumstances, was intended to guarantee the citizens political autonomy by institutionalizing an impartial opinion-and-will-formation. Here Elster's reconstruction tests and validates the discourse-theoretic reading of the constitutional state against its historical background.

From another perspective, however, Elster shows how the presuppositions of rational discourse strongly affect the course of debate, even when that course deviates from the ideal norm of democratic politics. Not all positions can be publicly advocated, for example, but the publicity of political communications presents the expectation that proponents are consistent and coherent in arguments. Under such a condition, concealing publicly indefensible interests behind pretended moral or ethical reasons necessitates self-bindings that can in the future expose somebody as inconsistent or, if one wishes to retain credibility, lead to the inclusion of other interests. Habermas's "subjectless" forms and rules of communication play a role here that goes beyond and supplements the actions and decisions of individuals and groups (339–41).

All of this is well and good and true, but I am concerned about the limits of Habermas's liberal interpretation of these issues, in contrast to a more radical interpretation. Howard Zinn, drawing on Charles Beard's book *An Economic Interpretation of the Constitution,* shows how the U.S. Constitution instantiates the general principle that the rich must, in their own interest, either control the government directly or control the laws by which government operates. Most of the fifty-five men at the Constitutional Convention were lawyers; most of them were very wealthy from land, slaves, manufacturing, and shipping; half loaned out money on interest; and forty held government bonds. Most had a direct economic interest in establishing a strong federal government because manufacturing required protective tariffs; moneylenders wanted to stop the use of paper money to pay off debts; land speculators wanted protection as they invaded Indian lands; slave owners needed federal security against slave revolts and runaways; and bondholders wanted a federal government strong enough to raise money by national taxation to pay off bonds. Many groups were not represented at the convention: slaves, indentured servants, women, and men without property. Consequently, the Constitution did not represent the interests of those groups, and it most certainly did not meet the criteria of Habermas's procedural democracy.[2]

Such observations do not invalidate Habermas's argument here, but they do serve to limit and qualify it more than he admits. Neither the U.S. Constitutional Convention nor, certainly, the French was an approximation to an ideal of discourse theory. Both were permeated with contradiction; classist, racist, and sexist bias and power; and illegitimate exclusion. We can say with Habermas that a piece of reason is inscribed in such constitutions, but, as with Habermas's critique and appropriation of Dworkin, this piece of reason coexists with many pieces of unreason.

Because of these realities, we easily see how an initial political definition of reason, as Hannah Arendt interprets the U.S. Constitution, very soon after turns into a dominantly economic interpretation that betrays the political version. The seeds of that betrayal are already present in the Constitutional Convention and in the Constitution itself; indeed, we would say against Arendt, there already is a good deal more of the economic sense of freedom than she admits. Probably we could say, correcting her, that in the convention and the Constitution, the economic and political senses of freedom coexist uneasily, and the economic takes over more fully after that.[3]

Moreover, this initially flawed Constitution contains the seeds for the emergence of a capitalist public sphere that only occasionally and in crisis situations can act as it should. Is not a radical interpretation of discourse theory here as it applies to history more comprehensive than

Habermas's liberal reformist, relatively benign reading? Should not a merely political interpretation of democracy have been rejected in favor of one that was and is economic, political, and social? Does not my hypothetical constitutional convention criticize and correct not only Habermas's liberal version but also the U.S. and French conventions? Using our radical version of discourse theory, we have not only shed a more critical, comprehensive light on such conventions but have also shown the seeds of an initially inadequate, merely political understanding of democracy grown up into the big capitalist oak tree of the present, where discursive democracy in the public sphere has only a chance of asserting itself occasionally. The economic meaning of democracy and freedom has triumphed almost totally, in a way that either vanquishes or seriously limits Habermas's valid but quite limited sense of democracy. History, radically interpreted, sheds light on the present, and vice versa.

THE CIRCULATION OF POLITICAL POWER

Willke takes up the issues of integration and legitimacy in the modern state from the perspective of systems theory. His view reads, according to Habermas, like a modern systems-theoretic version of the Hegelian state without the monarchical head. Concerted actions, roundtable arrangements, and coordinating committees arising in the gray areas between state and society are described by Willke as symptomatic bargaining systems. They should allow politics in a decentered society to play the role of a therapeutically trained supervisor preserving the social unity that the state can no longer represent or embody. On the one hand, the state has become one subsystem among others. On the other hand, Willke through the back door reintroduces the state as a guarantor of neocorporatist social integration. Habermas sees this surprising move as the result of the autopoetic turn taken by systems theory. The logic of the functional differentiation of society requires that the separate systems be reintegrated at a higher level. If such unity could not be preserved, then a decentered society could no longer profit from the gain in complexity of its parts and would be a victim of these gains in differentiation (342).

On the one hand, because each subsystem is enclosed within itself with its own picture of society and its own language, there is no common language in which the unity of society could be represented by all in the same way. Each system becomes insensitive to the costs it generates for the other systems. On the other hand, the trend toward social disintegration presents a challenge to the legitimation of modern societies. A legitimation problem is at least induced through the inadequate integration of the whole of society. Different systems need to be attuned with one another through a supervisory state that nonetheless cannot operate with any universal language but only its own language as a particular system (343–44).

Herein lies the problem. First of all, the supervisory state uses non-hierarchical bargaining systems to attune subsystems that either suffer disturbances in their operations or burden their environment with various negative costs and must be persuaded to "show consideration." The supervisory state pursues an "options policy" going beyond incentives and exerts influence on the system's self-steering through changes in context. The politics that advises systems must avail itself of the language of law, no longer in the form of conditional or goal programs but as "reflexive" law. An individualistic civil law must be transposed to the level of collective actors and be converted from personal preferences to system relations. Examples are legal protection of new collective goods such as the protection of the environment from destruction, radiation poisoning, or excessive depletion of resources. Although social integration shifts from the level of democratic opinion-and-will-formation to the level of intersystemic monitoring, Willke thinks that the essential content of constitutional democracy remains intact. He even speaks metaphorically of an "establishment of societal discourses" and "the attunement of autonomous actors through rational discourses." But the actors are systems, and the rationality is systems rationality. Does the transposition from one theoretical language to another work (344–45)?

Habermas thinks not. One difficulty is that the Hobbesian problem of how the egocentric perspectives of self-interested actors could form or even encourage a cooperative social order where each considers the interests of the others reappears in a different form in systems theory. How do self-enclosed systems, each one with its own grammar for interpreting the world, constitute an intersubjective or, more exactly, intersystemic world based simply on the achievements of individual systems? How does a universal intermeshing of perspectives emerge from systemic languages that are merely particular and merely express the perspective of each system? Willke, to solve this problem, can only implausibly have recourse to social evolution to account for the emergence of a universal language (346–47).

Another difficulty emerges to the extent that the burden of legitimation is borne solely by systems. What guarantee is there that intrasystemic bargaining will respect and preserve the right of the citizenry as a whole, especially those parts of the population that are unorganized and exist on

the periphery? What guarantee is there that increasing system complementarity and intrasystemic cooperation are, and will be, paralleled by
increasing democratic inclusion and participation by all citizens? What is
going to prevent systems from becoming ends in themselves, no longer
instrumentally serving citizens as individuals or as a whole? Contrary to
Willke, Habermas does not think that the essentials of the constitutional
state are preserved in such attunement of systems. What is left out, if you
like, is the necessary attunement of systems to the public of citizens "both
entitled and *in the position to* perceive, identify, and publicly thematize the
social intolerability of deficient or disturbed functional systems" (350). If
the discourse of experts is not occupied with democratic-opinion-and-
will-formation, then the experts will prevail against the citizens (350–51).

A further problem is that Willke's proposal is narrowly cognitive and
technical. There surely is a role for such technical expertise and for strategic and purposive-rational action and systems rational action, but these
are only parts, not the whole. Willke's mistake is to miss how these forms
of rationality need to be linked to moral and ethical aspects of social integration. One can ask about a policy or program not only whether it is
technically feasible but also whether it is right. Does it contribute to society as a whole or only a part of society? Yet Willke's theory has to exclude
such moral and ethical questions (351).

All of these objections point in the same direction; the integration of
complex societies cannot be carried out in a systems-paternalistic manner
that bypasses the public of citizens engaged in communicative action.
Semantically closed systems do not and cannot invent on their own the
common language necessary for articulating problems and standards of
evaluation to society as a whole. We already have a language in ordinary
language, which circulates throughout society and lies beneath the special
codes, which are founded on, or grounded in, such ordinary language.
For this reason, politics and law cannot be conceived as autopoetically
closed systems. The constitutionally structured political system is internally differentiated into spheres of communicative action and administration, is open to the life-world, and must use ordinary language as a unifying medium (352).

The life-world as a whole is a network of communicative actions. Within it, there are at least three action systems that communicate with one
another through ordinary language: those specialized for cultural reproduction, such as education; socialization, such as the family; or social integration, such as laws. These systems are not separated in their operations,
but each satisfies the needs of the other two and maintains a relation to
the totality of the life-world. The life-world also encompasses collectivi-

ties, associations, and organizations specialized for specific functions. Some of these specialized action systems become independent vis-à-vis spheres that are integrated through values, norms, and mutual understanding. Such systems develop their own codes, as the economy does with money and state administration does with power. Because such media are institutionalized, however, they remain anchored in society as a component of the life-world. The language of law brings ordinary communicative action from the public and private spheres and puts it into forms that can be received by special codes of autopoetic systems, and vice versa. Thus, from Habermas's point of view, Willke's account reduces the whole of the society to one of its parts, systems, mistakenly tries to account for that whole in the light of systems language, misses the pole of ethics and morality, misses the grounded or founded character of the system on life-world, and misses the role of ordinary language—a fivefold mistake (352–54).

This Habermasian humanism, if I may be so bold as to call it that, thus rigorously criticizes a German version of the tendency to reduce the life-world–system polarity to just one of its parts, and a founded, derivative, less important part at that. Habermas's criticism also plays, or can play, a similar role with postmodern, poststructuralist attempts to do the same thing: to reduce, minimize, or eliminate the life-world in favor of structures of language, the unconscious, and society. Both the German and the French attack critically an immediate humanism, which has little or no place for structure of any kind. Habermas convincingly shows how the standpoint reached by systems theory or poststructuralism is equally one-sided; we remain hung up on the dichotomy of immediate versus mediate, life-world versus systems, understanding versus explanation, first-person versus third-person perspectives on society. Habermasian humanism, however, resists this facile either/or by incorporating system as a part within a more all-encompassing social whole.[4] I note here again, nonetheless, the recurrence of the same kind of reified systems language criticized earlier. Some of the specialized systems, he says, become "independent" vis-à-vis the socially integrated sphere of action. Such systems develop their own codes, and law translates ordinary language into a language that can be received by the codes. As I argued, money and power as media are just aspects circulating in the economy and state, within which there is much conscious action of various kinds, communicative, purposive-rational, strategic, and compromising.

In concluding his discussion here, Habermas has recourse to Bernard Peters's model of society to give a more precise account of how power circulates. According to Peters's scheme, processes of communication and decision making lie along a center-periphery axis, are structured by a system of "sluices," and use two forms of problem solving. The core area includes state administration, the judiciary, and democratic opinion-and-will formation, which includes parliamentary bodies, political elections, and competition between and among parties. This center is distinguished from the periphery in virtue of formal decision-making powers and prerogatives. At the edge is an inner periphery, composed of various institutions like universities and professional agencies with rights of self-governance and other kinds of oversight and legislative functions. In contrast to the core area as a whole is an outer periphery that roughly divides into "customers" and "suppliers" (354–55).

On the side of customers, complex networks have arisen among public agencies, private organizations, labor unions, and so on. On the side of suppliers are groups, associations, and organizations that give voice to social problems and express demands and needs before parliament and through the courts. The spectrum here extends from organizations that express group interests through organizations with goals defined by party politics and cultural establishments such as writers' groups to political interest groups with public concerns such as the environment, nuclear arms, or animal rights. Although the distinction between customer and supplier is not a sharp one, the observable fusion between influencing policies that have already been adopted and influencing the formulation and adoption of policies is not constitutionally defensible (355–56).

If binding decisions are to be carried out with authority, they must pass through narrow channels of the core area. The center is a system of sluices through which many communicative processes must pass, but the center controls the direction and dynamics of the processes only to a limited extent. This sociological translation of discourse theory implies that binding decisions must be steered by communication flows that start from the periphery. Only in this way can we exclude the possibility that administration and economic power become independent vis-à-vis the communicative power that develops in the parliamentary complex (356).

To be sure, Habermas says, the normal business of politics as it occurs in western democracies does not and cannot satisfy such strong conditions. There is a countercirculation cutting across the official circulation that involves more than just a bad facticity, because it serves to relieve the burden of unavoidable complexity by breaking problems down into smaller components. Peters takes this circumstance into account by distinguishing between routine problem solving, such as happens when courts deliver judgments and legislatures pass laws, and problematic actions, which occur in crises. When this happens, the attention of the citizenry increases, and the courts and the parliament, the two branches of government that are formally required to deal constructively with normative questions, can actually determine the direction in which communication circulates. "When conflicts become this intense, the political lawgiver has the last word" (356–57, quotation from 357).

Nonetheless, the distinction between normal and extraordinary modes of posing and solving problems can be rendered fruitful for a sociological translation of discourse theory only if we introduce two further conditions. The periphery can play its role in relation to the core area, first, only if it has a specific set of capabilities and, second, if it has sufficient occasion to exercise them. The second condition is easier to satisfy, because of the growing need for integration between autonomous social systems and democratic communication, formal and informal. The first is more problematic because it refers to the capacities for ferreting out, identifying, and thematizing latent problems. The periphery can satisfy such strong demands and conditions, however, only insofar as networks of noninstitutionalized public communication make possible more or less spontaneous processes of opinion-formation. These in turn are anchored in voluntary associations of civil society and embedded in a liberal political culture; "in a word, they depend on a rationalized life-world that meets them halfway" (358). Life-world meaning is a scarce resource that can be stimulated, but it eludes legal regulation, administrative control, and political steering. It is not at the disposal of the members' will. How much is such meaning still operative and present in the civil society and public sphere, to the extent that they can be counted on to play their role of intervention, and how much is this spontaneity compromised by forms of administrative and corporate control? It is to this question that we now turn (358–59).

CIVIL SOCIETY, THE PUBLIC SPHERE, AND THE POWER OF CAPITAL

The discussion here will have three parts: a description of the public sphere, a description of civil society, and a critical reflection on how they function in late capitalist society. Up to now, Habermas has dealt with the public sphere as a communicative structure rooted in the life-world through the associational network of civil society. The public sphere has been described as a political sounding board and warning system that indicates problems that must be processed by the political system because they cannot be solved elsewhere. The public sphere, however, not only must detect and identify problems but must also convincingly and influentially thematize them. Although the public sphere cannot solve problems on its own, it must play an essential role in a process that begins with detection and thematization, applies pressure, passes laws, executes decisions, and passes judgments. Without this initial stage, a genuinely democratic system is present in name only (359).

The public sphere is neither an institution nor an organization nor even a framework of norms. Rather, it is best conceived as a network for communicating information and points of view, in which streams of communication are filtered and synthesized in such a way that they can become public opinion. Communicative action reproduces the public sphere, and for this task the mastery of ordinary language suffices, because this is tailored to the general comprehensibility of everyday communicative practice. Indeed, specific action systems requiring expertise are founded on the public sphere. These fall into two categories: systems such as religion, education, and the family, linked to the general functions of the life-world such as cultural reproduction, social integration, and socialization; and systems such as science, morality, and art, which take up and develop different aspects of everyday communicative truth such as truth, rightness, and sincerity. The public sphere is not specialized in any of these ways. Rather, it has a communicative structure referring neither to the function nor to the content of everyday communication but to the social space generated in such action (360).

Whenever two or more people encounter one another not in the success-oriented attitude of strategic action but communicatively, pursuing the truth together, they constitute a situation or space that is open and diffuse. This starts in small local situations but expands into a larger public, taking the form of assemblies, performances, presentations, debates, and so on. Public opinion formed in these areas can influence the voting behavior of citizens or their will-formation in parliamentary bodies, administrative bodies, and courts. Such influence is converted into power only when it affects the beliefs and decisions of authorized members of the political system and the behavior of voters, legislators, judges, and administrative officials (360–63).

A tension between an ideal and a real public sphere runs throughout Habermas's discussion here. In many sentences it is hard to tell which is which. In a heroic attempt to reconcile the two, Habermas, deliberately or not, trades on this ambiguity. When he says, for example, that "the diffusion of information and points of view is not the only thing that matters in public processes of communication, nor is it the most important" (362), this claim is perhaps true ideally because "the rules of a *shared* practice of public communication are of greater significance for structuring public opinion" (362). The discursive level of such communication, the quality of the arguments and reasons, is what *should* be important, but is it not really true descriptively, I ask, that the content of what is said in major media is often most important and most effective? Negative political campaigning, for example, quite reprehensible from the point of view of the ideal public sphere, is often highly effective and important in the real public sphere.

Indeed, normatively one can say that the "structure of a power-ridden, oppressive public sphere excludes fruitful and clarifying discussions" (362). The presence or absence of such discussions qualifies as an empirical variable that can be said to measure the legitimacy of influence. Yet, moving back to reality, "actual influence coincides with legitimate influence just as little as belief in legitimacy coincides with legitimacy" (362–63). Would not, and should not, taking seriously his prescription of reasonable, open discussion and linking it with his empirical admission lead Habermas to say that the public sphere as it actually exists is unacceptable, because it is "power-ridden and oppressed"? Yet Habermas mostly does not take that course, although he makes occasional empirical admissions that he should do so (362–63).

Who are the major players within the public sphere in the political struggle for influence? This struggle involves not only influence already acquired, such as that enjoyed by experienced political leaders, but also the influence of groups of persons and experts who have built up their reputations within the public sphere, such as religious leaders, artists, scientists, intellectuals, and articulate activists. These groups are distinguished from those who occupy an already situated space, such as large and well-organized interest groups anchored in various subsystems that affect the political system through the public sphere. These cannot use bribes or threats involved in bargaining but must use arguments that can mobilize convincing reasons and shared value orientations.

Maybe some groups should behave this way, but do they actually behave this way? Has Habermas never heard of political advertising employed by candidates, or commercial advertising employed by firms, or fictional entertainment favoring the status quo and rarely bringing up questions, because questions would offend the sponsor? Perhaps the ideal public sphere is totally free of such manipulative strategic action, but the real public sphere is shot through with it. Habermas may be falling into a tendency mentioned earlier of reifying an aspect and making it the whole story. Here the aspect is communicative action, one aspect of the real public sphere that is reified abstractly into the whole of the ideal public sphere. And, of course, the dominant players are the major media them-selves, such as CBS, NBC, ABC, CNN, the *New York Times,* and the *Washington Post.* These do not enter the public sphere from without but are already within it, and their aim is primarily to pursue capitalist ends and exclude or minimize perspectives that criticize or threaten capitalist priorities. As pursued by these firms, strategic action and manipulation are at least as dominant as communicative action in the real public sphere, if not more so. Here is another instance of trading on the ambiguity between real and ideal. If he recognizes them at all, Habermas certainly under-states the reality, importance, and effect of these firms in the public sphere.

Of course, Habermas has heard of such advertising and manipulation, but he does not advert to them here and elsewhere because of the ambiguity between real and ideal. He further comments that interest groups are vulnerable to criticism because undeclared infusions of money or organizational power lose their credibility as soon as they become public. Again, perhaps such a claim is true of an ideal public sphere confronted by an ideal public that has not regularly been brainwashed. But what about the situation when it is generally well known that political candidates receive large amounts of money from the rich and corporations and this seems not to hurt the candidates at all? Indeed, the public seems to expect such practices, and such candidates are often nominated and elect-ed. Such was true of both George W. Bush and Al Gore in the U.S. presidential campaign of 2000 (363–64).

Again, Habermas states that "public opinion can be manipulated but neither publicly bought nor blackmailed" because the public cannot be "manufactured" as one pleases (364). It must develop out of its own resources with a structure that stands on its own and reproduces itself out of itself. Has such development occurred in a way that can be verified, or is it not the case that capital can more and more take over the public sphere, perhaps not totally, but sufficiently to achieve its interests (360–64)?

Such is the burden of Habermas's early book on the public sphere, which he seems to have forgotten here. In that book he argues that a decline of the public sphere occurred as capitalist democracies moved from the eighteenth to the twentieth century in such a way that advertis-ing, propaganda, and strategic action serving capitalism more and more took over from and supplanted communicative action. But, balancing the ideals at the beginning of the paragraph, is some realism at the end. "This lawlike regularity governing the formation of the public sphere remains latent in the constituted public sphere—and takes effect again only in moments when the public sphere is mobilized" (364). There is a tension here between an ideal and "a really existing" public sphere that is not easily resolved.[5]

Civil society is a related but distinct concept. It is no longer now, as it was in the time of Hegel and Marx, the economy as constituted by private law and steered through markets in commodities, labor, and capital. Its institutional core includes nongovernmental and noneconomic connections and voluntary associations that anchor communication structures in the society component of the life-world. These associations and movements, because they are sensitive to how social problems resonate in private life, transmit and distill such reactions to the public sphere. "The core of civil society is a network of associations that institutionalizes problem-solving discourses on questions of general interest inside the framework of organized public spheres" (367). These organizations have an open, egalitarian form that mirrors the communicative action around which they crystallize and to which they give permanence and continuity. I interpret these sentences to mean that the public sphere is form and civil society is content, the organizations and movements that operate within the framework of the public sphere (366–67).

Borrowing from Cohen and Arato, Habermas lists the following aspects of civil society: plurality, a multiplicity of groups and associations allowing for different forms of life; publicity, institutions of communication and culture; privacy, a sphere of individual self-development and moral choice; legality, structures of basic rights and law demarcating privacy, plurality, and publicity from the state and the economy. The constitution of this sphere through such rights as freedom of assembly, freedom of speech, and freedom of association gives some indications of its social structure. Crucial also here is the protection of privacy through rights of personality, freedom of conscience, freedom of movement, and so on. The network of associations draws on and presumes the autonomy and privacy of this sphere and expresses its needs, especially when there is dislocation and suffering. The political system, which must remain sensitive to public opinion, is intertwined with civil society and the public sphere through the activity of political parties and general elections. Such intertwining is guaranteed by the positive right to contribute to the political will-formation of the people, the citizen's active and passive voting rights, and other participatory rights (368).

We thus have here a network of the private sphere, civil society, the public sphere, and the formal, legal political systems. Basic constitutional rights and guarantees, of course, cannot by themselves preserve civil society and the public sphere and keep them active. Rather, an active, communicative, collective agency must preserve, reproduce, and stabilize from its own resources the political public sphere. Habermas here focuses on the dual, reflective character of the public sphere and civil society; citizens not only try to influence the political sphere with their programs and proposals but also enlarge and revitalize these domains and confirm their own identities and capacities to act. Habermas sees this dual politics most promisingly instantiated in social movements such as the environmental, feminist, and antinuclear movements (369–70).

This idea of fruitful interplay "of a public sphere based in civil society with the opinion-and-will-formation institutionalized in parliamentary bodies offers a good starting point for translating the content of deliberative politics into sociological terms" (371). Nonetheless, the concept does not mean or imply the programming, direction, or control of society as a whole. Rather, civil society and the public sphere are linked in the following ways. First, they presuppose a liberal political culture, patterns of socialization that undergird and support that culture, and a robust private sphere. Second, activism in civil society and the public sphere can only achieve influence, not political power. Political power emerges only from legitimate lawmaking, judicial decisions, and administrative implementation of laws. Finally, Habermas reminds us again that law and administrative power have a limited effectiveness in functionally differentiated societies. Political steering can only be indirect and must leave intact the mode of operations that are internal to functional systems and other highly organized spheres. A consequence is that movements emerging from civil society have to give up holistic aspirations to a self-organizing society, such as that present in some Marxist versions' idea of a social revolution (371–72).

Here is, perhaps, another reason for Habermas's reformism. The idea of a market democratic socialism with a minimal state, worker-owned and -controlled firms, and full economic, political, and social democracy escapes Habermas's idea of a macrosubject creating a revolution and controlling and programming the whole of society. Or, to put it another way, the idea of revolution is not exhausted by this earlier idea of revolution based on a macrosubject. Neither here nor anywhere else has Habermas satisfactorily addressed this more nuanced model of socialism (371–72).[6]

In any event, Habermas goes on to say that the concepts of civil society and the public sphere are not merely normative but have empirical relevance. Additional postulates, however, are necessary to translate the discourse-theoretic reading of "radical democracy" (373) into sociological terms and reformulate it in an empirically verifiable manner. "I would like to defend the claim that *under certain circumstances* civil society can acquire influence on the public sphere, have an effect on the parliamentary complex (and the courts) through its own public opinions, and compel the political state to switch over to the official circulation of power" (373). Interestingly, the claim is that only under certain circumstances, not as a general rule, does civil society have an influence. Moreover, the official route of power from below upwards does not operate as a rule. We are tempted to ask whether such a state of affairs is an adequate translation of the system of rights, the discourse theory of democracy, and the normative reading of civil society and the public sphere. If "only under certain circumstances" generally obtains, why does this not falsify, rather than verify, the discourse theory of democracy? If such a state of affairs does not falsify the discourse theory of democracy, what would falsify it? Why could the normative theory of democracy be used here not to falsify itself but fundamentally to criticize a state of affairs in which it can only operate "under certain circumstances"? Such a path is open to Habermas, but he refuses to take it (373).

Habermas says further that the public sphere is differentiated into levels: the episodic level found in taverns and coffeehouses or on the streets; the occasional publics of particular presentations and events such as rock concerts, theatrical performances, academic conferences, or church congresses; and the abstract public sphere of isolated readers, viewers, and listeners scattered across the globe and brought together through the mass media. Despite such differentiation, however, all of these remain open to one another and porous to one another. The one text of the public sphere can be divided into arbitrarily small texts, but hermeneutical bridges can always be built from one to another text. Segmented public spheres constituted by exclusion mechanisms cannot harden into organizations or systems, because there is no exclusion rule without a proviso for its abolition. Boundaries remain permeable in principle because the rights to unrestricted inclusion and equality built into liberal public spheres prevent or overcome exclusion mechanisms of the Foucauldian type and ground a potential for self-transformation. The labor movement and feminism are examples of discourses that arose to shatter structures that had rendered them "other" to the bourgeois public sphere.

Even if one agrees with Habermas about Foucault, does he answer Marx, who makes the critique of capitalism as *essentially* unjust and irrational? Does he overstress the positive aspects of the public sphere in a liberal way? One can agree with him against Foucault, on the one hand, that there are positive forward moves and structures in modernity and yet argue that the public sphere and the democratic capitalist society of which it is a part are in principle ridden with contradictions. And, on the other hand, if there is a potential for self-transformation, why does Habermas arbitrarily limit it to *reformist* forms? Why is not a radical socialist form possible and desirable, even on Habermas's own grounds? And yet he says no; "Only the reformist path of trial and error remains both practically available and morally reasonable" (373–75, quotation from 57).

Returning to our reflections on the public sphere, Habermas distinguishes those who emerge from the public sphere from those who emerge "before the public." The latter have resources, power, and sanctions available to them from the start. Such actors are the large political parties and large interest groups. A third group is journalists, publicity agents, and members of the press who select programs and control the entry of contributions, topics, authors, and agenda into the mass media. As mass media become more complex and expensive, they become more centralized. To this extent, there is increasing pressure of selection on both the supply and demand sides. Such media are not sufficiently reined in by professional standards and only in fits and starts by legal regulation. As a result, the image of politics on television is predominantly made up of issues and contributions that are professionally produced as media input and then fed through news conferences, public relations campaigns, and so on. These are more successful the more they can rely on trained personnel, financial and technical resources, and a professional infrastructure. Collective actors operating outside the political system or large organizations have many fewer opportunities to influence the content of the media. Such a claim is especially true of messages that fall outside a narrowly defined center of opinion. Moreover, information-processing strategies are deployed to attract and manipulate viewers, facts are reported as human-interest stories, entertainment is mixed with information, and complex relationships are broken down into smaller, easily reportable fragments in such a way as to depoliticize public communication (376–77).

This rather negative empirical picture is still understated by Habermas. It is not just that "actors in the public sphere *depend* on the support of 'sponsors' who supply the necessary resources of money, organizations, knowledge, and social capital." Such a claim makes it seem as though an "inside" and "outside" distinction operates between the public sphere and systems of money and power. I would insist, however, that big media like CBS and ABC are already capitalistic, very wealthy in their own internal resources, very powerful, and, therefore, able to constrain free, unlimited expressions from within. Like all capitalist firms, their quantitative aim is profit measured in money. But their qualitative social function, their "use value" for capitalism as a whole, is to defend and promote capitalistic moneymaking as a way of life and, therefore, to limit criticism of it. Their aim is not to promote but to deter democracy and to convince a massive viewing population that an unjust economic system not functioning in their interests is just and is in their interests. Otherwise, left to its own devices or having resort to a really free, democratic form of expression, this population might start to question, criticize, and revolt.[7]

This empirical picture can be measured and criticized by normative requirements rooted in the idea of deliberative politics. These include surveillance of sociopolitical encroachment, reporting developments likely to impinge, positively or negatively, on the welfare of citizens; meaningful agenda setting; dialogue across a diverse range of views and between actual and potential powerholders and the public; mechanisms for holding officials accountable for how they have exercised power; incentives for citizens to become intelligent, active participants in the political process rather than its passive objects; and a principled resistance to forces outside of the media that threaten intelligent, reasonable, responsible citizens who do or can make sense of what is going of politically.

These principles express a single idea: the media ought to understand themselves as serving the interests of an enlightened public, retaining independence from political and social pressure, and they should block the tacit conversion of administrative and social power into political power. Actors should be able to use the media only insofar as they make contributions to solving problems put on the agenda by the public. Contrary to the usual practice in the United States, money should not be the primary determinant of whether a view is represented or presented. Political parties should participate in the opinion-and-will-formation from the public's own perspective rather than simply patronizing the public and extracting loyalty through propaganda, political advertising, and so on (378–79).

This expression of the normative idea of the media is impressive. How close do mass media come to satisfying these norms? Habermas has already indicated that *empirically* they do not even come close. He confirms the point by admitting that only occasionally, in crisis situations, do forces at the periphery of power get their agenda considered. Generally, the initiative for putting issues on the agenda for discussion comes from officeholders, while the broader public is excluded from the process or does not have any influence; or the initiative comes from the political system, and proponents of the issue must mobilize the public sphere to obtain formal consideration or to implement successfully an adopted program (379–80). Habermas summarizes thus:

In the normal case, issues and proposals have a history whose course corresponds more to the first or second model than the third [the normatively desirable one]. As long as the informal circulation of power dominates the political system, the initiative and power to put problems on the agenda and bring them to a decision lies more with the government leaders and administration than with the parliamentary complex. As long as in the public sphere the mass media prefers, contrary to their normative self-understanding, to draw their material from powerful, well-organized information producers and all along they prefer media strategies that lower rather than raise the discursive level of public communication, issues will tend to start in, and be managed from, the center rather than follow a spontaneous course originating in the periphery. . . . [I]n a perceived crisis situation, the actors in civil society thus far neglected in our scenario can assume a surprisingly active and momentous role. (380)

In other words, the public sphere as it should function normally is not operative and acts contrary to its own normative understanding (379–80).

At this point, the tension between normativity and facticity turns into a full-fledged contradiction. Facticity and normativity fall apart and conflict dialectically in ways that cannot be easily smoothed over or harmonized. By Habermas's own criteria and in his own words, modern democratic capitalist societies do not act justly and democratically *as a rule.* Only in rare instances and in crisis situations does the public *have a chance* of getting its issues on the agenda; and even then, influence does not automatically translate into power. Capitalist class power and other kinds of power as well—racist, sexist, heterosexist—can intervene further up the legislative, judicial, or administrative line, as it often does, or threaten to derail citizen initiatives. This has happened over the years with citizen efforts to limit military or campaign spending, to reduce poverty, or to limit environmental damage. These issues get on the agenda for discussion and are considered sometimes, but influence often is translated imperfectly or not at all into power and effective legislation. Legislation, too, can be derailed by powerful interests in the way it is interpreted and applied or not applied. The public sphere, democracy's last best hope and refuge, turns out to be undemocratic and unjust, as much a part of the problem as of the solution.

Yet Habermas seems curiously not to be bothered by this state of affairs. He seems satisfied to have shown that democracy has a chance of arising in certain crisis situations. What seems to be going on here, among other things, is a subtle weakening of the normative requirements of democracy as they occur in the first part of the book and throughout the book. According to a fairly straightforward reading of the requirements, "only a public sphere that has emerged from the confines of class and thrown off the millennia-old shackles of social stratification" (308) can realize its full potential. Otherwise, "structures of a power-ridden, oppressed public sphere exclude fruitful discussions" (362). In fact, his empirical admissions show that the public is for the most part influenced, internally and externally, by class and social stratification and is so power-ridden and oppressed that only "occasionally" and "in crisis situations" does democracy "have a chance." Yet tacitly Habermas shifts from a strong normative requirement and critique that points to radical social transformation as a necessary and sufficient condition to realize those ideals to being content to show that "under certain circumstances" (373) civil society has a chance to have an influence.[8]

There is a movement back and forth between a stronger normativity and a weaker, between an opposition between normativity and empirical reality and a tacit softening of normative demands so that they seem to be realized and verified in such reality. Demands are softened to such an extent that Habermas says later in the chapter that the "crises can at most be explained historically. They are not built into structurally differentiated societies in such a way that they would intrinsically compromise the project of self-empowerment undertaken by a society of free and equal subjects who bind themselves by law" (386). Yet, much of what he has said in *Beyond Facts and Norms* implies the opposite. If democracy is so constrained that it only has a chance to become operative occasionally, why is there not a problem in principle?

There are further, related problems. Prior normative and conceptual analyses prepare the way for the set of alternating contradicting claims in this chapter: for example, his narrow political conception of democracy, his occasionally reified use of "system," and his refusal to make the distinction between modern complexity as such and complexity rooted in capitalist exploitation and domination. Such claims prepare the way for him to say or intimate that the nature of modern democracy and modern complex societies implies that we cannot do any better. Such a claim would further imply that there is a problem in principle, not just historically, with realizing more democracy. The nature of modern complex societies implies that we cannot do any better because there is a necessary informal circuit of power starting from above that runs counter to, and indeed renders inoperative for the most part, the official circulation of power starting from the periphery. Yet, if we admit the possibility of a fuller sense of democracy, economic, social, and political; reject a reified sense of system; and distinguish between complexity as such and capitalist versions of it, then we do not have to become resigned to just occasional

manifestations of democracy. The way is open to serious reform and, finally and fortunately, radical social transformation.

A further related contradiction is not just that between communicatively based norms and recalcitrant empirical reality but also that between
two ideas of rationality: moral and normative, and socially scientific and
empirical. Communicative action gives rise to normative demands that
shoot beyond the empirical reality of capitalism and bring it into question.
Even Habermas, sometimes in spite of himself, does that. But social analysis, often based on bourgeois social science and borrowing much, sometimes too much, from systems theory, gives rise to problematic accounts
of modern, complex, differentiated societies. Such an analysis does not
distinguish, as we have seen, between differentiation as such and its capitalist form. As a result, we are led to the conclusion, implied or explicit,
that "this is the best we can do." Social scientific analysis counsels resignation, and normative reflection leads, if one is consistent and goes all the
way with it, to critique.

If I am correct, however, the problem is not in social reality as such but
in the mistaken conceptual and empirical analysis. A move Habermas
makes with other social theorists I make with him. I do not think that he
has sufficiently criticized and transformed the bourgeois social scientific
theory, including systems theory, upon which he has drawn. If one does
so, complex social differentiation can be linked to a project of radical
social transformation, and we do not have to conclude that capitalism is
the best we can do. Again, Habermas does not distinguish in his account
among the four possible ways of putting issues on the public agenda—the
two proceeding from the center of power and the other from the periphery—and a socialist form of democratic agenda setting. As a result, the
public sphere as such is conflated with the form that it takes in later capitalism, and real democracy only "occasionally" has a chance to operate.
The conservatism is in the beholder, not in the social reality.

The contradictions and tensions in this chapter are so intermixed that
they are not easily distinguished. Another problem still operative in
Habermas's book is the notion that the public sphere is somehow pure
within itself and only external factors prevent its successful functioning.
Habermas uses the language of resistance "to the effect of forces outside
the media" (378) and says that "mass media . . . ought to preserve their
independence from political and social pressure" (378). These quotations
are instances of the inside-outside dichotomy. But I would suggest that it
is the mass media themselves, operating as capitalist firms pushing capitalism as a way of life and, therefore, hostile to democracy *in principle,* that
are the major players within the public sphere. Because effectively demo-

cratic media function at the margins of the public sphere and are not major players within it, neither is democracy. The accumulation-legitimation tension, which Habermas recognizes in earlier works operates in the state, also exists in the public sphere. The big capitalist firms within the public sphere, whose reality Habermas misses or understates, are the major obstacles to its successful democratic functioning; they are not interested in the full range of opinions and possibilities of a fully open public sphere that would or could challenge capitalist priorities. That question is never, or rarely, allowed to come up.

The problem in principle, then, is the contradiction between accumulation and legitimation within the public sphere, between dominant firms at the center that are interested in in deterring democracy and publicly owned and financed firms in the periphery that are committed to democracy in principle. Yet democracy, normatively understood, should be central and not peripheral. Habermas smudges over this conflict in principle by affirming a public sphere that should be "pure" normatively and then sliding over into a description that implies that it is or could be pure in practice. This going back and forth between normative prescription and empirical description contributes to obfuscation and mystification.

Supporting these points about mass media as capitalist and not interested in democracy are two examples from Chomsky and Herman's discussion of mass media. One is the example of the obscure Polish priest killed in the 1980s, before the fall of the Berlin Wall, by a communist regime to which our government and economy were hostile. This killing was given more time and space in the *New York Times* and the *Washington Post* and on CBS, NBC, and ABC than several other incidents taken together and with many more victims, such as the assassination of Archbishop Romero in El Salvador, whose government we supported and which did our bidding. A second example is the favorable reception of these same media to undemocratic elections in the 1980s in El Salvador, Guatemala, and Honduras, regimes that we supported, contrasted to the unfavorable reception to the much more democratic elections held in Nicaragua during the same period, under a regime that we opposed because it was anticapitalist and anti-imperialist. By all the criteria of a democratic election—absence of terror, absence of pressure to vote, ability of media to freely express different opinions, and multiplicity and diversity of candidates—the Nicaraguan elections were far more democratic than these others. Yet the media presented the Nicaraguan election as undemocratic and the others as virtual showplace exercises of democracy. Such treatments of issues are very typical of the mass media.[9]

These examples show it is not system complexity as such that is the problem, but capitalist class bias and power operating in and through the media inside and outside of the public sphere. Because it so operates, it must present unjust, capitalist regimes that we support in a favorable light and present more just, democratic regimes in an unfavorable light. What would happen if we excluded the operating of such bias and power in principle by socially transforming and democratizing the corporation within and without the public sphere?

I am wary of appearing to overstate my argument here. It is never the case that capitalist or capitalist-controlled media are totally dominant over the public sphere or over the rest of society in such a way that no resistance is possible. Capitalism in all spheres is always contradictory, and thus more or less contestation is possible depending on time and context. Rather than speaking of total control or total administration, the totally administered society, we should speak of hegemony exercised by capitalist media; such hegemony is always contested and is more or less dominant, depending on the epoch. Douglas Kellner has shown that in the United States in the 1960s and 1970s there was a great deal of protest and dissent that broke through into mainstream, popular programming and news. In the 1980s and 1990s, however, such contestation was significantly beaten back, and a more thoroughgoing hegemony of capitalism obtained.[10]

That such lessening of hegemony is more than a pipe dream is proved by the presence of media that are fairly extensive and yet operate freely and openly every day, not just in crisis situations. WBAI, a listener-supported radio station in New York City, is part of Pacifica Network, which has stations in Washington, D.C.; Houston; Berkeley, California; and Los Angeles. WBAI and Pacifica forbid corporate sponsorship and advertisements, and the result is a stunning difference in the range of questions asked, opinions offered, and alternatives proposed. Specific examples in the last several years include the thoroughgoing criticism of the NATO intervention in Yugoslavia; the coverage of the fate of Mumia Abu Jamal, the black journalist railroaded by the Philadelphia and Pennsylvania criminal justice system into a death penalty; the coverage given to the killing of Amadou Diallo by four police officers and the questions raised about the repressiveness of the New York Police Department as part of the prison-industrial complex. Such a range of opinion has been significantly absent in coverage of these same issues by the mainstream corporate media; these media generally have functioned as cheerleaders for the status quo and for the white corporate power structure that benefits from it. Indeed, I would venture to say that WBAI as a matter of course satisfies Habermas's normative criteria in a way that capitalist media do not and cannot. What would happen if the major networks were similarly democratized and listener owned and supported? Would not all this Habermasian talk about "unavoidable system complexity" and "necessary informal circuits of power" cease to have much relevance?

CONCLUSION

This chapter, in spite of is insightfulness and its struggle to reconcile what is in principle irreconcilable, ultimately fails. But we can learn from that failure.

Habermas, in summing up, makes four points. First of all, the political system, because of its internal relation to law, considers problems affecting society as a whole, even though it is only one system among others. Collectively binding decisions, if they are to be legitimate, must be interpreted and must be a realization of rights such that structures of recognition built into communicative action are transformed, via the medium of law, from the level of simple interactions to the abstract and anonymous relationships of strangers. This is a marvelous intuition and ideal that can serve as a norm for a just, democratic society. Unfortunately, such a norm is realized only imperfectly and in a contradictory way in late capitalist society. Second, because it takes on the task of integration that others cannot take on, the political system is asymmetrically related to other subsystems. As a functionally specified action system, it runs into limits on its administrative power from other subsystems, which obey their own logic. But what if some of those other subsystems include corporations that are inherently undemocratic and unjust and that in turn affect the administrative system adversely, turning it into an instrument, more or less, of class power? Because the political system depends on the public sphere as its enabling condition, the conditions making the production of legitimate law are not at its disposal. But what if the public sphere itself, because of the influence of big corporations, does not and cannot play such an enabling role (384–85)?

Third, the political system is subject to disturbances from subsystems that can reduce its effectiveness and achievements and from the public sphere, which reduces the legitimacy of its decisions.

> The constitutionally regulated circulation of power is nullified if the administrative system becomes independent of communicatively generated power, if the social power of functional systems and large organizations (including the mass media) is converted into illegitimate power or if the lifeworld reasons for spontaneous public communication no longer suffice to guarantee an uncoerced circulation of social interests. (386)

An independence of illegitimate power from communicative praxis, along with the weakening of civil society and the public sphere, can degenerate into a legitimation dilemma, which, under certain circumstances, can develop into a vicious circle. Legitimation deficits and steering deficits reinforce one another in a downward spiral (386).

We see here a marvelous admission by Habermas. Such a downward spiral, which he reveals almost in spite of himself, is rooted in late capitalist democracies as capitalist and should be expected. Yet, instead of using this admission as a basis for developing a critique of such societies in principle, he says, fourth, that "such crises can at most be explained historically" (386). They do not compromise intrinsically the project of self-empowerment undertaken by a society of free and equal subjects bound under law. Thus, even in these last few pages of the chapter, normative criticism and empirical, historical resignation coexist uneasily in Habermas's argument. He gives and he takes away; he makes claims that are stunningly right normatively but refuses to follow where they lead. Finally, late capitalist societies are legitimate and marvelous, at least in principle.

The chapter fails, but we can learn something from the failure. Negatively, we learn that communicative action, discursive democracy, and the rule of law exist only very uneasily and inadequately within a capitalist situation. The public sphere cannot play its role because it is dominated from within and without by corporations that are intentionally undemocratic both in their internal structure and in their influence on society. Their essential role is to deter or subvert democracy, subordinating or sacrificing it to economic profit, because such democracy threatens class domination, injustice, and marginalization. As a result, we see such corporations using mechanisms, some of which Habermas has described, such as mixing news with entertainment and human-interest stories, to derail democracy and to depoliticize the public sphere. The dependence of mass media on advertising revenues from other big corporations outside the public sphere ensures that little or nothing appears on either news or entertainment that brings into question the capitalist agenda. This point is overwhelmingly verified in the ordinary, day-in and day-out operation of the mass media.[11]

Positively, the failure shows once again the way communicative action, discursive democracy, and the rule of law point beyond capitalism as a form of life. I take seriously Habermas's claim that only a public sphere free from the shackles of class domination and stratification can and should function as an effective basis for democracy. As the examples of WBAI and Pacifica show, this kind of public communication is possible.

What prevents it from being generalized to the whole of the public sphere is not anything "in the nature of functionally differentiated societies." This kind of claim just amounts to obfuscation and mystification that inhibits and blocks real social change.

NOTES

1. Jürgen Habermas, *Between Facts and Norms*, trans. William Rehg (Cambridge: MIT Press, 1996), 329–30. Page numbers in parentheses throughout this chapter refer to this book.

2. Howard Zinn, *A People's History of the United States*, rev. ed. (New York: HarperCollins, 1995), 89–95.

3. Hannah Arendt, *On Revolution* (New York: Viking Press, 1965). As Arendt interprets the Constitution, it is significant as a step forward in the institutionalization of political reason and leaves out or minimizes the strategic and economic senses of reason and action. As we have seen in chapter 4, Arendt's notion of political power very much influenced Habermas's conception of communicative praxis.

4. Jürgen Habermas, *The Philosophical Discourse of Modernity*, trans. Fred Lawrence (Cambridge: MIT Press, 1987).

5. Jürgen Habermas, *The Structural Transformation of the Public Sphere*, trans. Thomas Burger, with the assistance of Frederick Lawrence (Cambridge: MIT Press, 1989), 181–235.

6. See my model of democratic socialism in *Critique, Action, and Liberation* (Albany: State University of New York Press, 1995), 313–30.

7. Douglas Kellner, in *Television and the Crisis of Democracy* (Boulder: Westview Press, 1990), 80–90, describes the enormous wealth, power, and extent of the big corporate media.

8. William E. Scheurman suggests such a shift from strong to weak normativity in his "Between Radicalism and Resignation," in *Habermas: A Critical Reader*, ed. Peter Dews (Oxford: Basil Blackwell, 1999), 153–77.

9. Noam Chomsky and Edward Herman, *Manufacturing Consent: The Political Economy of the Mass Media* (New York: Pantheon, 1988), 37–142.

10. Kellner, *Television and Democracy*, 17–20, 71–177.

11. See Douglas Kellner, *Persian Gulf TV War* (Boulder: Westview Press, 1992) for a fine, very thoroughly empirically documented discussion of the way capitalist class bias functioned in the reporting and discussion of the Persian Gulf War in 1990–91. According to Kellner's point of view here and in *Television and the Crisis of Democracy*, the media have become even more enthusiastic cheerleaders for U.S. policies and capitalist practices in the last decades than they were in the 1960s and 1970s. From Habermas's point of view, things are getting worse rather than better. This same point of view is shared by William McChesney, *Rich Media, Poor Democracy* (Chicago: University of Chicago Press, 1999).

8

The Different Paradigms of Law
and the Difference They Make

We come now to Habermas's final chapter reflecting on the paradigms of law and arguing that his own proceduralistic paradigm represents a step forward from the earlier paradigms of bourgeois formal law and the welfare state. Habermas here makes his argument more explicit. If Habermas wants to argue for his paradigm as both a necessary and a sufficient condition for democratizing modern industrial society, I will question that conclusion. It may be necessary but it is not sufficient. The sufficient condition has to be a socialist, revolutionary transformation of modern society. A radical, socialist version of the new paradigm, providing for, among other things, full, economic, political, and social democracy, and, therefore, a fully democratic public sphere would be both necessary and sufficient.

To the extent that Habermas simply repeats conclusions from earlier chapters about the necessity of avoiding an overly concrete understanding of the separation of powers or the importance of the public sphere in relationship to the formal processes of legislation, administration, and judicial decision making, I will question such conclusions insofar as they remain tied to a capitalist context. Finally, insofar as there is appropriation of feminist insights to develop and instantiate his model, I applaud that but argue that his appropriation is limited by his reformist stance and leaves unaddressed the deeper issues of both sexist and capitalistic class power.

Habermas begins his discussion in this chapter by pointing out how important legal paradigms are in making, interpreting, and applying law. The objectifying gaze of the historian of law focuses on the social context in which law is embedded and from which the background assumptions of adjudication and legal doctrine are nourished. We can understand what legal actors are responding to only if we recognize their implicit or explicit image of society and know which structures, achievements, potentials, and dangers actors ascribe to the society of their time as they struggle to realize a system of rights.[1]

Habermas in this chapter tries to examine the adequacy of his proceduralist paradigm of law geared to complex societies but retaining significant normative components. We do not need, in the face of such societies, to give up on a normative understanding of law and move to mere efficiency. In the first part of this chapter, Habermas considers how materialization of law has taken place in several areas of private life and how, consequently, the status of legal persons must be realized in different ways. In the second part of this chapter, Habermas shows how the undesirable effects of the welfare state can be countered only by politically guaranteeing private and public autonomy simultaneously. In the third part of the chapter, Habermas shows how the changed catalogue of government tasks and the expanded role of the administration, which give rise to problems for the separation of powers, can be met by shifting the functional separation of powers onto the administrative system itself through new elements of participation and control (391).

THE MATERIALIZATION OF PRIVATE LAW

Developing the point about the importance of paradigms of law as part of a necessary background knowledge in contemporary societies, Habermas asserts that even legal practitioners and commentators have become aware of this phenomenon. Even specialized legal commentary cannot avoid the question about the correct paradigm, once we lose the innocent ignorance of a background knowledge that operates behind everyone's backs. Private law must explain and justify its relation to society as a whole, because the old liberal or social welfare models of law no longer are persuasive (392–93).

> The desired paradigm should satisfy the best description of complex societies; it should illuminate once again the original idea of the self-constitution of a community of free and equal citizens; and it should overcome the rampant particularism of a legal order that, having lost its center in adapting to the *uncomprehended* complexity of the social environment, is unraveling bit by bit. (393)

The required background knowledge can be reconstructed neither by relying solely on legal theorists or experts nor by having recourse only to the public as client. Because the public has the constitutional role of author as well as client, and therefore can function as a critic of any claim by experts, all of the involved actors must form an idea of how the normative content of the democratic state can be fully and effectively exploited and understood within the horizon of existing social structures and emerging developmental tendencies. The question about the correct paradigm is a political issue, to be decided by all of the people. In this discussion, experts have a privileged role, but the citizenry as a whole must be convinced (393–94).

The paradigm shift was noticed first, especially in Germany, in the domain of private law. In organizing a privately separated domain of a depoliticized economic society immune from state intrusion, the negative legal freedom of subjects was guaranteed. Public law was reserved to the sphere of the authoritarian state in order to keep a rein on an administration that reserved for itself the right to intervene. With the establishment of the Weimar Republic in Germany, the separation of private from public law effectively ended. The subsequent priority of the democratic constitution over private law meant that the normative content of basic rights had to unfold within private law itself through an active legislature and courts (396).

A similar social transformation occurred in other societies as well. Such changes made it necessary to conceive the relationship between private and public autonomy not as contradictory but as complementary. Individual negative freedom was initially guaranteed by a certain set of rights and institutions, including personal rights and protections from torts, freedom of contract in exchange for goods and services, and property rights. This situation was altered through the emergence of new areas of law, such as labor law, social legislation, and commercial law, as well as the materialization of contract law, tort law, and property law. The whole of private law appeared to go beyond the goal of safeguarding individual negative freedom in order to ensure the realization of justice. In many cases, principles hitherto relegated either to private or to public law merged. The new goal of social justice seemed to demand new ways of conceiving formally equal but materially different legal relationships (397–98).

Enter the social welfare model as a result of the critique of bourgeois formal law. This model was tied to the assumption of an economic society institutionalized in the form of private law defining negative liberties against the state and assuming that this legal arrangement was sufficient for the interpenetration of legal freedom with the universal right to equality. This assumption relied on assumptions about the equilibrium of market processes, equal distribution of wealth and social power, and equal opportunity to exercise the power conferred by private law. If freedom is the capacity to have and acquire, then an equality of legal capacity must exist if justice is to be attained.

When these assumptions became untenable because of the gross inequality in resources, wealth, income, and power, it became necessary to specify the content of existing norms of private law and to introduce a new category of basic rights that grounded claims to a more just distribution of wealth and income and more effective protection from socially produced dangers. Materialization of private law and social entitlements become relatively necessary and justified from the perspective of an absolutely equal distribution of individual liberties. Because legal freedom to do as one pleases is worth nothing without actual freedom, the real possibility of choosing between the permitted alternatives, materialization of private law is necessary. Because the freedom of a large number of rights bearers does not have its material basis in an environment they control, but requires government intervention, social entitlements are necessary (401–3).

Changes in property law and contract law are prime examples of the materialization of bourgeois formal law. Property rights have been extended beyond material property to include entitlements and rights affecting income, such as membership rights, pension rights, and pension eligibility. In contract law rightness no longer depends on the fiction of free declaration of intention linked with the freedom to enter into contracts. Rather, regulations emerge that guarantee compensations for those in weaker market positions, such as employees, tenants, and consumers; and structural advantages in information, power, and authority are subject to empirical analyses and legally binding evaluation (403–4).

The premises underlying these examples reveal a changed interpretation of social processes. Statutory limits on property and judicial interventions into the framing and concluding of contracts seek to compensate for asymmetries in economic power positions. The equal opportunity to exercise liberties is used to justify rejection of the liberal market model of rights and the acceptance of the welfare state model. The new background understanding has two components: an increasingly complex society of specific domains of action that pushes individual actors into the position of clients handed over to the contingencies of independently operating systems, and the expectation that these contingencies can be normatively tamed through administrative power operating through redistributive measures in either a preventative or a reactive manner (404–5).

Habermas, using Steiner's reflection on American adjudication of accident law, constructs the following table. The contrast here is between a liberal and welfare state view of the way cases of liability in business are described and interpreted.

The Liberal View	Today's View
unique	statistical
individual, personal	category, impersonal
occasional, random	generalized, purged of detail
isolated conduct	recurrent, systemic
unforeseeable (in the particular)	predictable (in the aggregate)
wait and see, fatalism	manageable, planning through insurance and regulation

If one reads the table in sequence from top to bottom, there are shifts in perspective from a first-person point of view on the left side to an impersonal, system level of description on the right. If one reads the table in reverse order, from bottom to top, the difference is a shift in the actor's perspective. According to the liberal model, society represents the result of spontaneous forces resisting the influence of individual actors. From the point of view of the regulatory welfare state, however, society loses this quasi-natural spontaneous character. As system conditions vary beyond acceptable limits, the state is held accountable for crises seen to result from its decisions and policies (405–6).

Nonetheless, as long as the administration remains bound to individual rights, both readings assume a competition between two agents, the state and those subject to it. The more individual freedom and rights obtain, the less state intervention is possible or legitimate, and vice versa. Welfare state paternalism has raised the question whether the new paradigm is compatible with legal freedom at all. The welfare state provides services that guarantee a natural base for a dignified human existence, such as employment and education, but in so doing, it runs the risk of impairing the very freedom it is supposed to defend. We seem to be in a bind. The justified critique that the welfare paradigm levels against bourgeois formal law precludes a return to the liberal paradigm. Habermas gives no ammunition here to those who wish to cut back on the welfare state or "end welfare as we know it" in favor of a supposedly more basic or important individual freedom or state right. At the same time, weaknesses of the welfare state model might lie in its being too close to the premises of its liberal counterpart (406–7).

Both paradigms, Habermas tells us, share the "productivist image" of capitalist industrial society. In liberal terms, this image takes the form of private pursuit of personal interests; in the welfare state view, such private pursuit blocks and frustrates justice. Both views focus on how a legally protected negative status functions in a given social context. Is private autonomy guaranteed through a mere protection of negative liberties, or must the condition for genesis of private autonomy be secured by welfare entitlements? Both views lose sight of the internal relation between private and public autonomy and of the democratic meaning of communal self-organization. Because both views focus on material preconditions or rights, on what can be had privately or what can be shared, they run the risk of seeing the citizen merely or primarily as a passive recipient of protection or services and not also and equally as an active subject and author of the law (407–8).

Habermas argues here and through the rest of the book that private autonomy secures public autonomy, and vice versa. This mutual dependency is manifest in the genesis of valid law, because it reproduces itself only through the forms of a constitutionally regulated circulation of power nourished via the networks of civil society by the communication of citizens in an unsubverted public sphere rooted in the private sphere of an undisturbed life-world. Here the burden of normative expectations shifts from the level of the actor's qualities, competencies, and opportunities to the forms of communication in which informal opinion-and-will-formation take place. In place of the zero-sum game between private and governmental actors, "we reckon instead with the more or less intact forms of communication found in the private and public spheres of the lifeworld, on the one hand, and those in political institutions, on the other" (402–9, quotation from 409).

This claim does not mean that the law's internal relation to actors is ignored; all rights stem from the system of rights that free and equal legal subjects mutually accord one another. The reference to communicative structures and relations from which political power arises and the reference to the forms of communication direct our attention to the structures of mutual recognition stretching "like a skin" around society as a whole, within which private and public autonomy mutually influence and condition one another. A legal order owes its legitimacy to these forms of communication, in which alone the autonomy can express and prove itself. Once a formal guarantee of private autonomy and social intervention has been proved to be insufficient, the only solution consists in "thinking the connection between forms of communication that *simulta-neously* guarantee private and public autonomy *in the very conditions from which they emerge*" (409).

I reflected on some of this discussion in a preliminary way in chapter 1, using Habermas's contrast between a bourgeois formal law and a social welfare model sharing a productivist image of capitalist society and his proceduralist model to formulate my notion of basic contradiction in the book. How, on the one hand, does the proceduralist model find an ade-quate material embodiment in a society that is even more virulently capi-talist and productivist? On the other hand, does not the proceduralist model hang uneasily over such a society, pointing toward a postcapitalist society that has overcome in principle the dominance of "having" and that adequately embodies and institutionalizes the reciprocity between private and public autonomy? How does the proceduralist model, attempting to transcend productivism, not lie in fundamental contradiction to a capital-ist society that is more than ever devoted to possession, commodification, reification, and the treatment of human beings as things?

On the basis of what he says here, Habermas could say there is in con-temporary society at least a partial real referent of his proceduralism, namely, the communicative structure and forms that stretch around soci-ety like a skin. But, I would argue, contemporary capitalist society embodies such forms in a contradictory way. The communicative skin surrounds a society suffused with the productivist, capitalist image and reality; communicative form contradicts capitalist content.

Not only is there this kind of contradiction, but also the capitalist con-tent overwhelms and breaks through the communicative skin. The forms of communication are not pure, undisturbed, or "more or less intact," as Habermas keeps saying in this section, but are shot through with capital-ist productivism, propaganda, and manipulation. The major players in the public sphere are big corporations such as ABC, CBS, and NBC, which are engaged in selling capitalist production as a way of life. Advertise-ments and fictional programs teach us that being is really having, pro-ducing, and resorting to murderous defense programs to defend this way of life, and news programs teach us that there is nothing better than cap-italism linked to democracy nationally and internationally. It is as though, to keep to Habermas's simile, the communicative skin is overwhelmed with diseased capitalist content, which makes the skin break out in sores, abscesses, and boils.

Moreover, short- and long-run empirical trends indicate that late capi-talist society is moving away from communication and toward produc-tivism. If it is true to say that the media within capitalist society will

always be characterized by a tension between accumulation and legitimation, capitalist productivity and communicative oneness, then in some
periods that tension more virulently favors capitalism than in others. In
the 1960s and 1970s, for example, in the United States, leftist, progressive
groups and movements and causes were more successful in getting their
protests covered and their agenda presented on major media than in the
1980s and 1990s. Part of the reason the public turned against the Vietnam
War had to do with the critical coverage the war received in the 1960s and
early 1970s. Programs such as *The Smothers Brothers, That Was the Week
That Was,* and *East Side, West Side* were strongly critical of national and
international capitalist injustice.

In the 1980s and 1990s the lid went on as the emphasis shifted toward
accumulation and away from legitimation, away from open, critical discussions of issues. Programs such as *Dynasty* and *Dallas* presented the
lives of the rich and famous as basically moral and righteous. Only char-
acters like J. R. Ewing on *Dallas* stood out as villains, exceptions to the
generally moral, normal capitalist rule. The safe, bland, largely apolitical
humor of *Saturday Night Live* contrasted starkly with the sharp, biting,
critical humor of *The Smothers Brothers* or *That Was the Week That Was.* NBC
was sold to General Electric and ABC to Westinghouse, and coverage of
the Gulf War was severely restricted, to reflect a positive, uncritical view
of that conflict. Newscasters like Dan Rather on CBS and Tom Brokaw on
NBC became little more than cheerleaders for government and corporate
policies, and such behavior contradicted what they should have been
doing, which was to ask hard questions about what we were doing in
areas like the Persian Gulf.[2]

These trends became part of a larger, longer-range trend in the 1980s
and 1990s toward a different capitalist regime, away from Fordism, in
which there is a tolerably moderate approach to welfare and democracy
somewhat approximating Habermas's ideals, albeit in a contradictory
way. Even during the Fordist era, approximately 1930–70, there were still
massive poverty, huge gaps in income and wealth between rich and poor,
and disproportionate corporate influence and domination of the political
process. Habermas's system of rights was not, and could not have been,
adequately embodied even then. But in the 1980s and 1990s in the United
States and Western Europe, we have moved away from the welfare model
ethically and politically. We have cut back programs benefiting the inner-
city poor and increased by hundreds of billions of dollars a year direct
and indirect subsidies for the rich and corporations. These subsidies
include tax breaks and write-offs, reductions in capital gains taxes, and
other changes in the tax code that hurt the poor and middle class and ben-

efit the rich, as well as subsidies, through spending for the Pentagon, for the development of innovations such as the Internet, which are passed on at little or no charge to corporations that profit greatly from them.[3]

Thus, neither short-range empirical nor long-range structural trends justify much optimism about realizing Habermas's proceduralist model, much less achieving a society that is morally and politically free of basic contradictions. Ethically, politically, and communicatively, late capitalist society is regressing even from where it was at the end of the 1970s in relation to his normative ideals. Now we have the fullest realization ever of international capitalism, and unjust interventions in the Persian Gulf and Yugoslavia take place with Habermas's approval. Rather than using his norms to bring such trends into question critically and radically, Habermas is either curiously silent or approving. Apparently, from his point of view, things are not that bad, and we can reasonably hope that they will be better. The critical theorist views the empire through rose-colored glasses.[4]

I disagree with Habermas's stance here. His system of rights and democratic theory have legitimate reformist and revolutionary uses, to which he refuses to put them. They could be used to begin the long march through institutions to create a more decent society, supplemented by extrainstitutional protests and street demonstrations, blending an ever more disenchanted labor movement with social movements, and resorting to alternative media.[5] Private formal autonomy, the welfare model, and communicative forms all fall to the ground dramatically in the face of the ongoing capitalist assault against people and their institutions everywhere. But his theory has another possible use in creating a fourth alternative, reformist in the short run, revolutionary in the long run, that would lead us to a postcapitalist society, one that would be communicative all the way through, not just on the skin, because democracy is present in the content as well as in the form of economic, political, and cultural institutions. Consequently, in this fourth alternative, the content-form dichotomy is overcome in principle, as is the accumulation-legitimation tension, and a society emerges in which private and public autonomy genuinely support and enhance one another.

THE FEMINIST POLITICS OF EQUALITY

In the beginning of the next section, Habermas admits that the contours of the proceduralist paradigm that would lead us out of the dilemmas of the welfare state model are vague. He states three premises: the way back to formal civil law administered by neoliberalism is blocked; the call for the rediscovery of the individual is blocked by a welfare state that threatens to turn autonomy into its opposite; and the social welfare project must be neither continued at the same level nor broken off but must be pursued at a higher level of reflection. Rather, the "intention is to tame the capitalist economic system, that is, to 'restructure' it socially and ecologically in such a way that the deployment of administrative power can be simultaneously brought under control" (410). From the standpoint of effectiveness, this taming "means training the administration to employ mild forms of indirect steering; from the standpoint of legitimacy, it means linking the administration to communicative power and immunizing it better against illegitimate power" (410). We have already seen how plausible such a project of taming is, both from the standpoint of effectiveness and legitimacy. Capitalist power in recent years has been much more successful in tipping the accumulation-legitimation tension in its favor and thus reducing democratic legitimation, and communicative media, one means of linking communicative power to administration, are themselves shot through with illegitimate power.

Habermas goes on to say that there is no specific legal form—reflective law—that the proceduralist paradigm would privilege in the same way that the liberal and welfare paradigms favored their corresponding forms, formal and material law. A radical or potentially radical procedural paradigm must be bound to a status quo that offers it no adequate possibility for embodiment. Choice of legal form must remain bound to the original meaning of the system of rights, which attempts to secure each citizen's private and public autonomy at once. Each legal act should be understood as a contribution to a process of constitution building. In other words, rather than radicalism or radical reform leading to a distinctly new legal paradigm embodied in a distinctively new way, tinkering is recommended. The communicative, legal gnat tries to move the capitalist elephant (410).

Habermas gives examples of such tinkering, dilemmas flowing from them, and feminist reflections on these dilemmas. One kind of proposal for escaping welfare state paternalism devotes attention to the actionability of rights. Such an approach begins with the observation that materialized law requires conflicting parties to possess a high level of competence. In addition to normal formal education, social background, and other kinds of expertise, the ability to use materialized law requires parties to be able to analyze their everyday problems regarding work, leisure, consumption, and so on into highly specialized legal constructions abstractly related to real-life contexts. A compensatory approach to legal protection becomes necessary and desirable, using not only forms of legal insurance and legal aid but also collective modes of implementing law. Such forms of redress as class action and community complaints will be effective, however, only if the affected citizens experience organization of legal protection as a political act in which they themselves take part (410–11).

Another approach, developed by Rudolf Wiethöilter, strengthens the positive legal status of the individual not by way of collective implementation but in forms of cooperative will-formation. The legislature is supposed to make procedures and organizational forms available for the internal constitutionalization of different spheres of action, modeled after self-governing bodies and arbitration boards. Such forms are supposed to help involved parties manage their own affairs and resolve conflicts by themselves. In this way, private autonomy is supplemented by a kind of social autonomy.

Both social autonomy and active procedural status run the risk of too quickly reducing private and public autonomy to a common denominator. The right to free collective bargaining, for example, although it can facilitate participation and achieving citizenship rights, can also undermine individual self-determination. Phenomena such as rigid gender- and age-specific limits, protective norms for women employees, and regulations for part-time work indicate a tendency to satisfy social claims at the cost of dictating from above. Such normative controls have the effect of normalizing and restricting freedom (412–13).

Discourse theory explains the legitimacy of law by having recourse to communicative procedures and presuppositions that, when institutionalized, justify the supposition that processes of making and applying law lead to rational outcomes. Rationality is proved by equality of treatment and protection of individuals in their integrity. What is equal in all relevant aspects should be treated equally, and what is unequal should be treated unequally. Criteria of just equal and unequal treatment need to be arrived at under discursive conditions in which citizens act as authors of the legal order. Legitimate law closes the circle between the private autonomy of the addressees, who are treated equally, and the public autonomy of enfranchised citizens who, as equally entitled authors of the legal order, must decide on criteria of equal treatment (414–15).

Involved in ascertaining such criteria is determining the boundary between the public and private spheres. Indeed, the dispute between the liberal and welfare paradigms is a dispute about the boundary and the criteria of equal treatment. Now that the dispute has become reflective and thematic, neither can any longer be dominant or unquestioned. It must be decided from case to case whether and in what respects factual and material equality is required for the legal equality of addressees. But in addition to the equality of addressees, equality among the authors and agents is the concern of the proceduralist paradigm. Here what comes up for discussion are not only situations where requirements of equal treatment are contradicted by those inequalities that discriminate against specific persons or groups by reducing their opportunities to utilize equally distributed liberties but also those situations in which equality in power and living situations is achieved only by limiting the exercise of individual freedom. This point is reached, for example, when regulation of work or family life forces employees or family members to conform to a standard pattern of socialization, and the right to unionize leads to representation of interests only at the cost of the members' freedom to decide. Authorization for the use of freedom turns into custodial supervision (415–16).

Even though materialized law is stamped by an ambiguity of guaranteeing freedom and taking it away, the ambiguity is not necessarily structural. The criteria for identifying the point at which legitimate empowerment is turned into illegitimate supervision are not arbitrary. Here the intuitive normative ideal is the idea of complementarity between private and public autonomy, such that each draws upon and sustains the other. Communication in the public sphere depends on spontaneous input from a life-world in which private domains are left intact, and individual citizens' rights must be guaranteed through materialized law and sufficient material resources to permit them to participate as public citizens. This ideal of reciprocity between private and public autonomy allows us to determine which regulation results in formal legal discrimination or welfare state paternalism. A legal program is discriminatory if it is insensitive to how actual inequalities have debilitating side effects restricting the use of liberty, and it is paternalistic if it is insensitive to the side effects of the state's compensations for these inequalities (416–17).

The mistake in both the liberal and welfare paradigms lies in seeing the legal constitution of freedom as having to do with distribution, either of private or of public goods. Justice cannot be reduced to redistributive justice but also manifests itself in the exercise of those rights derived from legitimately produced norms. Drawing on Iris Young, Habermas argues that rights are not possessions but relationships specifying what people can do to one another. Habermas uses the history of feminism to develop this point. Problems connected with the equal treatment of women make us realize that equal treatment of men and women requires more than redistribution. Feminism aims at structural inequalities concealed by a paradigm geared to social redistribution. "Welfare capitalist society creates specifically new forms of domination. Increasingly the activities of everyday work and life come under rationalized bureaucratic control, subjecting people to the discipline of authorities and experts in many areas of life" (419–20, quotation from 420).

A history of feminism relevant to these concerns is concealed in the feminist charter of 1977 adopted in Houston. There are historical layers of still outstanding concerns of the feminist movement. Liberal demands refer to a more extensive inclusion of women, such as abolition of all gender discrimination or the implementation of basic rights, either in social domains involving spheres of special power relations that require, for example, government support for battered women, or in view of new legal definitions surrounding such domains as reproductive freedom, pornography, and consensual homosexual activity. Social welfare demands, such as those for an adequate standard of living for all individuals, including income transfer for indigent homemakers with dependent children and child-care services accessible to families at all income levels, are still relevant. A reflective or procedural approach requiring attention to agency as well as redistribution comes out in a demand such as that for full employment, with increased opportunities for flexible and part-time schedules (420–21).

This complex layering indicates the necessary reciprocity of distribution and participation in defining issues and solutions. False classifications occur because of the assurance that equal treatment of the sexes can be achieved within the existing institutional framework and within a culture dominated and defined by men. Consequently, efforts meant to promote the equal status of women end up benefiting only one category, wealthy as opposed to poor women or white as opposed to black women. When women from all social classes, ages, and races have an equal voice in defining the problems, boundaries, and solutions, progress can be, and has been, made (422–23).

What is one to think of this ingenious use of feminist theory by Habermas, which he sees as confirming and instantiating his proceduralist paradigm of law? One can only applaud his opening to feminism here, long overdue in critical theory, and agree with him that developments in feminist theory, minus its radical account and implications, do indeed confirm and develop discourse theory. Earlier we considered Nancy Fraser's feminist, socialist critique of Habermas's conception of the public sphere and Habermas's inadequate response. We quoted him here quoting Young on late capitalist "welfare dependencies." Can one overcome these without addressing the issues of capitalism itself? Because Habermas does not confront these issues, or does so inadequately, his limited appropriation of feminism here does very little to tame the capitalist economic system (410).

I would insist more than Habermas does on the *reciprocal* relationship between distribution and participation. Not only is participation essential for adequate distribution to take place, but no adequate participation is possible without sufficient provision of resources. And this, of course, capitalism makes impossible in any full sense, because it is a society in which the top layers have the most wealth, income, and power, leaving the rest of the population insufficiently provided for and, therefore, unable to participate fully (410).

The proceduralist move beyond the liberal and welfare paradigms is good, but Habermas's version leaves proceduralism anchored insecurely in capitalist "having" as that occurs in the economic system and as it affects the political system and the public sphere. So the question recurs about the adequacy of Habermas's use of the proceduralist paradigm, which, as he intends it, can be applied only in a partial, contradictory way. Would not a fully active and materially sufficient democratic agency have to be present across the board, politically, economically, and culturally? How can full participation occur when democracy is restricted to the informal and formal political realm? Even this realm has been effectively disempowered under capitalism.

Not only is Habermas's appropriation of feminism inadequate, but also he does not consider other uses of the proceduralist paradigm in liberatory race or class theory. Here Habermas would undoubtedly admit the pertinence of discourse theory up to a point but then limit its extension and application reformistically. The claim that capitalism uses race to discourage, divide, and distract resistance, for example, is not discussed, nor is the problematic character of a society in which the average CEO makes more than two hundred times as much money a year as the average worker. Here the dialectic between formal legal equality and material equality turns into a contradiction. Do citizens' private life-worlds remain intact with that kind of inequality or with the kind of propaganda dinned into their homes every evening by capitalist media? With such material inequality, how can the public citizen participate equally and fully? Is not the conceptual overcoming of "having" in favor of "agency" more than a little moot? Can it not function perhaps to cover and legitimize the material inequality ideologically?

The conflict between private formal law and public welfare law, between the private person and the public citizen is an old story for Marxists. Marx in *On the Jewish Question* makes this point, explaining it by rooting it in the already divided and dividing character of capitalist social relations. Of course, there is going to be alienation and division when most citizens are effectively and structurally denied a public voice and when private capitalist interests rule the public domain, using it for their own well-being and profit. That claim is even more true today than when Marx wrote it. Yet Habermas thinks he can reconcile and integrate private and public autonomy merely by tinkering, leaving unaddressed the major cause of the division.[6]

Habermas himself, in earlier works, updates Marx's point. In *Legitimation Crisis*, he describes civic privatism, political abstinence combined with an orientation to family and career, as the way the capitalist buys off the citizens in creating a depoliticized public realm. In other words, capitalism structurally and intentionally works against an active, participatory approach on the part of citizens and rewards them with private "goodies," with having. The 1977 Trilateral Commission report, for example, argued that an excess of democracy in the 1960s had endangered the safe, effective maintenance of the capitalist system. In other words, citizens who try to be active and participatory the way Habermas recommends are guilty of going too far. Anything more than a merely formal democracy, in which citizens vote every two or four years for candidates chosen by elites, is undesirable. It is better to return to a passive, depoliticized citizenry that leaves the system unchallenged. Can anyone seriously doubt that the aims of the Trilateral Commission were largely achieved in the 1980s and 1990s? The dangers of creeping democracy in the West have been beaten back.[7]

CRISIS THEORIES AND PROCEDURALISM

Habermas begins the third section of his chapter by turning again to the issue of complexity, law, and legitimation. The procedural paradigm of law is concerned not only with the realization of rights but also with how constitutional democracy can be consolidated in complex societies. Here again Habermas considers the ambivalent consequences of welfare state materialization and an overly concrete reading of the separation of powers, focusing on the form that takes in state administration. His recommended solutions shift the functional separation onto the administration itself, recommend new avenues of client participation, and argue for public spheres specific to the administration (427–30).

Habermas is again trying to reconcile democracy and the capitalist state, which in function, intention, and structure is meant to repress democracy. The capitalist state, like the economy and media, functions over and above and against the population as an alien force, because most of the population is not meant to participate meaningfully in governance.

That would be to risk an "excess of democracy." This deprivation of, and alienation from, political power echoes and reinforces the deprivation of, and alienation from, economic wealth in the economic sphere and from communicative accessibility and influence in the public sphere. We have here, therefore, a threefold kind of alienation that includes and builds on Marx's economic account.[8]

This is not to deny that Habermas has useful insights here. There are issues relating to modern complexity as such and to the modern democratic state about which one has to think seriously and which will not simply dissolve in a democratic socialist transformation of the capitalist state. What is missing is the distinction between modern complexity as such and its contingent, capitalist version, which, despite Habermas's attempt, cannot be reconciled or integrated with democracy.

With the growth and qualitative transformation of governmental tasks and the enlistment of law as a means of political steering and planning, the burden of legitimation to be borne by the democratic genesis of law has grown. Law has a purpose of its own that cannot be used for just any purpose. If policy formation uses the law for whatever purpose it pleases, then conditions for legitimate lawmaking and administration are violated. Here Habermas points to a danger resulting from the simple multiplication of tasks that an administration must undertake: the danger that the sheer quantity of political tasks will overburden the legal medium and lead to the substitution of efficient implementation for legitimate political opinion-and-will-formation. In fact, however, legitimation problems cannot be reduced to administrative steering, because that would be to reduce the full range of reason, especially its moral, communicative dimension, to one of its modes, the scientific and technical (427–30).

This is a real danger in modern capitalist states. One is reminded of Habermas's last essay in *Toward a Rational Society*, in which he argues for a correlation between the dominance of the scientific, technical rationality in the modern state and the capitalist economy, and the tendency to substitute it for communicative, democratic, moral reason. A one-dimensional reason that is oriented to quantity rather than quality, fact rather than value, and that cheapens and dominates labor through development of technology rather than enriching and empowering labor corresponds to a one-dimensional society. How convenient for capitalist firms and the capitalist state that have no use for any moral critique or challenge to rule it out ahead of time as "irrational" and "unscientific." If science and technology are the only forms of reason and if they correspond perfectly with capitalism as productive force and ideology, then it is hard not to conclude that capitalism is perfectly rational.[9]

Habermas, in a way that I do not find plausible, backs away in *Between Facts and Norms* from the earlier more critical stance into one that tries to overcome the dominance of scientific, technical rationality within the state with reformist measures that refuse to break with or criticize capitalism. He wants to overcome scientism and technocracy and their tendency to do in communicative reason but without doing anything about the capitalism that is their source and goal. This reminds me a little of Proudhon's attempt to do away with money in capitalism while retaining capitalism, which Marx criticizes in *The Grundrisse.* Habermas's attempt is equally plausible, or implausible. Money is to the capitalism that Marx criticizes what scientism and technocracy are to late capitalism. Just as one cannot get rid of money without getting rid of the capitalist social relations that necessitate the use of money, so also one cannot get rid of technocracy without getting rid of the capitalism that requires technocracy, making it the privileged, dominant form of reason. Habermas once knew but now has apparently forgotten it; he gives no arguments for rejecting his earlier criticism. Why is that criticism not as true now as when he wrote it, if not truer?[10]

Let us take up now the main threads of Habermas's argument in this section. He goes on to say that in past chapters he had dealt with a criticism of the judicial development of law that endangers the rationality of adjudication as well as the basis of judicial legitimacy. Here he deals with the lack of constitutional controls on administrative activity. The formerly authoritarian relation between the administration and clients was replaced, even in Germany, by a reified relation monitored by the courts and binding on both sides. Also, the area covered by judicial review has been broadened by expanding the requirement of statutory authorization. Such changes, however, do not compensate for weaknesses in the binding force of regulatory law, because in fulfilling its tasks the administration often does not need to intervene in the technical legal sense.

These problems are aggravated by expansion of the temporal horizon in which policy unfolds, because the state is increasingly involved in the production of new risks connected with science and technology, such as those arising from nuclear technology and genetic engineering. Future generations have to be taken into account. Moreover, the state continually has to bargain with large social subsystems and organizations, which resist legal imperatives and can be dealt with only through persuasive means. In such contexts, big corporations can emerge as equal or superior in power to the state and can exercise political authority. Here is one example of where the distinction between modern complexity as such and capitalist complexity is relevant. If big corporations were broken up and democratized, the problem would be less severe (430–34).

Even political parties have moved from being instrumental in forming political will to taking possession of core areas of the political system without fully fitting into the functional separation of powers. They exercise paragovernmental, integrative functions by recruiting personnel with powers that extend to the administration, judiciary, mass media, and other social domains; by shifting political decisions from committees with formal responsibility to the back rooms of informal agreement; and by instrumentalizing the public šphere to gain access to administrative positions (434).

Habermas thinks this crisis tendency should be responded to neither by appeasement nor by a return to the liberal model of the constitutional state. Such crises are not insoluble in principle, and thinking that they are results from an understanding of law that is biased toward functionalism and overly preoccupied with administrative processes. This mistaken interpretation is based on a mistaken periodization of the history of growing state complexity: taming absolutist power in the liberal state, overcoming the poverty generated by capitalism in the welfare state, and taking precautions against the risks created by science and technology in the security state. As one moves from the liberal state into the other two forms, these are less regulated by law and rely increasingly on other resources such as money, economically valuable intrastructural activity, information, and technical expertise. But that the tasks are less and less legal in nature does not demand that they are not subject to legal regulation. Such a state of affairs simply means that the conditions of effectiveness do not coincide with the conditions of legitimacy, as they did in the liberal period. Moreover, from the point of view of legal doctrine, new risks to legal certainty do not pose new problems but rather exacerbate old ones having to do with the diminishing binding power of statutory law that is already beginning to be an issue in the welfare state. Preventative norms create a new problem only in regard to a long-overdue extension of protection from the individual to the collective (434–36).

The proceduralist paradigm has both normative and descriptive components that can be useful in diagnosing the contemporary situation. The discourse theory of law sees constitutional democracy as institutionalizing the procedures and presuppositions for a discursive opinion-and-will-formation making plausible the exercise of political autonomy and legitimate lawmaking. The communicative theory of society conceives the political system as one subsystem among many but also as being able to serve as a backup surety for problems of overall social integration through an interplay of institutionalized opinion-and-will-formation with the informal processes of the public sphere. A specific conception of law establishes a relationship between normative and empirical analyses such that the structure of recognition of communicative action can be transferred from the level of simple interaction to the abstract level of organized relationships. Indeed, law mediates between simple, ordinary communication and organized, systemic complexity. Moreover, the proceduralist paradigm results from a contest of paradigms that construes the realization of rights in overly concrete terms and conceals the relationship between private and public autonomy. Under these premises, the crisis tendencies of the modern state appear in a different light—an excessively reformist light resulting from a departure from Habermas's earlier diagnoses of such crises as rooted in capitalism Yet, he has not argued for this departure (437–38).

From a proceduralist viewpoint, according to Habermas, it is not a matter of replacing one type of law with another but merely providing the occasion for the dissolution of a specific historical form of the separation of powers. Today, the political legislator must choose from formal, material, and procedural law, according to the matter requiring regulation. No one of these forms should be privileged. Here, as before, Habermas distinguishes between institutional and functional separation of powers. As the liberal state gives way to the welfare and then to the security state, the functional separation of powers of necessity coincides less with their institutional separation, although they did not fully coincide even in the liberal period. What is required is a different institutionalization of the principle of the separation of powers, such that different sorts of reasons and arguments become available, regardless of the local context (438).

Habermas has some specific recommendations about how to go about this task. Dealing with the law reflexively requires, first, that parliamentary legislators must make metalevel decisions concerning whether they should decide at all, who could decide in their place, and, if they do want to decide, what the consequences will be for their broad legal programs. If the legislature does employ regulatory law, it must take precautions to compensate for the weak binding force of such law in the judiciary and administration. According to the proceduralist paradigm, the procedural conditions of democratic process are what primarily deserve protection. Citizens participating in political discourses to fill vacancies left by the private market participant and welfare state client must be able to express violated interests, articulate new needs, and collaborate in developing standards for treating like cases alike and different cases differently. If legal programs need further specification in the courts, juristic discourses of application must be supplemented by elements taken from the discourse of justification. Such an additional burden of legitimation requires institutionalization of a legal public sphere going beyond the culture of experts and sufficiently sensitive to focus on important court decisions (439–40).

Second, administrative decisions are no longer simply those of technical implementation and application of law, but rather involve the weighing of collective goals, the choice between competing goals, and the normative evaluation of individual cases. Consequently, procedural law must be used to build a legitimation filter into the decision making of an administration oriented primarily to efficiency. In a sense, the administration must be democratized in a way that, going beyond special obligations to provide information, would supplement parliamentary and judicial controls on administration from within. Means for achieving this end include participation of clients, use of ombudspersons, quasi-judicial procedures, and hearers. Such democracy from within must not render superfluous reactive controls from without by the legislature and the judiciary, especially in matters of individual legal protection. Legal remedies need to be developed that focus on the conditions for mobilizing law; the most important of these is enabling individuals to exercise their rights by developing and articulating interests, perceiving these in common with others, and bringing them to bear on the processes of governmental decision making (440–41).

Third, and finally, we need to deal with the neocorporatist relation of administration to those organizations and subsystems whose social power and complex internal structure make them largely inaccessible to legal imperatives, a fact making them different from other clients. Here Habermas does little more than repeat points and arguments made earlier, which have as much or as little plausibility as they did then. In bargaining with such organizations, the state must not see itself as merely one system among others but must defend the interests of society as a whole. The last recourse must be an alert, alive, and vital public sphere. "This brings us to the core of the proceduralist paradigm. . . . [T]he universal combination and reciprocal mediation of legally institutionalized and institutionalized popular sovereignty is the key to the democratic genesis of law" (441–42, quotation from 442).

This argument, even though it is more specified and developed, is not any more plausible here than it was in the last chapter. Because the public sphere is capitalized, dominated primarily by big corporations that are not only uninterested in, but hostile to, democracy and desirous of repressing or containing it, it does not protect democracy against corporate interests. It is one, or more, of these interests. The basic role of these big corporate media is to deter democracy through propaganda, advertising, biased news reporting, fictional programs that promote bourgeois values and leave the status quo unchallenged, and the presentation of an array of phantasmagoria that seduce us into worshipping the commodity or capital fetish.[11] The role of the public sphere is to prevent an excess of democracy in which popular participation asserts itself against these interests and prevails against them. Since the public sphere is part of the core on which defense of constitutional democracy rests, Habermas's whole argument is shaky at best and in ruins at the worst. If the public sphere is part of the problem rather than part of the solution, and is intended by its capitalist masters to be such, then that condition seriously affects its capacity to beat back capital all the way up the line as it involves the legislature, judiciary, and administration. The state remains a contradictory, bland, or oppressive capitalist state, in relation to which the public sphere, which should be a bulwark against both it and corporations, is as contradictory and flawed as they are.

I wish to avoid misunderstanding here. Because the capitalist state and the public sphere are flawed and contradictory, caught between the two goals of accumulation and legitimation, there is always the possibility of reform. Here Habermas's suggestions for such recommended changes as expanded citizen participation are relevant. My quarrel with Habermas is that for him such reforms are the best that we can do, and capitalism is beneficent and just. Even at best in his scheme the situation still remains contradictory and irrational both from a moral, communicative point of view and from the point of view of a social theory working for a rational, coherent, sane society. But moves toward greater reform and participation are always good.

Rather than relating to the public sphere reformistically, I would use Habermas's recommendations for reform radically. What if the democratic citizenry, in trying to tame the capitalist state and corporation, itself began to think and act instead to transform capitalism into a socioeconomic system that would in principle and in a noncontradictory way, relying on extensive alternative media, fully embody the system of rights. In such a changed context of revolutionary praxis, reforms and reformists would be necessary first or even second steps, especially in the public sphere, because part of what has to emerge is a revolutionary consciousness, and that can and should democratically and communicatively unfold within and without the public sphere. Rather than a contradictory "reformist reformism," therefore, that fails to realize Habermas's deepest values and intentions, we have a "radical reformism" or "revolutionary reformism" that consistently and comprehensively fulfills these intentions.[12] Taking Habermas fully seriously, in a way that he himself does not do, means being revolutionary. Revolutionary reformism saves Habermas from himself.

CONCLUSION

We have confronted in three different ways Habermas's articulation and defense of the proceduralist paradigm of law as a step beyond the liberal and welfare paradigms. First, we have argued that the proceduralist paradigm, essentially communicative, is in conflict with, and hovers uneasily over, a capitalist society still dominated by "having." At best, communicative forms inadequately encircle such a society and at worst are subordinated and sacrificed to such a society.

Second, Habermas appropriates in a reformist way the feminist critique of the welfare state. In so doing, he shows feminism to substantiate the proceduralist paradigm and its superiority over liberal and welfare paradigms. Equals should be treated equally and unequals unequally. I argue that such an appropriation should be expanded to a radical reading of the proceduralist paradigm that would be much more critical of class and racial, as well as sexual, injustice.

The proceduralist unity of participation and distribution falls apart on both sides in late capitalist society. Because democracy is, and can be, only political, in a contradictory, depoliticized, manipulated manner, most of the citizenry remains passive, alienated objects of a cultural, economic, and political process of rule from above that is out of their control. Because most citizens are inadequately provided for distributively, they are unable to participate in any fully adequate, even roughly equal, manner. A formal democratic freedom is contradicted by little or no material, real *worth* of liberty. Habermas's conceptual reconciliation of participation and distribution is contradicted by their real antagonism and lack in real capitalist society, still dominated by a having that makes full participation and distribution impossible.

Third, Habermas, as he has done before, argues against an overly concrete reading of the separation of powers and for an expansion of communicative action into the judiciary and administrative spheres. This move is laudable as a way of dealing with complexity as such, but it is inadequate as a way of dealing with capitalist complexity, since the corporations functioning as media undermine and contradict the informal democracy in the public sphere that is supposed to be a basis and guarantee of the democracy and justice of the whole system.

In his conclusion, Habermas makes one claim that has fruitful, if contradictory, implications. In arguing against procedural rationality as implying a form of life, he says that "the paradigm of law, unlike the liberal and welfare models, no longer favors a particular ideal of society, a particular vision of the good life, or even a particular political opinion. It is 'formal' in the sense that it merely states the necessary conditions under with legal subjects in their role of enfranchised citizens can reach an understanding with one another about what their problems are and how they are to be solved" (445). I am tempted to say, in response to this point, "Since when?" All the way through this book Habermas has linked the system of rights and democracy to late capitalism as its privileged milieu. Insofar as he wishes to back off from that claim, there is an opening to conceive in his terms other, possibly more privileged, milieus. We sense a dilemma here. Either the procedural paradigm should be taken in the purely formal sense argued for here, in which case it opens onto possibilities other than capitalism. But that runs against much of the argument of *Beyond Facts and Norms*—for example, Habermas's antirevolutionary orientation. Yet, if the procedural paradigm is linked implicitly and explicitly to capitalism, which is the dominant strain of this argument, all of the anomalies and contradictions that we have mentioned result.

It is an interesting, dubious claim. If we take Habermas at his word here, against the dominant tenor of this book, and read the system of rights, democracy, and procedural paradigm of law as pertaining to modern society as such, rather than simply or primarily privileging the capitalist form of such modernity, then an opening presents itself for other possible, more privileged, more adequate embodiments of his vision. It is that question that we will take up in the next chapter.

NOTES

1. Jürgen Habermas, *Between Facts and Norms*, trans. William Rehg (Cambridge: MIT Press, 1996), 388–89. Page numbers in parentheses throughout this chapter refer to this book.

2. Douglas Kellner, *Television and the Crisis of Democracy* (Boulder: Westview Press, 1990), 25–68.

3. James L. Marsh, *Critique, Action, and Liberation* (Albany: State University of New York Press, 1995), 293–308.

4. Jürgen Habermas, *The Past as Future*, trans. Max Pensky (Lincoln: University of Nebraska Press, 1994), 5–31. Ulrich Rippert, "How Jürgen Habermas Defends the Balkan War," 1–6, World Socialist Web Site, www.wsws.org, June 5, 1999.

5. See Marsh, *Critique, Action, and Liberation,* 345–55, for a further development of this proposal to link social movements with that of the working class.

6. Karl Marx, *On the Jewish Question,* in *Karl Marx: Selected Writings,* ed. David McClellan (New York: Oxford University Press, 1977), 39–62.

7. Jürgen Habermas, *Legitimation Crisis,* trans. Thomas McCarthy (Boston: Beacon Press, 1975), 37.

8. Karl Marx, *The Economic and Philosophical Manuscripts of 1844,* ed. Dirk J. Struick, trans. Martin Milligan (New York: International Publishers, 1964), 106–19. See Marsh, *Critique, Action, and Liberation,* 265–89, for an updating of this analysis and its application to late capitalism. Marx's economic concept of alienation has four aspects: labor's alienation from the object, not only the product produced but also the means of production and means of consumption keeping labor alive; from the process of work, in which the enjoyment and self-realization of the worker in work is subordinated and sacrificed to capitalist efficiency, division of labor, and use of technology; from species life, in which the worker is not an end in herself in work but a mere means to capitalist profit; and from other people, so that the worker becomes either a means or an obstacle to the capitalist's path to Wall Street and enrichment there.

9. Jürgen Habermas, *Toward a Rational Society,* trans. Jeremy Shapiro (Boston: Beacon Press, 1970), 81–122.

10. Karl Marx, *The Grundrisse,* trans. Martin Milligan (New York: Vintage, 1973), 115–28.

11. Walter Benjamin, *The Arcades Project,* trans. Howard Eiland and Kevin McLaughlin (Cambridge: Harvard University Press, 1999), 14–15.

12. "Radical reformism" is a phrase used by Habermas in *Toward a Rational Society,* 49.

9

The Achievement and Limits
of Habermas's Philosophy of Law

We now come to the conclusion of this long and detailed study. In it, I have attempted to combine interpretation and critique, sympathetic reconstruction of Habermas's argument and reflection on the limits of that argument. I continue to believe that *Between Facts and Norms* is an enormously important book, even, with all of its flaws, a great book. Since when, we might ask, are great books necessarily without contradiction, without anomaly, without difficulty? Can such a claim be made of the *Critique of Pure Reason, Phenomenology of Spirit,* or the book that is perhaps closest to *Between Facts and Norms* in importance and greatness, Hegel's *Philosophy of Right*? Not if Marx is correct, as I think he largely is, about the *Philosophy of Right*.[1] Indeed, part of Hegel's greatness, like Kant's, is that he allows into his framework of analysis, interpretation, and critique questions, insights, and empirical evidence that give trouble to his argument and tend to burst it asunder.

SUMMARY OF RESULTS

Even though, therefore, I resist the equation of importance and greatness with positive insight and truth alone, there is much of both in the book with which we may agree in whole or in part. Habermas has put philosophy of law on a new, more methodologically conscious and rigorous, albeit troubled, foundation. It is a prolegomena to any future philosophy of law. The general argument for linking communicative power and administrative power, life-world and system through law has much to recommend it. The horizontal and vertical genesis of rights in its general orientation and direction has much validity to it, even though that argument requires a radical corrective to work fully. The social theoretical argument, made mostly in chapters 4 through 8, that democracy is feasible within modern complex societies is true. Habermas very convincingly answers skeptical social scientific doubts about the possibility of such democracy.

On more specific issues as well, such as his dialectical overcoming of the splits between liberalism and communitarianism and between the liberal and welfare state models, Habermas has taken an enormous step forward. We also need to note more specific intellectual advances such as his correction of Dworkin's Hercules in favor of a communicative model of adjudication, the importance of the public sphere and the way it intersects with formal democracy centered in the state and systemic power, and the procedural model that functions as a step forward beyond the liberal and welfare state models.

And yet, at the same time there is a negative side, a limit to the achievement. My response to *Beyond Facts and Norms* most closely parallels my experience of Sartre's *Being and Nothingness* and *Critique of Dialectical Reason I*, books in which there was also a frustrating and maddening blend of insight and oversight, clarity and obfuscation, brilliant claim and contradiction, something to agree with and something to disagree with on almost every page.[2]

At the outset of this book, I hypothesized that the basic contradiction is that between a procedural, communicative model that in principle transcends "having" in relation to a capitalist society that is still dominated by having. That hypothesis has been overwhelmingly verified in my interpretation and critique. Contradiction after contradiction and anomaly after anomaly have emerged.

To try to be helpful to the reader who might otherwise be overwhelmed by, or forgetful of, the analytical detail of the last seven chapters, I sense the need to bring all of this together synthetically. If the first chapter functions as identity, presenting the sketch and outline of my book and the major contradictions, the next seven chapters present analytical and critical difference, and this current chapter presents identity in difference. The first two, or fundamental, contradictions are supplemented and further instantiated by eleven other significant contradictions, anomalies, and difficulties, within some of which are subcontradictions, anomalies, and difficulties, so we have thirteen major contradictions and anomalies. This summary account on my part may not be exhaustive, either in my text or in Habermas's. Maybe there are others in my and his texts, and maybe other critical and sympathetic readings of his text will discover two or three or ten more.

The reader will then have encountered the following material four times: the first time in the first chapter, at least in outline; the second time in some detail in the next seven chapters; the third in the summary at the end of the chapters; and the fourth in this chapter. The reader is invited to return to earlier chapters, if necessary, where there is more detailed development and argumentation.

Let us return briefly to the first major contradiction, that of the procedural model hovering above a capitalist society devoted to having. Everything in *Between Facts and Norms* and everything that I have discovered in my reading supports the validity of that claim. In chapter 9 Habermas says that the procedural paradigm has a partial referent in the communicative form that fits around society like a skin. But, I argue, this skin tends to be overwhelmed by the capitalist society that it encircles; the communicative form enters into contradiction with capitalist content.

A second, equally general formulation of the basic contradiction is that between democracy and capitalism. This contradiction is present in every part of Habermas's presentation: the genesis of horizontal and vertical rights; the legislative, judicial, and administrative operation of the constitutional state; the public sphere; and the articulation of the procedural paradigm.

A third contradiction running through the book is that between Habermas's account in *Between Facts and Norms* and his own past work. Here perhaps the major instance is the notion of a legitimation crisis in the modern state rooted in capitalism and Habermas's current claim that there are no problems in principle in the modern state and economy. Other subinstances include those between a technocracy rooted in capitalism present in *Toward a Rational Society* and the tendency in *Between Facts and Norms* to think that such technocratic tendencies can be reformed away; between the vocational, civic privatism discussed in *Legitimation Crisis* rooted in capitalism's buying off citizens for not participating in politics and the more benign notion of, and hope in, citizen participation in *Between Facts and Norms*; and between the "radical reformism" of *Toward a Rational Society* and the "reformist reformism" of the later book. In all of these instances, I have argued for the superiority of the earlier account, because it is more adequate and, therefore, points to a more radical solution. *Between Facts and Norms* is also weakened by Habermas's failure to give a sufficient account, if any at all, for why he prefers the latter, more benign version. His earlier interpretations and arguments are not reconciled with the newer. This conflict suggests a troubled, ambiguous future: the radical future that is the most adequate outcome of the Habermas text, and a perpetually worsening capitalist future that backs further away from the welfare paradigm and moves toward one that is even more cruel, heartless, and irrational.

A fourth contradiction lies in the genesis of right outlined in chapters 4 and 5 of *Between Facts and Norms*: within and between principles 4 and 5, and between the horizontal and vertical genesis of rights. The major problem with principle 4, affirming equal opportunity to participate in processes of opinion-and-will-formation, is that it confines democracy to its political form and thus excludes as possible and desirable economic and social-political democracy. Such an approach seems arbitrary and question-begging in light of communicative openness to all possible questions and seems implausible and wrong in light of what a community would and should choose in setting up its constitution. If democracy is good, why should not and would not a community choose full political, economic, and social democracy rather than just the limited political version here? At the very beginning of his argument, Habermas cuts off possibilities arbitrarily and with no explanation. At the very beginning there is a tacit, dogmatic adherence to capitalism that is at odds with full, democratic, communicative openness. These problems are especially telling for a thinker like Habermas, so committed to the force of the better argument. This arbitrary, dogmatic restriction, often functioning tacitly and implicitly, runs throughout the book, taking new forms at each step along the way.

Principle 5, concerning the provision of ecological, social, and technological conditions necessary to exercise the first four rights, is more acceptable as stated but is flawed by Habermas's restricting it to the capitalist version of the welfare state, arbitrarily excluding consideration of a democratic socialist alternative. Why is there no reflection on these two alternatives as possible instantiations of principle 5? Again the arbitrary preference for capitalism is in tension with communicative openness and runs through the book both as basic premise and as part of each further step.

Moreover, principle 5 is in contradiction with principle 4 since the confinement to political democracy in principle 4 makes possible, likely, and necessary an enormous material inequality that contradicts the material provision demanded in principle 5. Because the economic inequality rooted in economic oligarchy makes full political democracy even in Habermas's liberal sense impossible, principle 4 is in conflict with itself and with principle 5. The system of rights on a horizontal level is internally incoherent, arbitrary, and dogmatic, and all of these traits inherently conflict with the orientation toward communicative rationality, which brings into question and overcomes incoherence, arbitrariness, and dogmatism. Since capitalism is the fly in Habermas's ointment here, we are invited even at this early point to conceive of an alternative formulation of right and an alternative social system that would not be incoherent, arbitrary, and dogmatic.

Because the horizontal genesis of rights is internally and inherently flawed, so is the vertical genesis of rights based on it. It is similarly contradictory, incoherent, dogmatic, and arbitrary, because the tension between democracy and oligarchy already present in the horizontal genesis of right asserts itself as possibility and actuality all the way along the line, in the legislature, judiciary, and administration. The possibility of corporations and the rich interfering in the formal operation of government is fully actual and verifiable empirically. Such interference is not accidental but is built into Habermas's system of rights as possibility.

In chapters 5 through 8, I move from the ethical genesis of rights to Habermas's social theoretical linking up of the normative and the empirical reality of modern law. A fifth area of concern is Habermas's social, theoretical, and empirical inadequate theorizing of modern capitalist society. This has several aspects. One of them is failing to make distinctions such as that between system as such and the capitalist version of system. Another is the benign reading of the American and French Revolutions, in contrast to the much more adequate and radical understanding of these. Another is to underplay the moral and systemic irrationality of late capitalism by focusing just on colonization, ignoring other aspects of injustice such as exploitation, domination, marginalization, and tyranny. Habermas also fails to note the problems that the prison-industrial complex presents for the benign character of law and legal systems in modern capitalist societies.

He also speaks of corporate power as operating outside the public sphere, endangering it through colonization, whereas such power is actually the major player within the public sphere. He ignores the enormous empirical evidence concerning the class position and influence of those in the legislature, judiciary, and administration. Another aspect of his inadequate theorizing is his failure to distinguish between facticity-validity tension and facticity-validity contradiction; in the latter, aspects such as capitalism and democracy are not reconcilable. Another is the shift from Fordism to flexible accumulation, in which modern capitalist societies are moving away from the norms of the welfare and procedural paradigms. One result of such undertheorizing is to make the situation in late capitalism appear more benign than it really is; thus Habermas makes it too easy for himself to achieve a reconciliation between moral and legal validity and capitalist facticity.

Nonetheless, facticity and validity fly apart in Habermas's theory and in capitalist society. A sixth contradiction is that between the implicitly utopian aspirations of communicative action and its capitalist embodiment. In spite of itself, Habermas's theory points beyond itself to a more adequate democratic embodiment. The implicit utopianism conflicts with the explicit realism and resignation before a corrupt, degraded status quo.

A seventh contradiction echoing and instantiating this last contradiction is that between the requirements of a fully democratic public sphere and what is actual and possible in the capitalist public sphere. Taking the democratic requirements strictly, we simply have to reject the capitalist public sphere as contradictory to the imperatives of democracy. Taking such requirements loosely in such a way that they can fit current reality, the public sphere can be called adequately democratic if "occasionally" the people can assert its will in crisis situations. A prima facie reading of the requirements of the public sphere shows them to be incompatible with capitalism; only by adjusting these requirements implausibly can they be rendered compatible with the really existing capitalist public sphere. Habermas's theory alternates between contradiction, abject resignation, and unity between "ought" and "is."

Habermas shifts uneasily between the strict and loose meanings of democracy, between legitimate utopianism leading to incompatibility with the status quo and illegitimate realistic adaptation. Such an alternation is part of a general problem in chapter 8, where Habermas shifts ambiguously back and forth between description and prescription. Is the public sphere being described as it actually is, or is it being normatively prescribed? The effect of this ambiguity is to blur the difference between the normative and empirical definitions. As a result, Habermas argues that democracy as actually practiced, "really existing democracy," may be the best we can do. Yet, if we preserve the distinction between strict and loose definition and drop the loose definition, and between description and prescription, the bourgeois public sphere cannot and does not meet the normative definition. The normative and empirical dimensions of Habermas's social theory fall apart, in spite of the heroic attempt to keep them together. He can keep them together only by watering down the requirements of the normative theory, so that democracy becomes whatever the current practice is or whatever is compatible with the practice.

An eighth, and related, problem is the contradiction between a conceptual reconciliation between facticity and validity and a real contradiction. Real social facticity in late capitalism is undertheorized so that it appears to be compatible with the requirements of communicative interaction. From the side of validity, Habermas reduces the meaning of "socialism" or "radical democracy" to one that is merely formal and that obtains in principle in late capitalist society. The tension between facticity and validity, which includes real contradictions, is reduced to a harmonized reconciliation between the two. Meanwhile "really existing" capitalism goes on its own way in flat contradiction to the imperatives of right and legality.

A ninth problem is that Habermas's theory turns into a modernist, ideological justification for late capitalism in all of its injustice. Everything is really all right in principle; a merely formal socialism is compatible in principle with late capitalist society, which is the best we can do; and a critical theory that began historically as a critique of ideology turns into, in Habermas's hands, a form of modernist ideology.

A tenth area of concern is the inconsistency between Habermas's claim that his procedural model is not linked to any specific kind of society and the implicit and explicit linking of the model all the way through the book with capitalist society. Thus, the system of rights; the genesis of the state; the reflection on the interplay between legislative, judicial, and administrative aspects of the state; and the theorizing of the public sphere all take their bearings from capitalist society, articulating dimensions of this society and justifying it. If the proceduralist model shoots beyond this society in possibility, meaning, and aspiration and is truly independent of particular forms of society, the question again arises of a possible postcapitalist empirical embodiment. If it does not, then the problems about the proceduralist model in a capitalist context surface again.

An eleventh problem has to do with the way the inadequate conceptual, legal constitution of the system of rights leads into, makes possible, and undergirds an inadequate socioempirical account in chapters 5 to 8. The contradictory, dogmatic, inadequate conceptual genesis leads into, and is completed by, a similarly flawed empirical analysis, and vice versa. Thus, a narrowing of democracy to political democracy leads into, and helps make plausible, an equally narrow empirical conception of democracy. A tacit, dogmatic moral-legal acceptance of a capitalist status quo leads into, and is apparently confirmed by, a similar social theoretical acceptance and resignation. A split in the genesis of rights between communicative praxis oriented to utopia and really existing capitalist society gives way to, and is mirrored by, a social theoretical split between norm and reality. Similarly, a heroic, inadequate attempt to bring norm and reality together in the genesis of rights is mirrored and confirmed by social theoretical analysis, as we have just seen in discussing the public sphere. The system of rights and social theory constitute a contradictory, dogmatic, divided whole, which can be described in Hegelian-Marxist terms as "essence" in relation to "appearance."

A twelfth problem lies in the inadequate overcoming of the liberal-republican split. Habermas, up to a point, is impressive on this issue, but finally deontology tends to trump teleology too much. My recommended alternative is a reciprocal interaction on the universal level between right and good, duty and happiness, deontology and teleology, while still retaining Habermas's distinction between a universalistic morality, system of rights, democracy, and communicative action and particular ethical traditions.

A thirteenth issue is the incompatibility not only between capitalism and democracy but also between capitalism and the rule of law. Law is the middle term between democratic communicative action and administrative and economic systems. But because law in this sense is rooted in, and expressive of, communicative action oriented toward democracy and justice, and because capitalism is essentially undemocratic and unjust, it is incompatible with the rule of law in a full, coherent, substantive sense. Because capitalism is essentially undemocratic and unjust, it is also essentially lawless.

This is not to say that the rule of law is not present in western capitalistic societies in a contradictory, divided, incomplete way. Capital has a tendency to use law to legitimate its domination but resists the law insofar as it tends toward full democratic participation and justice. Thus, we have the tension between accumulation and legitimation in the modern state and culture; between a law that is ostensibly universal and impartial and one that is actually separate and unequal in legislation and application to the rich and poor; between a public sphere that is legally open to all points of view and one that is actually dominated by one point of view, that favoring the wealthy and corporations; between principle 4 and principle 5; , between a legal commitment to democracy and actual structural tendencies to undermine democracy through unequal participation and influence; between laws that favor private ownership of the means of production and those that contest such laws implicitly or explicitly; between a constitution that is ostensibly "of, by, and for the people" and one that actually is of, by, and for capital. We, the citizens of North America and Western Europe, have the best government money can buy, and such rule is, implicitly or explicitly, opposed to the rule of law. The capitalist says, "If the law serves my interests, I support it. If it threatens my interest, I will oppose it or render it null and void. If it contests my interests, I will not apply it."

In general terms, then, law in capitalist society is either contradictory or is not applied and administered, or it is applied and administered unequally, or it exists merely formally or merely on the books, in contrast to what goes on. When all else fails, the law is broken or subverted, sometimes violently, through bribes, payoffs, illegal wiretaps, or police brutality and killings.All these lead to an unjust legality or legal injustice that contradicts the inherent telos of law.

At least these problems are in the Habermas text, and perhaps there are others as well. The first two are general formulations of the basic contradiction, and the last eleven are more specific instances of it. The first two are related to the last eleven as universal to particular, claim to justification and proof. Occasionally in this critique I have had recourse to my own systematic theory to provide an adequate context and justification for particular claims, as in my account of other kinds of injustice in addition to colonization.But, for the most part, my approach has been that of immanent critique, measuring Habermas's achievement against his own standards and claims and finding it wanting.

WHERE DO WE GO FROM HERE?

What would be a more coherent alternative to what Habermas has presented?

My first recommended change is in the system of rights, basically in principles 4 and 5. We intend the notion of democracy to include all the institutions in which human beings exercise a social role. The principle would thus read: "Basic rights to equal opportunity to participate in processes of opinion-and-will-formation in which human beings exercise their autonomy, in all institutions in which they participate, economic, social-cultural, and political, and through which they generate, administer, apply, or conform to legitimate law."

Principle 5, which basically is on the right track, could perhaps be specified more. Hence, from my own ethics articulated in *Critique, Action, and Liberation*, I add: "Inequalities are not to exceed levels that will seriously undermine equal worth of liberty or the good of self-respect."[3] Therefore, principle 5 restated and reformed reads: "Basic rights to the provision of living conditions that are socially, technologically, and ecologically safeguarded, insofar as the current circumstances make this necessary if citizens are to have equal opportunities to utilize the civil rights listed in 1 through 4. Inequalities are not to exceed levels that will seriously endanger equal worth of liberty and the good of self-respect." Enormous differences in material resources make equal opportunity, equal worth of liberty, and the good of self-respect impossible, but we desire some difference, some legitimate inequality. We do not want a univocal, homogeneous equality, but rather a complex equality. After a basic level of material equality is achieved, we allow for some legitimate inequality in terms of need and merit. Also, self-respect is endangered if there is enormous material inequality. It is impossible for me to have equality of self-respect in relation to somebody who earns four hundred to six hundred times more than I do and therefore can exercise much more influence socially and politically, as well as having access to a lifestyle that is closed to me.

These changes have several effects. First, principle 4 is made consistent with itself because political democracy is no longer in conflict with economic and social oligarchy and resulting material inequality. Second, principle 4 is made consistent with principle 5 because the idea of equal opportunity is no longer undercut by an economic and social oligarchy and material inequality present directly or by implication in principle 4. Third, the contradiction between principle 5 and Habermas's implicit confining of its meaning and instantiation to welfare state capitalism is overcome. Fourth, the arbitrary restriction of democracy to its political version is overcome in a way that respects better the unrestricted range of communicative action, which resists and overcomes inconsistency, arbitrariness, and dogmatism. Fifth, the link between democracy and material equality, formal opportunity and material equality is affirmed while allowing for legitimate difference and inequality.

Next, we move from the horizontal genesis of rights within a self-constituting community to the vertical genesis of rights within the state. Thus far the case of democratic socialism as ethically, economically, socially, and politically superior to capitalism has been implicit. I propose to make it explicit by adding another constitutional principle: "All social and economic firms and organizations should be worker owned and controlled." Class difference within and without the firm is abolished in principle. I propose to add an equal rights amendment that would render other kinds of discrimination illegitimate: "All discrimination on the basis of race, sex, or gender is forbidden." The full self-constituting community is sensitive to issues of race, sex, and gender, as well as class, and it is open to the full radical implications of being committed to justice on these issues.

We have positively institutionalized in the horizontal and vertical genesis of rights the internal link among communicative action, democracy, law, democratic socialism, and racial, sexual, and gender justice. Habermas's account points inconsistently and incompletely toward that connection but then backs off and ends up in contradiction, anomaly, and inadequacy. My reconstruction respects, however, the basic insight concerning the relationships among democracy, law, and the economic and political system. It does so by extending democracy into the firm, which is defined inadequately as "system" by Habermas.

We have thus far been dealing with a reconstructed system of rights and the genesis of the state. What happens when we move from this ethical, legal, and political level to an empirical, pragmatic, social theoretical level, as Habermas does in chapters 4 through 8, in which he seeks to develop a theory of democracy that has empirical relevance and applicability? We have seen how he tries to achieve a reconciliation between "ought" and "is," ideal and real, and how he fails, in that ideal and real fall apart in a contradictory manner. I believe we can do better.

The major problem in the theory of rights, class division and the resulting material inequality and lack of democracy, has been removed in principle. Consequently, the major reason for the social theoretical contradictions, anomalies, and inadequacies has been removed in principle. Because our recommended form of democracy is socialist—full economic, social, and political democracy; a minimal welfare state; worker-owned and -controlled firms; markets forbidding exchange between capital and labor; and social, regional, and national planning commissions to monitor abuses and employ resources for needed investment—the problem of disproportionate class, racial, sexual, and gender influence on the legislature, judiciary, and administration is removed in principle. There is no reason for rich, white males to have a disproportionate presence in, or influence on, government. Class division, domination, exploitation, tyranny, and marginalization have been abolished in principle. Moreover, the domination of the public sphere by capitalist firms is abolished in principle because capitalist firms have been abolished in principle in the horizontal and vertical genesis of rights. The contradiction in the state and public sphere between legitimation and capitalist accumulation has been overcome because capitalism has been abolished in principle.[4]

We are dealing with a paradox here. Because Habermas's ethical and normative theory is in fact and in principle in its more progressive aspects incompatible with capitalism as a social system, the best way to achieve a reconciliation between ought and is, real and ideal, is not reformist adaptation but radical critique and transformation.Habermas would certainly have some questions to ask me about that, to which we will return in a bit. But first, let us focus on my social theoretical model and the way it mediates between real and ideal.

My model picks up and redeems Habermas's valid theoretical insights such as law mediating between communicative praxis and administrative and economic systems, and the legitimate and necessary interplay between formal democracy in the state and informal democracy in the public sphere. These legitimate ideas obtain somewhat in late capitalist society, in contradiction with other aspects of that reality and Habermas's theory. These ideas point toward ways to reform that society, such as minimizing the influence of the rich and corporations on elections and legislation, but such limiting is always a matter of degree and does not remove disproportionate capitalist power in principle. There are different ways of dealing with a contradictory reality. We can just stay with the contradiction, while trying to contain its destructive side-effects, as Habermas does; we can abolish it by removing the positive contradictory pole, democracy or law or the public sphere; or we can abolish it by removing in principle its negative pole, capitalist injustice. Now I submit that the most rational and realistic way, and from the perspective of communicative action the only way, is the third alternative, overcoming the contradiction in principle by removing its negative pole. Radical realism, therefore, starting reformistically but working toward a radical social transformation, is the only kind of realism that is not a cop-out. It meets the normative exigency of communicative action because it moves toward full democracy and abolishes capitalist injustice in principle, and it satisfies the social theoretical exigency because it argues for a fully coherent society, one that is not in principle antagonistic.

The democratic socialist state, economy, and society are in principle fully coherent, principled, democratic, and open to difference. Such difference arises initially in the private and public spheres: legitimate sexual, racial, and gender difference; differences in lifestyle, forms of dress, and forms of expression; and different forms of religion and ethical belief. The way has been paved for these differences by our equal rights amendment, and interplay among such differences is one of the most significant implications of Habermas's emphasis on the importance of the public sphere. Habermas hints at this implication but then backs away from it because he is unwilling to criticize and transcend capitalist homogeneity and commodification. Freedom or the play of difference in this context means the freedom to choose among fifty different kinds of toothpaste or ten different Victoria's Secret bras or two nondescript candidates representing the two different wings of the business party in the United States.

The play of legitimate difference, then, can emerge only in a fully just, liberated society, and this society is only possible with some universality and identity; commitment to communicative praxis; a system of rights; a just, democratic socialist state, economy, and society; and a fully liberated public sphere. Recognition of individual dignity in all of its radical, sexual, and gendered difference is possible, legitimate, and necessary, but only in a society animated by a justice in distribution and production that is first of all economic. There can be no adequate cultural-political recognition without economic justice, and no full economic justice without cultural-political recognition. Recognition is an important aspect of justice especially pertinent, perhaps, to gays, lesbians, women, and people of color but also to the poor, exploited, and economically disenfranchised. On the one hand, full recognition of the dignity and reality of the poor is the first step toward achieving economic justice for them, and lack of such recognition legitimates injustice towards them. On the other hand, mere paper equality and recognition without full material equality is meaningless.[5]

What about the issues of paradigm? I recognize a validity to Habermas's procedural paradigm but want to radicalize it by arguing for its embodiment in a democratic socialist state and economy that would resolve the contradiction between communicative form and anticommunicative content in late capitalist society. Second, because of the connection between right and good in my ethics, I want to argue that such a paradigm is not purely procedural. It is procedural-liberatory, linked to an idea of a fully democratic society as good; legitimate distribution of goods as a component of material equality; the play of aesthetic and cultural and political difference in the public sphere as a good; and finally liberation from racial, sexual, heterosexual, and class injustice as a good. These modifications of the procedural paradigm remove the major contradiction within the paradigm and in the whole of *Beyond Facts and Norms*.[6]

In conclusion, I wish to return to the paradox of radical realism or realistic radicalism and allow Habermas to question me. "Professor Marsh," he might say, "you have continually focused on the contradiction between my notion of democracy, communicative action, and law and existing capitalist society. You have pointed out how the United States and Western Europe are regressing from the form of welfare state capitalism achieved from 1930 to 1970 as capitalist society has moved from Fordism to flexible accumulation. Why are you not more flagrantly guilty of a contradiction between your sense of socialist democracy as a more desirable future and really existing capitalist society? My work, while it may have difficulties, at least has the merit of trying to relate to, understand, and do something about our lived present, inadequate as that is. If really existing capitalist society is moving away from my conception of the procedural paradigm, is it not moving even more obviously away from your liberatory paradigm?"

This objection is serious and needs addressing. First of all, there is a sense in which Habermas is right. If flexible accumulation is moving away from his liberal, proceduralist paradigm, it is certainly moving away from, and is even more incompatible with, my liberatory, socialist paradigm. But the meaning and consequences of that tendency are different from, and less destructive for, my theory than for his, because I am not defending the status quo as adequate in principle and use the fact of "moving back" as part of my argument for moving forward. Second, Habermas cannot exempt himself from the claim that he is utopian. Communicative action projects contrafactually a future society based on true, full consensus. His starting point and mine are the same; both of us are utopian because both of us start with communicative action; both are open and committed to unrestricted questioning; and we both project a system of rights, a just state, and a public sphere free from illegitimate intrusion of powers.

Nor can Habermas take the evasion, which he and Marcuse earlier criticized, of a positivism or technocracy that identifies rationality with technology or science and therefore rules out any ethical, apolitical, and legal form of rationality and critique that would transcend a problematic present endorsed by scientism and technocracy. Up to the present, Habermas has been concerned to articulate and defend legitimate, nonscientific, and nontechnical forms of rationality, such as the moral and aesthetic, that are specifically, qualitatively different from science and technology. This approach is in contrast to post-1989 forms of bourgeois realism, which defend the status quo as the best we can do, often by having at least implicit recourse to scientism and technocracy.

It is not, therefore, that I am utopian and Habermas is not. It is that he is inconsistently utopian, in a way that I am not. It is too late, I would argue, after he has taught us about communicative action, the ideal speech situation, the system of rights, and so on, to reject a democratic socialism as "unrealistic." Rather, his theory calls for an interplay between utopian, ethical reason and empirical reality that commits itself to transforming that reality reformistically or radically. If ethical, political, legal reason criticizes reality as contradicting and not measuring up to that reason, we have three choices. We can stay in that contradictory situation, simply adapting ourselves to the irrational, empirical reality (which I think Habermas is doing for the most part in this book); back away from those demands in a way that mitigates or removes those normative demands (fascism is the limit of this kind of conservative move); or move forcibly to transform that status quo. Radical realism emerges, then, as the true realism and criticizes bourgeois realism, of which Habermas's position is one form, as an ethical, philosophical, social theoretical, and legal cop-out. Such realism backs away from or softens the normative demands of reason in favor of an unjust present and remains stuck in a contradictory, irrational social system.

Reality, furthermore, is not only or primarily this contradictory, degraded present but also the historical present in the context of past, present, and future, which can transform and change that present. Reality is not this hard, empirical present, but communicative action emerging from, and rooted in, a past historical context and set of traditions responding to the situation in relation to a possibly more humane future.[7]

"But," Habermas might say, "the situation today is not one that is revolutionary, and even you, Professor Marsh, have admitted that we are moving away from that." I would reply by saying that if that is true, and I think that it is true, then the appropriate response is not just to give up in resignation but to create the conditions for revolution by organizing, talking to people, raising consciousness; organizing demonstrations, strikes, sit-ins, and teach-ins; using and supporting alternative media that contest capitalist media; having recourse in a radical reformist way to this very public sphere that Habermas sees rightly as important. I see it as important also, because of the possibility of such reformism and the revolutionary transformation that should follow from it. Such transformation, if it is to be ethically legitimate, should be consensual and democratic, and for that to obtain, interaction between the public sphere and the state and economy is essential. If the end is democratic and socialistic, then the means and the way to that should be also.

"But," Habermas might say, "capitalism has won out over Soviet socialism worldwide." It has won, I would say, empirically and strategically, but not in such a way that makes capitalism either systemically rational in a noncontradictory way or entirely acceptable. Why should "winning" in that way give any more ethical comfort to a citizen of conscience than would storm troopers from the Third Reich marching down the streets of Berlin after returning from a victorious battle in World War II? They were winning also. Once again, the distinction between ethical, communicative reason and scientific, technical reason is crucial.

But has not the triumph of capitalism over communism shown the validity of mediated forms of economic organization over forms of immediate or state-directed, nonmarket socialism? I agree that this has happened, but I deny the equation between free-market society and capitalism; between socialism and state, nonmarket socialism; and between socialism and immediate, nonrepresentative socialism. State socialism, because it is not democratic, and therefore not what Marx was talking about, is not the kind of socialism I would defend.

Again, I do not equate complex, market society with capitalism, a mistake that Habermas makes continually in his book. A market socialism, drawing on his distinction between system and life-world, is possible and desirable. Again, I think socialism is compatible with representative democracy; indeed, that is the political form that democratic socialism would take. Finally, expertise and mediation are possible and desirable in a worker-owned and -controlled firm, as they are in a capitalist firm. The difference is that in a socialist firm all major decisions about organization, investment, and design proposed by experts would be made by all of the workers in the firm. The technological experts in a socialist firm propose; they do not dispose or decide.[8]

Finally, on the most concrete level of praxis, it seems to me that we can have recourse not only to social movements whose life-world has been colonized by system and to nonviolent civil disobedience endorsed by Habermas but also to movements arising from labor, the poor, the unemployed, the homeless—in general from those who have been more and more economically disenfranchised since 1980 in the United States and Western Europe through flexible accumulation. Habermas's argument in *Legitimation Crisis* that economic crisis is unlikely and motivation and legitimation crises are more unlikely was truer under the regime of Fordism in western capitalist countries from 1930 to 1970 than for flexible accumulation, which has been rolling back progress made by labor and the poor during Fordism and which has internationalized capital in a way that leaves it less under any political control. Consequently, under flexible accumulation economic and rationality crises and motivation and legitimation crises flowing from them become more likely.[9]

What needs discussing, then, is a unity or identity in difference; feminists, gay rights groups, environmentalists, antinuclear groups, antimilitaristic groups, labor, the poor, the unemployed, and the homeless should join forces in national and international forms of resistance to the New World Order. The internationally organized demonstrations against the World Trade Organization in Seattle in the fall of 1999 and the World Bank in Washington, D.C., on April 19, 2000, are encouraging manifestations of these recommended forms of resistance, as are the many successful social movements in the United States for a living wage, resistance against police brutality, and the campaign on behalf of Mumia Abu Jamal, which dramatizes the evil of the prison-industrial complex.

In a curious way, Habermas not only understates how bad things are, thus giving the impression that late capitalism is easily compatible with the rule of law and democracy, but also understates the positive structural forms of possible and actual resistance against the New World Order. Such forms of resistance as they have been occurring during the last decades are evidence of the way the public sphere can be used to achieve significant social change. Because such resistance is increasing significantly throughout the western capitalist world, and in the Third World as well, it constitutes a final bit of evidence for my claim that I am being "realistic" in a legitimate, radical sense.

CONCLUSION

One final objection to what I am proposing in this book is that of inconsistency; am I not making contradictory claims? On the one hand, Habermas's system of rights, because it is finely tailored to capitalism, is or seems to be consistent with capitalism and justify it. His confining of democracy to political democracy, for example, is consistent with a social theoretical version of that in late capitalist society. On the other hand, I say that his system of rights, concept of democracy, and the public sphere point beyond the capitalist status quo. Are not these claims inconsistent?

I do not think so. First of all, as reconstructed and made fully consistent and nonarbitrary, his system of rights, state, democracy, concept of law, and public sphere is incompatible with late capitalism. Second, parts of his theory—for example, principle 4—link up to and justify capitalism but are incompatible with other parts, such as principle 5. Third, parts of his account are directly contradictory and point beyond late capitalist society: the idea of a public sphere free from influence or power; a state that functions in its legislative, judicial, and administrative operations in a totally fair, just manner; or the idea of a society that would provide the requisite material provision called for in principle 5. Finally, other claims that Habermas makes implicitly point beyond capitalism as a form of life. Since political democracy in capitalism is compromised by the role of money in legislation, campaign financing, and the media, political democracy even as he defends it is incompatible with capitalism. Finally, empirical descriptions such as the public sphere only "occasionally" and "in crisis situations" functioning from the bottom up contradict the strong meaning of democracy in that sphere.

NOTES

1. Karl Marx, "Critique of Hegel's *Philosophy of Right*," in *Karl Marx: Selected Writings*, ed. David McLellan (New York: Oxford University Press, 1977), 26–35.

2. James L. Marsh, *Post-Cartesian Meditations* (New York: Fordham University Press, 1988), 96–99, 144–48. James L. Marsh, *Critique, Action, and Liberation* (Albany: State University of New York Press, 1995), 87–93.

3. Marsh, *Critique, Action, and Liberation*, 162–63. I take this reformulation of

principle 5 to be a more proximate and determinate version of the "roughly, approximately, sufficiently equal, material" recommended revision in chapter 3.

4. Marsh, *Critique, Action, and Liberation,* 316–26.

5. Two books are instructive. Nancy Fraser's *Justice Interruptus* (New York: Routledge, 1997) is on the right track when it insists on an interplay between recognition and economic distribution. My misgiving here is that the issue is one not merely of distribution but also of capitalist ownership and control of the means of production. Thus, I insist on economic justice as an issue of distribution-production.

Axel Honneth's book *The Struggle for Recognition* (trans. Joel Anderson [Cambridge: MIT Press, 1996]) takes a step back from Marx to recover Hegel's concept of recognition, but then there is not a step forward to retrieve Marxian and post-Marxian theory on issues of economic justice. Consequently, the overall impact of Honneth's book is regressive and conservative; it decidedly is not *liberating* or even particularly *critical* social theory.

6. Marsh, *Critique, Action, and Liberation,* 113–24.

7. Marsh, *Critique, Action, and Liberation,* 331–34.

8. Marsh, *Critique, Action, and Liberation,* 173–74, 331–35.

9. James L. Marsh, *Process, Praxis, and Transcendence* (Albany: State University of New York Press, 1999), 308–20.

Select Bibliography

Albert, Michael. "Seize the Day." *Z Magazine,* November 1999, 5–14.

Arendt, Hannah. *On Revolution.* New York: Viking Press, 1965.

Avineri, Schlomo. *The Social and Political Thought of Karl Marx.* Cambridge: Cambridge University Press, 1970.

Benjamin, Walter. *The Arcades Project.* Trans. Howard Eilad and Kevin McLaughlin. Cambridge: Harvard University Press, 1999.

Berrigan, Daniel. *Ten Commandments for the Long Haul.* Nashville: Abingdon, 1981.

Bohman, James. *Public Deliberation.* Cambridge: MIT Press, 1996.

Burnham, Walter Dean. *Critical Elections and the Mainsprings of Politics.* New York: Norton, 1970.

Calhoun, Greg, ed. *Habermas and the Public Sphere.* Cambridge: MIT Press, 1992.

Carnoy, Martin, and Derek Shearer. *Economic Democracy: The Challenge of the 1980's.* Armonk, N.Y.: M. E. Sharpe, 1980.

Chomsky, Noam. "Rollback II." *Z Magazine,* February 1995.

———. *Profit over People.* New York: Seven Stories Press, 1999.

Chomsky, Noam, and Edward Herman. *Manufacturing Consent.* New York: Pantheon Books, 1988.

Cockburn, Alexander, and Jeffrey St. Clair. *White Out: The CIA, Drugs, and the Press.* New York: Versol, 1998.

Derrida, Jacques. *Specters of Marx.* Trans Peggy Kamuf. New York: Routledge, 1994.

Dews, Peter, ed. *Habermas: A Critical Reader.* Oxford: Basil Blackwell, 1992.

Forbath, William. "Short-Circuit: A Critique of Jürgen Habermas's Understanding of Law, Politics, and Economic Life." In *Habermas on Law and Democracy: Critical Exchanges,* ed. Michael Rosenfeld and Andrew Arato, 272–86. Berkeley and Los Angeles: University of California Press, 1998.

Fraser, Nancy. *Justice Interruptus.* New York: Routledge, 1997.

Habermas, Jürgen. *Toward a Rational Society.* Trans. Jeremy Shapiro. Boston: Beacon Press, 1970.

———. *Legitimation Crisis.* Trans. Thomas McCarthy. Boston: Beacon Press, 1975.

———. *Habermas: Autonomy and Solidarity.* Ed. Peter Dews. London: Verso, 1986.

———. *The Philosophical Discourse of Modernity.* Trans. Fred Lawrence. Cambridge: MIT Press, 1987.

———. *The Theory of Communicative Action.* Vol. 2, *Lifeworld and System: The Critique of Functionalist Reason.* Trans. Thomas McCarthy. Boston: Beacon Press, 1987.

———. *The Structural Transformation of the Public Sphere.* Trans. Thomas Burger, with the assistance of Frederick Lawrence. Cambridge: MIT Press, 1989.

———. *The Past as Future.* Trans. Max Pensky. Lincoln: University of Nebraska Press, 1994.

———. *Between Facts and Norms.* Trans. William Rehg. Cambridge: MIT Press, 1996.

———. *A Berlin Republic: Writings on Germany.* Trans. Steven Rendell. Lincoln: University of Nebraska Press, 1997.

———. "Bestialität und Humanität: Ein Kriegand der Grenze zwischen Recht und Moral." *Die Zeit,* April 29, 1999.

Hahn, Lewis Edwin, ed. *Perspectives on Habermas.* Chicago: Open Court Press, 2000.

Hahnel, Robin. "Going to Greet the WTO in Seattle." *Z Magazine,* November 1999, 5–14.

Harvey, David. *The Condition of Post-Modernity.* London: Basil Blackwell, 1989.

Honneth, Axel. *The Struggle for Recognition.* Trans. Joel Anderson. Cambridge: MIT Press, 1996.

Honneth, Axel, and Hans Joas, eds. *Communicative Action.* Trans. Jeremy Gaines and Doris L. Jones. Cambridge: MIT Press, 1991.

Ingram, David. *Reason, History, and Politics.* Albany: State University of New York Press, 1995.

———. "Individual Freedom and Social Inequality: Habermas's Democratic Revolution in the Social Contractarian Justification of Law." In *Perspectives on Habermas,* ed. Lewis Edwin Hahn, 289–307. Chicago: Open Court Press, 2000.

Kellner, Douglas. *Television and the Crisis of Democracy.* Boulder, Colo.: Westview Press, 1990.

———. *Persian Gulf TV War.* Boulder, Colo.: Westview Press, 1992.

Marcuse, Herbert. *One-Dimensional Man.* Boston: Beacon Press, 1964.

Marsh, James L. *Post-Cartesian Meditations.* New York: Fordham University Press, 1988.

———. *Critique, Action, and Liberation.* Albany: State University of New York Press, 1994.

———. *Process, Praxis, and Transcendence.* Albany: State University of New York Press, 1998.

———. "What's Critical about Critical Theory?" In *Perspectives on Habermas,* ed. Lewis Edwin Hahn, 555–65 . Chicago: Open Court Press, 2000.

Marx, Karl. *The Economic and Philosophic Manuscripts of 1844.* Ed. Dirk Struick, trans. Martin Milligan. New York: International Publishers, 1964.

———. *The Grundrisse.* Trans. Martin Milligan. New York: Vintage, 1973.

———. *Capital,* vol. 1. Trans. Ben Fowkes. New York: Vintage, 1977.

————. "Critique of Hegel's 'Philosophy of Right.'" In *Karl Marx: Selected Writings,* ed. David McClellan, 26–35. New York: Oxford University Press, 1977.

Moynihan, Dennis. "Anti-WTO Activist Jamboree." *Z Magazine,* November 1999, 5–14.

Nelson-Pallmeyer, Jack. *Brave New World Order.* Maryknoll, N.Y.: Orbis Books, 1992.

Parenti, Michael. *Democracy for the Few.* 2d ed. New York: St. Martin's Press, 1995.

Rawls, John. *A Theory of Justice.* Cambridge: Harvard University Press, 1971.

Rehg, William. *Insight and Solidarity: A Study of the Discourses on Ethics of Jürgen Habermas.* Berkeley and Los Angeles: University of California Press, 1994.

Ricoeur, Paul. *Oneself as Another.* Trans. Kathleen Blamey. Chicago: University of Chicago Press, 1992.

Rippert, Ulrich. "How Jürgen Habermas Defends the Balkan War." World Socialist Web Site, www.wsws.org. June 5, 1999.

Rosenfeld, Michael, and Andrew Arato, eds. Habermas on Law and Democracy: Critical Exchanges. Berkeley and Los Angeles: University of California Press, 1998.

Scheurman, William E. "Between Radicalism and Resignation: Democratic Theory in Habermas's *Between Facts and Norms.*" In *Habermas: A Critical Reader,* ed. Peter Dews, 253–77. Oxford: Basil Blackwell, 1999.

Sklar, Holly. *Chaos or Community.* Boston: South End Press, 1995.

————. "Imagine a Country." *Z Magazine,* July-August 1997, 65.

Sklar, Martin J. *The Corporate Reconstruction of American Capitalism, 1890–1916.* Cambridge: Cambridge University Press, 1988.

Street, Paul L. "The Economy Is Doing Fine, It's Just the People That Aren't." *Z Magazine,* November 2000, 30.

Taylor, Mark Lewis. *The Executed God: The Way of the Cross in Lockdown America.* Minneapolis: Fortress Press, 2001.

Walzer, Michael. *Spheres of Justice.* New York: Basic Books, 1983.

Webb, Gary. *Dark Alliance.* New York: Seven Stories Press, 1998.

Wolfe, Alan. *The Limits of Legitimacy.* New York: Free Press, 1977.

Zinn, Howard. *A People's History of the United States: 1492–Present.* Rev. ed. New York: HarperCollins, 1995.

Zwerdling, Daniel. *Workplace Democracy.* New York: Harper Colophon, 1980.

Index

About the Author

James L. Marsh is professor of philosophy at Fordham University. He is the author of several books, including *Modernity and Its Discontents* and *Critique, Action, and Liberation*.